Your Point Being?

# Your Point Being?

Graham H. Twelftree

MONARCH
BOOKS
Mill Hill, London & Grand Rapids, Michigan

Published by Monarch Books in the UK in 2003,
Concorde House, Grenville Place,
Mill Hill, London NW7 3SA.

Distributed by:
UK: STL, PO Box 300, Kingstown Broadway,
Carlisle, Cumbria CA3 0QS;
USA: Kregel Publications, PO Box 2607,
Grand Rapids, Michigan 49501.

ISBN 1 85424 592 9 (UK)
ISBN 0 8254 6217 7 (USA)

**British Library Cataloguing Data**
A catalogue record for this book is available
from the British Library.

Cover art: Ian Moore

Printed and bound in Great Britain by
Bookmarque Ltd, Croydon, Surrey

Designed and produced for the publisher by
Gazelle Creative Productions,
Concorde House, Grenville Place, Mill Hill,
London NW7 3SA.

# CONTENTS

To
Jeff and Glenda Mountford

# PREFACE

Story telling is as old as the camp fire. Story telling is also powerful and life-changing. We see this when God uses a well-chosen story in a talk to help people hear God's voice. However, I find the business of discovering good stories a relentless and difficult task. Therefore this book is designed to help other speakers find stories for effective communication.

The post-modern world of Twenty-Somethings, Busters or Generation Xers hears truth most clearly through the story – that powerful image maker. Today we are talking to people whose minds are frequently informed by television, videos, computer games and the Internet. Nevertheless people are not only learning primarily through seeing or hearing words and ideas. The clear, brief, high-impact image – conveyed by the story as effectively as by the screen – is still the diet of modern minds. Indeed, most of the books borrowed from libraries in Britain are novels with their stories.

We also share an era when objective truth and certainty are assumed to have been lost. No longer can anything be believed – except "my" story. And when we hear the story of another we are comforted; it orders and helps make sense of our story.

Further, until this one, there has never been a generation with an absence of meaningful relationships or so many broken relationships. Hope for new and meaningful relationships – with God and each other – can be conveyed through poignant stories. This can be seen, for example, in the "Testimony" stories that follow.

The story is, then, increasingly important if we are going to communicate our message. However, using (not reading out!) the stories that follow will require personalising, applying and retelling with conviction – or passion, to use a contemporary word.

What follows are the best stories from the two volumes *Drive the Point Home* and *Get the Point Across*. There are also many new stories: 3, 36, 43, 44, 45, 51, 72, 88, 90, 98, 105, 109, 125, 139, 149, 159, 168, 178, 179, 192, 213, 229, 239, 242, 252, 263, 272, all identified by a *.

To make this book as "user friendly" as possible there are themes and Scripture references appended to each story. Where a biblical passage is paralleled in more than one Synoptic Gospel, generally only Mark has been cited, and only Luke is cited for Q (passages common to Matthew and Luke but not found in Mark). These, as well as the headings, and many other key words and ideas, are collected in the extensive indexes (where incidentally references are to story numbers, not page numbers), helping readers to find appropriate stories quickly.

I first heard preaching that faithfully and consistently communicated the good news when I was on the staff of All Souls Church in London. Especially from Michael Baughen, Richard Bewes, John Stott and other staff members, I saw the importance and power of the story in communication. I remain thankful for what I learnt from them. To this list I add the late David Watson, whose use of stories and clear messages have been a great example to me.

I gladly record my gratitude to Megan Clark, Jeremy Smith and Andrew Whitaker for their help, as well to those who send me stories, often by e-mail. Despite her busy life, Barbara, my wife, has been particularly involved in the creation of this book. Thank you. I also pay tribute to Monarch Books, marvellously efficient publishers.

This book is dedicated to Jeff and Glenda Mountford in gratitude for their companionship through twelve years of ministry together. Thank you both.

Graham H. Twelftree
Regent University, Virginia Beach
February 19, 2003

# Stories

## ↷ ABORTION

To the Editor: In the annual report of the committee reporting on abortions notified in South Australia, the committee chairman, Professor L. W. Cox, states that, although abortion is a procedure associated with a known risk, in 96 per cent of the abortions performed in 1982 there were no complications.

I had an abortion in South Australia in 1982 and, seeing that I did not suffer from haemorrhage, sepsis or damage to the uterus (the complications about which the committee was concerned), I presume that I was included among the 96 per cent of women who suffered no complications following the procedure. I would like to tell a different story.

Although I was ambivalent about my pregnancy (it was unplanned), I did want to keep my baby. My husband, however, was very hostile to the idea. I had severe hyperemesis [vomiting], and because I was so ill I could not cope with my husband's anger towards my children and myself. At the time, to agree to his demands for an abortion seemed the only solution to the problem.

For the first four months after the abortion, I cried more or less all day and all night. I would wake myself up sobbing in my sleep, and, if I did sleep fitfully, would have terrible nightmares about dying children. During the day I would do things like going around the house rocking an imaginary baby in my arms, or scattering rose petals over the garden. I was haunted by the fact that my baby had no funeral, and I would play the same piece of sad music over and over again obsessively, each time mentally burying my baby. It was spring, and the sight and scent of flowers seemed to mingle with, and heighten, my grief. I had no one to share my grief with, and nothing to focus it on. I felt physically exhausted all the time.

Within a month of the abortion, my hair started turning grey. I almost lost my part-time job because I cried so often at work. When I drove the car I was frequently blinded by tears, and had several minor accidents, any one of which could have been more serious. I often had thoughts of killing myself and my children.

Then came the terrible anger which ate away at me for months, and finally the time of deep depression, when I just lay on the bed all day. I was absent-minded, lethargic and withdrawn.

Today, 17 months after the abortion, the grief, the anger and the depression, although diminished, are still there. I still find it difficult to cope with the sight of babies or pregnant women. I have several sexual and identity problems, my relationship with my surviving children has been damaged, my marriage is in ruins, and I am under the care of a psychiatrist.

Please, let all doctors be aware, if they are not already aware, that abortion is not "just a ten-minute procedure" but can have very serious and long-lasting psychological consequences.

(Name withheld by request.)

**Themes:**  *Family, Grief, Marriage, Medical ethics, Suicide.*
**Scriptures:**  Exodus 20:13; Job 31:15; Psalms 22:9, 10; 71:6; 119:73; 139; Ecclesiastes 11:5; Isaiah 49:1, 5; Jeremiah 1:5; Matthew 5:4; 2 Corinthians 1:3–4.

## 2 ABORTION

The story is told of a woman who went to a doctor in Bonn, Germany to ask for an abortion. The father had a sexually transmitted disease. They already had four children. The oldest one was blind. The second had died. The third child was deaf and dumb. The fourth child, as well as the mother, had TB. The doctor held out little hope of a healthy fifth child.

If you were the doctor, would you have agreed to an abortion? An abortion would certainly ease a great deal of suffering for the mother and the family.

If you had agreed to that abortion you would have killed Beethoven.

**Themes:** *Christians at work, Hope, Human life – value of, Medical ethics.*
**Scriptures:** Exodus 20:13; Job 31:15; Psalm 22:9, 10; 71:6; 119:73; 139; Ecclesiastes 11:5; Isaiah 49:1, 5; Jeremiah 1:5; 1 Peter 1:13.

## 3 ABSTINENCE *

I was holding a notice from my thirteen-year-old son's school announcing a meeting to preview the new course in sexuality. Parents could examine the curriculum and take part in an actual lesson presented exactly as it would be given to the students.

When I arrived at the school, I was surprised to discover only about a dozen parents there. As we waited for the presentation, I thumbed through page after page of instructions in the prevention of pregnancy or disease. I found abstinence mentioned only in passing.

When the teacher arrived with the school nurse, she asked if there were any questions. I asked why abstinence

---

3 Adapted from a story by Robert Layton.

did not play a noticeable part in the material. What happened next was shocking.

There was a great deal of laughter, and someone suggested that, if I thought abstinence had any merit, I should go back to burying my head in the sand.

The teacher and the nurse said nothing as I drowned in a sea of embarrassment. My mind had gone blank, and I could think of nothing to say.

The teacher explained to me that the job of the school was to teach "facts" and the home was responsible for moral training. I sat in silence for the next 20 minutes as the course was explained. The other parents seemed to give their unqualified support to the materials.

"Doughnuts at the back," announced the teacher during the break. "I'd like you to put on the name tags we have prepared. They're right by the doughnuts, and mingle with the other parents."

Everyone moved to the back of the room. As I watched them affixing their name tags and shaking hands, I sat deep in thought. I was ashamed that I had not been able to convince them to include a serious discussion of abstinence in the materials. I uttered a silent prayer for guidance.

My thoughts were interrupted by the teacher's hand on my shoulder. "Won't you join the others, Mr. Layton?"

The nurse smiled sweetly at me. "The doughnuts are good."

"Thank you, no," I replied.

"Well, then, how about a name tag? I'm sure the others would like to meet you."

"Somehow I doubt that," I replied.

"Won't you please join them?" she coaxed.

Then I heard a still, small voice whisper, "Don't go." The instruction was unmistakable. "Don't go!" "I'll just wait here," I said.

When the class was called back to order, the teacher looked around the long table and thanked everyone for putting on name tags. She ignored me. Then she said, "Now we're going to give you the same lesson we'll be giving your children. Everyone please peel off your name tags."

I watched in silence as the tags came off. "Now, then, on the back of one of the tags, I drew a tiny flower. Who has it, please?"

The gentleman across from me held it up. "Here it is!"

"All right," she said. "The flower represents disease. Do you recall with whom you shook hands?" He pointed to a couple of people. "Very good," she replied. "The handshake in this case is intimacy. So the two people you had contact with now have the disease."

There was laughter and joking among the parents. The teacher continued, "And with whom did the two of *you* shake hands?"

The point was well taken, and she explained how this lesson would show students how quickly disease is spread. "Since we all shook hands, we all have the disease."

It was then that I heard the still, small voice again. "Speak now," it said, "but be humble." I noted wryly the latter admonition, then rose from my chair. I apologised for any upset I might have caused earlier, congratulated the teacher on an excellent lesson that would impress the students, and concluded by saying I had only one small point I wished to make.

"Not all of us were infected," I said. "One of us abstained."

***Themes:*** *AIDS, Courting, Dating, Ethics, Fornication, Parenting, Sex, Sexually transmitted disease, Virginity.*

**Scriptures:** Exodus 20:14; Leviticus 18:20; Deuteronomy 5:18; Job 31:11; Proverbs 6:26; Matthew 5:27–29; Romans 1:18–32; 13:9; Colossians 3:5.

## 4 ABUSE

When the author Dr John White was in junior high, a young married Christian youth worker invited him to stay for a week in his home in the country. The first night he was there he and the youth worker had devotions in their pyjamas on their knees beside the double bed he and his wife normally occupied. His friend's wife, for a reason that it never occurred to John to question, was to sleep in a single room. John says: "What followed made me feel embarrassed, fearful to offend, helpless, angry and sexually aroused, all at the same time. I was too embarrassed to go on resisting his attempts to seduce."

John could not tell his parents for he did not have the language to describe what was happening to him and, after all, this man was a Christian leader.

John says that his encounter with the youth leader went on over a couple of years before he was able to break it off. Breaking it off was an important step for John and he says that his current sexual life is about as normal as it could be.

*Themes:* *Homosexuality, Immorality, Inner healing, Leadership, Sex, Sexual abuse, Youth ministry.*

**Scriptures:** Leviticus 18:22; 20:13; Romans 1:24–27; 1 Corinthians 6:9–18; Galatians 5:16–24; Ephesians 5:3; 1 Thessalonians 4:3; 1 Timothy 1:8–11.

## 5 ADOPTION

During a heated argument, an Arab struck and killed another man. Knowing the inflexible custom of his people, the young Arab ran across the desert until he came to the big sprawling tent of the tribal sheik. The young fellow confessed his guilt and asked for protection. The old sheik put his hand on one of the guy ropes of his tent, swore by Allah, and accepted the murderer into his tent of refuge. He was now safe.

The next day, others came looking for the fugitive. However, the sheik would not let the pursuers take the young man.

"But, do you know whom he has killed?" they asked.

"I have not the slightest idea."

"He has killed your only son!"

The sheik's heart and mind began to fill with confusion. Then the old sheik looked at the young man he had accepted. He said, "You have killed my son. But I am going to make you my son, and you will inherit everything I possess."

News of that particular story reached a nearby Christian hospital. Some of the patients who had heard about Jesus recognised that, just as the sheik had offered his son in death for the freedom of a stranger, so God has offered his Son's death in our place.

*Themes:* *Acceptance, Easter, Forgiveness, Grace, Love, Murder, Sacrifice.*

**Scriptures:** Mark 11:25; Romans 5:8; 8:14–17, 23, 32; 9:4; Galatians 4:5–7; Ephesians 1:5.

## 6 ADOPTION

During the Korean War a guerrilla fighter murdered the son of a Christian minister in order to undermine the Christian influence in the village. Later he was captured and put on trial. The grief-stricken father gave evidence against the man.

But then, to everyone's amazement, the minister pleaded – not for justice but for the life of the murderer of his son. The minister offered to adopt the murderer. In the confusions of wartime it was permitted.

As a consequence the guerrilla fighter in turn became a

Christian. The minister had turned his quite justifiable verdict of "guilty" into a verdict of "accepted". This stunning act is only a reflection of what God has already done for each of us.

*Themes:* *Accepted, Conversion, Easter, Forgiveness, Grace, Love, Murder, Sacrifice.*

**Scriptures:** Mark 11:25; Romans 5:8; 8:14–17, 23, 32; 9:4; Galatians 4:5–7; Ephesians 1:5.

## 7 ADOPTION – ANCIENT ROMAN

It was a serious step to take a child out of one *patria potestas* [father's power] and to put him into another. It was, however, not uncommon, for children were often adopted to ensure that some family should not become extinct, but should continue to exist. The ritual of adoption must have been very impressive. It was carried out by a symbolic sale in which copper and scales were used. Twice the real father sold his son, and twice he symbolically bought him back; finally he sold his lad a third time, and at the third sale he did not buy him back.

After this the adopting father had to go to the *praetor*, one of the principal Roman magistrates, and plead the case for the adoption, and only after all this had been gone through was the adoption complete. But when the adoption was complete it was complete indeed. The person who had been adopted had all the rights of a legitimate son in his new family, and completely lost all rights in his old family. In the eyes of the law he was a new person. So new was he that all debts and obligations connected with his previous family were cancelled out and abolished as if they had never existed.

7 William Barclay, *Ephesians* (Edinburgh: The Saint Andrew Press, 1958), pp. 92–93.

**Themes:** *Acceptance, Easter, Forgiveness, Sacrifice.*

**Scriptures:** Matthew 6:13; Mark 11:25; Romans 5:8; 8:14–17, 23, 32; 9:4; 1 Corinthians 6:20; 7:23; 2 Corinthians 5:15–19; Galatians 4:5–7; Ephesians 1:5–6; Colossians 1:13.

## 8 ADULTERY

Around a country school in South Australia there were about 20 acres of trees. Through them went a winding dirt track, locally known as "Lovers' Lane". On Saturday nights, young people would sneak through the dark and shine torches in the windows of the parked cars and there was great revelry on the part of the pranksters as young lovers were disturbed. One day, as some lads shone the torch in a car to give the lovers a fright, they got more than they bargained for. It was one of the lads who got a fright. In the car was his mother, caught in the very act of adultery.

**Themes:** *Ethics, Parenting, Sexuality.*

**Scriptures:** Exodus 20:14; Leviticus 20:10; Deuteronomy 5:18; Proverbs 6:32; Jeremiah 3:8; 5:7; 13:27; Hosea 2:1–5; Matthew 5:7–8; 19:9; Mark 7:21; 10:11, 19; John 8:1–11; 2 Peter 2:14.

## 9 ADVENTURE – SENSE OF

About 350 years ago a shipload of travellers from Europe landed on the northern coast of America. The first year they established a town site. The next year they elected a town government. The third year the town government planned to build a road five miles westward into the wilderness. In the fourth year the people tried to impeach their town government because they thought it was a waste of public funds to build a road five miles westward into a wilderness. Who needed to go there anyway?

Here were people who once had the vision to see 3,000

miles across an ocean and overcome great hardships to get there but had now lost their vision.

*Themes:* Certainty, Creativity, Faith, Leadership, Risk, Vision.

**Scriptures:** Proverbs 29:18; Matthew 28:19; Mark 11:22–24; Luke 7:1–10; Acts 1:8; 13:1–3.

## 10 **AIDS**

Earvin "Magic" Johnson is well over six feet tall. He is the all-American hero, worshipped like a god. He is a champion basketballer who has lived on a pedestal for years. But, on 7 November 1991, he announced his retirement from professional basketball. He had not long been married to his high school sweetheart, Cookie. Cookie was already pregnant.

A few weeks after they married Magic had a blood test. It showed he was infected with HIV, the virus that can cause AIDS. When Magic told his pregnant wife she was stunned. They had married just a few weeks earlier. She started to cry. The next moment she slapped him with her hand. He explained that he had slept with too many women to know who had infected him. In fact, after he had arrived in Los Angeles, in 1979, he had done his best to accommodate as many women as he could – most of them through unprotected sex.

"I told her that I'd understand if she wanted to leave me but she hushed my lips with a kiss," he said.

Cookie said, "We have been together on and off for the past fourteen years. Our love is so strong that I would never leave him to be alone with his pain. Not for one second did I consider packing my things."

There was one sad comment made by Cookie, "Everything's the same, except we can't have unprotected sex."

**Themes:** *Adultery, Fame, Heroes, Idols, Love, Marriage, Sex, Sexual ethics, Sport, Worship.*

**Scriptures:** Exodus 20:14; Leviticus 20:10; Deuteronomy 5:18; Proverbs 6:32; Jeremiah 3:8; 5:7; 13:27; Hosea 2:1–5; Matthew 5:7–8; 19:9; Mark 7:21; 10:11, 19; Luke 13:1–5; John 8:1–11; Romans 1:18–32; 13:9; 2 Peter 2:14.

## ⅄⅄ AIDS

A homosexual was dying of AIDS. Without disclosing his illness, he invited a minister to lunch. Halfway through their meal, the homosexual paused. He looked the minister in the eye, and blurted out, "I am dying of AIDS." Then, with tears in his eyes, the minister reached across the table and touched the homosexual's arm. "I am sorry, I am truly sorry," he said.

Later, the homosexual submitted his life to Jesus. He said this to the minister, "Do you want to know why I have decided to receive Jesus? When I told you I was dying of AIDS, I was watching your body language. I wondered if you would quickly lean back, away from my face. Or if you would surreptitiously move your glass and your plate... Instead of rejecting me, you reached out and touched me. Your eyes filled with tears... You accepted me. Then and there I decided that your God is the God I want to meet when I die."

**Themes:** *Acceptance, Compassion, Conversion, Evangelism, God – meeting, Homosexuality, Kindness, Life – after death, Love – God's, Parable – Good Samaritan, Witnessing.*

**Scriptures:** Leviticus 19:18; Mark 12:31; Luke 10:25–37; 13:1–5; Romans 1:18–32; 12:20–21; 13:9; Galatians 6:2; James 2:8.

## ⅄Ⅎ AIDS

An AIDS victim died. Sadly, no minister was interested in taking the funeral. Eventually the undertaker found a minister who was willing to conduct the ceremony. When the minister got to the funeral parlour he found about 25 to 30 homosexual men waiting for him. They were in the room with the casket, just sitting as though they were frozen in their chairs. Each one of them faced straight ahead with glassy, unfocused eyes. Their hands were folded on their laps as though some teacher had ordered them to sit that way. In all the various parts of the funeral, at the parlour and at the graveside, not a word was spoken by any of those men. As the minister left the graveside he realised that still the men were standing frozen in their places. He went back to one of them and said, "Is there anything I can do for you?" The man asked the minister to read the Twenty-third Psalm because he was hoping someone would read it at the funeral. So the Twenty-third Psalm was read. When he had finished, a second man spoke, and asked for another passage of Scripture. He wanted to hear the passage about nothing separating us from the love of God. For almost an hour the minister stood by the graveside reading passages of Scripture for those homosexual men.

**Themes:** *Acceptance, Bible – value of, Clergy, Compassion, Death, Evangelism, Funerals, Homosexuality, Kindness, Love, Parable – Good Samaritan.*

**Scriptures:** Psalms 23; Luke 13:1–5; Romans 1:18–32; 8:31–39; 13:9; 2 Corinthians 1:3–7.

## 13 ANGER

It is said that, when Leonardo da Vinci was working on his painting *The Last Supper*, he became angry with someone. Losing his temper, he lashed the man with bitter words

13 Adapted from Herbert V. Prochnow and Herbert V. Prochnow, Jr. *The Toastmaster's Treasure Chest* (Wellingborough: Thomas, 1979), #2062.

and threats. Returning to his canvas, he attempted to work on the face of Jesus, but was unable to do so. He was so upset he could not compose himself for the painstaking work. Finally, he put down his tools and sought out the man and asked for forgiveness. The man accepted his apology and Leonardo was able to return to his workshop and finish painting the face of Jesus.

**Themes:** *Character, Communion, Confession, Eucharist, Forgiveness, Humility, Last Supper, Reconciliation, Tongue.*

**Scriptures:** Genesis 4:5, 23–24; 27:43–45; 1 Samuel 18:8–9; 19:9–10; 20:30–31; Job 18:4; Psalms 4:4; 37:8; Proverbs 14:29; 16:14; 20:21; 29:22; Ecclesiastes 10:4; Matthew 5:22–24; Mark 11:25; Luke 18:9–14; Galatians 5:20; Ephesians 4:26, 31; 6:4; Philippians 2:3–11; Colossians 3:8; 1 Timothy 2:8; Titus 1:7; James 1:19–20.

## ᛝᛋ APPEARANCES

A few years ago, Adele Gaboury was reported missing. Concerned neighbours informed the police. But a brother told police she had gone into a nursing home. Satisfied with that information, Gaboury's neighbours began watching her property. Michael Crowley noticed her mail. It was delivered through a slot in the door and it was piling high. When he opened the door, hundreds of pieces of mail drifted out. He notified the police, and the deliveries were stopped.

Adele's next-door neighbour was Eileen Dugan. She started paying her grandson $10 a fortnight to mow Adele's lawn. Later, Eileen Dugan's son noticed Adele's pipes had frozen. Water spilled out the door. The water authority was called to turn off the water. What no one had guessed was that all the while they'd been trying to help, Adele Gaboury had been inside her home.

The police investigated the house as a health hazard. They were shocked to find her body. The press reported in

October that police believed Adele had died of natural causes four years previously.

*Themes:* *Death, Neglect, Neighbours, Old age, Parable – Good Samaritan, Servant evangelism.*

**Scriptures:** Leviticus 19:18; Mark 12:31; Luke 10:25–37; Romans 13:9; Galatians 6:2.

## 15 ATONEMENT

The story is told that Billy Graham, the great American evangelist, was once caught for speeding and received a ticket from the traffic cop. He went to the Sheriff's office to pay the fine. The Sheriff behind the desk took the piece of paper and did not react as he read the name William Franklin Graham. Then he looked up. He recognised Billy, for he also was a Christian. They began to converse about Christian things.

Eventually the Sheriff got down to business. He opened his book and asked, "How do you plead?"

"Guilty," said Billy.

The Sheriff recorded the verdict in his register. "That will be $150," he said. Then the Sheriff got out his wallet, took out $150, wrote paid in full in the final column, left the money in the book and shut it.

*Themes:* *Atonement, Cross, Expiation, Freedom, Jesus – work of, Ransom, Reconciliation, Redeemed.*

**Scriptures:** Exodus 6:6; Psalms 77:14–15; Mark 10:45; Luke 24:21; John 1:29; 8:31–36; 1 Corinthians 1:30; 5:7; 6:19–20; 7:22–23; Galatians 3:13; 4:4–5; 5:1; Ephesians 1:7; 5:2; Titus 2:14; Hebrews 9:15; 1 Peter 1:18–19; 1 John 2:2.

## 16 BEAUTY

Cher invests big in the body beautiful. Oscar-winning film star Cher has invested about $55,000 in the past decade in her quest for the body beautiful, says *Paris Match* magazine.

"The physical retouches are the secret of her magical youth and legendary silhouette at the age of 41," says *Paris Match*.

Cher says that in 1981 she spent $3,000 on removing traces of acne from her face. Another $4,200 was invested on having the size of her navel reduced and two ribs were removed, to give her torso that slender, boyish look.

Since her nose was "gigantic", Cher had that done too – at a cost of $6,000.

Her jaw has been rounded off and cheekbones made more prominent. She has also had her teeth capped ($4,200), a bust operation in 1969 ($7,500), followed by another round in this department in 1979 and, in 1983, her buttocks rounded ($7,500) and her thighs reduced ($6,000).

**Themes:** *The Body, Materialism, Self-esteem, Vanity.*

**Scriptures:** Romans 12:3–6; 1 Corinthians 12:12–27; Ephesians 4:12–16; Colossians 1:18; James 2:15; 3:6.

## 17 **BIBLE**

When Anatoly Rudenko was a student at the Moscow University in his late teens he was an atheist and a Communist. While he was doing economics at university, he began to ask the big questions in life. He wondered if there was some superior power above us, a God. In a certain situation he asked God for help. God answered his prayer. Anatoly said that he then wanted to find out more

---

16 *The Advertiser* (Adelaide) 23 April 1988, p. 7.

17 Adapted from *The Sower*, the magazine of The Bible Society in Australia (Canberra) Autumn 1991, p. 6.

about this God. He had heard that there was such a book as a Bible and he became very keen to read it.

Just to get one Bible he made a 72 kilometre journey from Moscow to Zagorsk. He found a monk in a Russian Orthodox church and pleaded with him for a Bible. It was 1976 and Bibles were scarce. Eventually, the monk agreed to give him one of these rare and valuable books. But Anatoly had his bag stolen at university and his Bible was gone. He so much wanted to read the Bible that he made yet another trip to pester the monk for another copy.

*Themes: Bible – value of, Doubt, God – his existence, Inspiration, Life, Perseverance, Prayer – answered, Russia, Students.*

**Scriptures:** Psalms 14:1; 53:1; Matthew 5:18; 8:26; 14:28–31; John 10:35; 2 Timothy 3:16–17; Hebrews 11; 2 Peter 1:20–21.

## 18 BIBLE

In 1787 Captain Bligh took the ship, the *Bounty*, on a voyage around the world to collect breadfruit trees. When he reached Tahiti in the central southern Pacific he found a veritable paradise. Soon every sailor had a girlfriend. There was quite a deal of grumbling when Bligh announced that after a few months in this heaven on earth they were leaving.

Not many days out of Tahiti Bligh woke up to find himself looking down the barrel of a gun. Bligh and 18 officers were put in a small boat without maps. Fletcher Christian and eight mutineers took the ship back to Tahiti and the pretty women. There they convinced not eight but twelve girls to go with them. They set off again in fear of being caught. They had no plans and came across Pitcairn Island. It was another island paradise. They took as many

18 Adapted from Tom Rees, *Can Intelligent People Believe?* (London: Hodder and Stoughton, 1971), pp. 29–32.

of their things as possible on to the island and then set fire to the ship.

What looked like a paradise turned out to be ten years of hell. One of the sailors used a copper kettle to make a distillery. They drank the "fire water" made from tree roots. The men spent days, weeks and months on end "plastered" by the spirits. Some of the men went mad and became like animals. They fought amongst themselves. One jumped off a cliff. After several years there were only two men left, Edward Young and Alexander Smith. Young was old, ill and an asthmatic.

One night the women seized the guns and barricaded themselves and the 18 children off from the men. Neither the women nor the children would go near the two men.

One day Young went to the ship's chest and, at the bottom among the papers, he found a book. It was a leather-bound, old, mildewed and worm-eaten Bible. He had not read for years and Smith could not read at all. So, Young taught him. The two men, frightened, disillusioned and utter wrecks, together read the Bible. They started at Genesis. They saw from the Old Testament that God was holy and that they were sinful. They did their best to pray.

The little children were the first to come back to the men. They noticed a change in the men. Then the children brought the women. They sat and listened to them read. During this time Young died. Then Smith came to the New Testament. Something important happened to him as he read the story of Jesus in the Bible.

"I had been working like a mole for years," he said, "and suddenly it was as if the doors flew wide open, and I saw the light, and I met God in Jesus Christ, and the burden of my sin rolled away, and I found new life in Christ."

Eighteen years after the mutiny on the *Bounty*, a ship from Boston came across the island of Pitcairn and the captain went ashore. He found a community of people who were godly. They had a love and peace about them that he had never seen before. When the captain got back to the United States he reported that in all his travels he had never seen or met a people who were so good, gracious or so loving. They had been changed by the message of the Bible.

*Themes: Conversion, God – holy, Holiness, Human nature, Jesus – Light, Light, Love – of others, Paradise, Prayer, Suicide.*

*Scriptures:* Genesis 1:3–4; 1 Samuel 2:2; Job 10:22; Psalms 14:1; 27:1; 53:1; Isaiah 9:2; Habakkuk 1:13; Matthew 5:18; Luke 10:27; 16:8; John 3:19–21; 8:12; 9:5; 10:35; 12:36, 46; 13:1, 34–35; 17:11; Acts 4:30; Romans 7:14–25; 8:29; 12:2; 1 Corinthians 13; 2 Corinthians 3:18; 4:6; 6:14; Galatians 5:19; Ephesians 5:8; Colossians 3:10; 1 Thessalonians 5:5; 2 Timothy 3:16–17; 1 Peter 1:13–16; 2:9; 2 Peter 1:20–21.

## 19 BIBLE

Mr Yang, a builder of Shen Yang Province in north-east China, once owned more than one Bible. However, during the cultural revolution he had to stand by despairingly as his Bibles were taken from him and burnt.

Later, he was delighted to hear some good news. A man not far away had been able to hide his Bible successfully. The same man had, for some time, been asking Mr Yang to take his son as an apprentice.

With a twinkle in his eye, Mr Yang said, "At the time I was a builder. I did not normally take on apprentices, but when I heard that man had a Bible, I agreed to take the boy as an apprentice, if he would let me borrow the Bible!"

When he got the Bible, Mr Yang began to copy it by hand. But he was tired at night after his long, hard days of

---

19 Adapted from *The Sower*, the magazine of The Bible Society in Australia (Canberra) Summer 1991, p. 12.

labouring, so he asked his 16-year-old daughter to help him.

"That was a good move," said Mr Yang, "because after she had copied out some of the Scriptures she became a Christian, and she is now studying the Bible in seminary."

They persisted with their laborious task for two long years and completed the four Gospels, Revelation, the Psalms and Proverbs. The manuscripts were then circulated among the members of Mr Yang's village who had been attending church in his house. In this way church members were able to study and obey God's Word, despite the terrible upheaval in their country.

*Themes: Bible – translation, Bible – value of, China, Church growth, Church planting, Conversion, Persecution.*

**Scriptures:** Psalms 1:2; 14:1; 53:1; 119; Matthew 5:18; John 10:35; 2 Timothy 3:16–17; 2 Peter 1:20–21.

## 20 BIBLE

A wealthy young man fell in love with BMW cars. As an expression of his devotion he bought a manual for one of the current models. He so much enjoyed reading it that he decided to get up early each morning to read it more carefully, section by section. There were some sections that seemed particularly interesting; those he underlined, sometimes with different-coloured pens. What seemed to be the more important sentences he began to memorise. In turn, there were a few lines he wrote out on small cards. He laminated them and put them on his mirror so he could see them when he shaved in the morning.

There were other people in his area who also had BMW handbooks. Our young man joined a group of these folk who met once a week in each other's homes to study their manuals. They would each bring different editions of the manual to compare what they said about various aspects of the BMW car.

In time, our young man decided it was time to go the next step. He enrolled in a night course to study German. He wanted to be able to read the manual in the original language. Yet, he had never bought a BMW car.

*Themes: Bible – inspiration of, Bible – memorising, Bible reading, Bible study, Personal devotions, God – knowing.*
**Scriptures:** Psalms 14:1; Matthew 5:18; John 10:35; 2 Timothy 3:16–17; 2 Peter 1:20–21.

## 2 ㄱ BIBLE

Marion was doing English at university. In second term she had to write an essay on a particular modern writer. She found his work boring, to say the least. She could not get into his novels or short stories and the deadline for her essay loomed closer and closer with little good work done.

Glad to have the chance to get away from study she went with some of her friends from her year to a party at their tutor's home. Amongst the clatter of glasses and thump of loud music she enjoyed the conversations. During the evening her tutor introduced her to a very good-looking man in his early thirties. He seemed to know a lot about literature and was very interesting. Marion could feel herself falling for him.

During the conversation, to her surprise, Marion discovered him to be the modern writer who was the subject of her essay. That night she went home and in the small hours started to read page after page of his work and found it exciting and worthwhile.

*Themes: God – knowing, Students, Study, University.*

*Scriptures:* Psalms 14:1; 53:1; Matthew 5:18; John 10:35; 2 Timothy 3:16–17; 2 Peter 1:20–21.

## 22 BIBLE – INFLUENCE OF

A Russian teenager, living in Paris around 1930, was aggressively anti-Christian and hated everything to do with God. After listening unwillingly to a talk by a priest, he decided to read a gospel to check whether the priest's picture of Christianity – which the young man found repulsive – was supported by the gospel account. Not to waste time unnecessarily, he chose Mark, the shortest gospel. Before he reached the third chapter, he suddenly became aware that on the other side of his desk stood the risen Jesus. His hostility crumbled and he became a disciple of Christ. He became Metropolitan Anthony, the Russian Orthodox Archbishop in London.

*Themes: Conversion, Visions.*

*Scriptures:* Psalms 14:1; 53:1; Matthew 5:18; John 10:35; 2 Timothy 3:16–17; 2 Peter 1:20–21.

## 23 BIBLE – LIFE-CHANGING

In January 1994, 24-year-old Leon Booth of Runaway Bay, Queensland, Australia threw himself in front of a fast-moving car. "I couldn't see any point in living," Leon said. The suicide bid resulted in several broken bones, a series of skin grafts and a period of deep pain for his family who had already suffered through Leon's times in prison.

"I was tired of having no money and being unemployed. I drank away my problems, and then took every drug I could lay my hands on – pot, hash, marijuana – anything I could get," says Leon.

22 Stephen H. Travis, *Getting to Know the New Testament* (London and Oxford: Mowbray, 1987), pp. 1–2.

During one prison term, he saw a psychiatrist for the first time. "We knocked on every door looking for help, and Leon's suicide bid was a further desperate cry for help," says Pam, his mother.

On his release from hospital Leon again visited a psychiatrist. But this one contacted the Revd. John Tully, founder of New Life Ministry at Street Level Inc on Queensland's Gold Coast. John visited the family and introduced them to the Serenity New Testament with its integrated Twelve Steps to Recovery.

A week later he received a phone call from Leon's psychiatrist. "I'm very impressed", were the simple words used by the psychiatrist to describe what had been a dramatic turnaround in Leon's life.

"I always believed in God, though I didn't want anything to do with Bible bashers." Then Leon added quickly, "But what I am reading in the New Testament applies so much to my own life that my whole outlook has changed." And Leon's mother says, "Leon no longer hates us as he did before."

*Themes:* Bible – importance of, Conversion, Life, Suicide, Testimony, Twelve Steps to Recovery.

**Scriptures:** 1 Kings 22–23; Psalms 14:1; Matthew 5:18; John 10:35; 2 Timothy 3:16–17; 2 Peter 1:20–21.

## 24 BIBLE – LIFE-CHANGING

Ted McDonough lives in Moree in New South Wales. One day Ted was dumping some of his rubbish at the local "tip". He noticed a small New Testament in very good condition. Ted was not a religious man, but he picked it up, saying to himself, "You're too good to be left on a scrap heap." And he put the book in his pocket.

Years later, when Ted's personal life and marriage

problems caused him to question the meaning of life, he decided to go to church. So, one Sunday morning, he got up early, got dressed very carefully and went off to the local church. Ted then lived in a small town and the Christians did not have church every week and the church was shut. He went home and hunted for and found the New Testament he picked up in the dump years before. In its pages Ted found forgiveness and a new life.

*Themes: Bible – influence of, Bible – value of, Conversion, Forgiveness, Life – meaning of, New life.*

**Scriptures:** 1 Kings 22–23; Psalms 14:1; Matthew 5:18; John 10:35; 2 Timothy 3:16–17; 2 Peter 1:20–21.

## 25 BROKEN

The royal palace in Tehran, Iran, is breathtakingly beautiful. A visitor stepping into the palace is surrounded by millions of pieces of glittering sparkling glass. It appears as if the domed ceiling, the side walls and columns are diamond covered and not cut glass; however, they are all small pieces of mirrors. The edges of the myriad of little mirrors, like prisms, reflect light, throwing out the colours of the rainbow. Spectacular!

Here is how it happened. When the royal palace was planned the architects ordered mirrors to cover the entrance walls. When the mirrors arrived, it was found that they had all been broken in transit. There were thousands of pieces of smashed mirrors. They were going to dispose of them all when one creative man said, "No, maybe it will be more beautiful because they are broken."

He took some of the larger pieces and smashed them also and fitted them together like an abstract mosaic. Today, the palace is beautiful beyond words, awash with sparkling rainbow colours.

**Themes:** *Beauty, Creation, Creativity, God – his creativity, Healing, Inner healing, Opportunities, Past hurts, Recreation.*

**Scriptures:** Genesis 1:1–2; Job 38:4–7; Psalms 19:1–4; 33:6, 9; 90:2; 102:25; Isaiah 40:22, 26, 28; 42:5; 45:18; Jeremiah 10:12–16; 18:1–12; Amos 4:13; Acts 17:24; Romans 1:20; 12:2; 2 Corinthians 4:16; 5:17; Galatians 6:15; Ephesians 2:1–10; Titus 3:5.

## 26 CALL – GOD'S

Every June, when the National Basketball Association holds its annual draft of college players, hundreds of players, good enough to be eligible for the draft, sit by their telephones anxiously awaiting a call that will inform them that they've been picked by one of the pro teams. Very few athletes receive a call. An article on the sports page of the Seattle *Post-Intelligencer* (29 June 1986) states that only one in 12,000 basketball players gets a call that will land them on the starting five of a pro basketball team. That means that, for every athlete chosen, 11,999 basketball players do not receive a call.

**Themes:** *Assurance, Discipleship, Election, Evangelism, God – his call, Life – purpose, Mission, Prayer – answers, Predestination.*

**Scriptures:** Isaiah 6:1–13; Jeremiah 1:4–19; Matthew 10:1–16; 28:16–20; Mark 3:13–15; 6:6–13; Luke 6:12–13; 9:1–6; 10:1–20; 24:44–49; Acts 1:8.

## 27 CANCER

A TV producer wanted to create a very special programme. He obtained permission from a cancer specialist to place cameras in his clinic. He also gained approval from three patients – two men and a woman. He captured on film the moment each of them learned they were afflicted with a malignant cancer in its later stages. Their initial shock, disbelief, fear and anger are all there, graphically recorded in detail.

Then the documentary team followed these three families through the treatment process. The film records the ups and downs, the hopes and disappointments, the pain and the terror. What is interesting is the different ways the three people faced their suffering. Two of them reacted with anger and bitterness. They not only fought their disease: they seemed to be at war with everyone else. Their personal relationships, and even their marriages, were shaken – especially as the end drew near.

But the third person was different. He was a humble black man from the inner city. His love for the Lord was so profound it was reflected in everything he said. When he and his wife were told he had only a few months to live, they revealed no panic. They quietly asked the doctor what it all meant. When he had explained the treatment programme and what they could anticipate, they politely thanked him for his concern and departed. The camera followed this couple to their old car. The camera eavesdropped as they bowed their heads and recommitted themselves to the Lord. In the months that passed the man never lost his poise. Nor was he glib about his illness. He was not in denial. He simply had come to terms with the cancer and its probable outcome. He knew the Lord was in control, and he refused to be shaken in his faith.

The cameras were present on his last Sunday in church. He spoke in church. He said, "Some of you have asked me if I'm mad at God for this disease that has taken over my body. I'll tell you honestly that I have nothing but love in my heart for my Lord. He didn't do this to me. We live in a sinful world where sickness and death are the curse man has brought upon himself. And I'm going to a better place where there will be no more tears, no suffering and no heartache. So don't feel bad for me..."

Then, this frail black man began to sing unaccompanied. He sang about his confidence in God and the better life ahead for him.

*Themes: Anger, Bitterness, Confidence – in God, Death, Fallen creation, Heaven, Hope, Love – for God, Love – God's, Marriage, Pain, Peace, Prayer, Recommitment, Relationships, Shock, Suffering.*

**Scriptures:** Matthew 5:12; John 1:2–4; 14:6; Romans 4:18; 5:1–5; 8:9–25; 12:12; 15:13; 1 Corinthians 13:13; 15:19; 19:20–28; 2 Corinthians 1:10; 4:17; Galatians 5:5–6; Ephesians 1:8; 2:12; 4:4; Colossians 1:5, 27; 3:4; 1 Thessalonians 1:2–3; 4:13; 5:3; Hebrews 3:6; 6:10–12; 10:36; 13:14; 1 Peter 1:3–9, 13, 21; 2 Peter 1:3–21; 2:9; 1 John 2:28; 3:2.

## 28 CHRISTMAS

Jim Prince was a tall, strapping 18-year-old who loved to play football. On his first day in the trenches in Belgium, in 1914, he passed some bread to a fellow-soldier. The fellow, rising to take the bread, stuck his head above the parapet. A German sniper's bullet killed the soldier instantly. Some quarter of a million people were killed in that area of Belgium in just a month.

That Christmas Eve, the First World War became bogged down in deadlock. The opposing sides were hidden in cold, water-logged trenches extending from the English Channel to the Swiss border.

Graham Williams, aged 21, of the London Rifle Brigade, peered over the parapet towards the German lines. As it was moonlight, he expected to see figures darting here and there trying to recover the dead and wounded. But an eerie stillness hung in the crystal-clear air.

Then he saw a light in the air above the German trenches. It was too low to be a star. Then he saw another, then another. Suddenly, there were lights all along the enemy trenches as far as he could see.

---

28 Adapted from Roul Tunley, "The Christmas that Stopped a War", *Reader's Digest* (December 1983), pp. 21–25.

"By God, the Jerries have Christmas trees!" Williams shouted. Then, from a German trench not more than 50 metres away a beautiful baritone chorus began singing "*Stille Nacht, Heilige Nacht*" – "Silent Night, Holy Night."

When the carol finished, the whole of Williams' regiment cheered and sang "The First Noël". For an hour the opposing troops sang to each other. In between the carols, there were cries for each side to come over to the other. No one dared move. But, in Jim Prince's part of the front, amazingly, the Germans – with hands in their pockets – started walking towards the British. Then the British started climbing out of their trenches too. Five metres from a German, Prince stopped. Here was a man he had been shooting at.

The German said simply, "I am a Saxon. You are an Anglo-Saxon. Why do we fight?" Years later Prince said that he still did not know the answer.

Peace was now sweeping through no-man's-land. Soldiers met and shook hands, laughed together and promised to continue the peace throughout next day.

Christmas Day dawned cold, clear, sparkling – and peaceful. No-man's-land was soon filled with thousands of soldiers from both sides, walking arm in arm and taking photographs. Several soccer matches were held. Most of them were with tin cans. But one Scotsman managed to produce a real soccer ball. The sportsmanship was amazing. One solder said, "If a man got knocked down, the other side helped him up."

Some men cut buttons off their uniforms as Christmas presents. A German handed over his spiked helmet. A Brit handed over a tin of bully beef in return. An English hairdresser gave free haircuts. A juggler from the German side enthralled the audience.

Then, soldiers from both armies dug graves side by

side. There were joint funeral services. By sunset there had been almost no firing along the entire front for 24 hours. No birds had been seen on the front for months. But now there were sparrows everywhere.

In some places the truce lasted until New Year's Eve. One German said in a letter home, "We had to have it last that long. We wanted to see how the pictures they took turned out."

The general agreement was that when one side was forced to break the truce, they would fire shots into the air. In Jim Prince's section the shots were fired into the air on 29 December. Men scrambled back into the trenches to cries of "Go back, Tommy!" or "Go back, Jerry!"

Jim Prince died in 1981 at the age of 85. He said that he could never hear "Silent Night" without tears streaming down his cheeks.

*Themes:* *Joy, Peace, Reconciliation, War.*

**Scriptures:** Psalms 34:14; Isaiah 9:6; Luke 2:14; 10:20; John 14:1–4; 15:11; 16:33; Romans 5:1–5; 1 Corinthians 7:15; Ephesians 1:9; Philippians 4:6–7; 1 Thessalonians 5:13; 2 Timothy 2:22; 1 Peter 3:11.

## 29 **CHRISTMAS**

Christmas 1971, John McCain's peace was broken and mended. His navy plane had been shot down over Hanoi during the Vietnam war. Then, for five-and-a-half years he was to be a prisoner. On this particular Christmas Eve, John and two dozen other freezing prisoners huddled together to celebrate Christmas in their tattered clothes. For some of the men, who had been in isolation, it was the first time they had been together for seven years. Physically, they were skin and bone, mere shadows of their former selves. Some were too weak or too sick to stand. But their frail and croaky voices gladly forced out the carol:

> Hark! The herald angels sing
> glory to the newborn king,
> peace on earth,...

At one point, they even exchanged imaginary gifts they had pretended to collect from the barren prison cell. John read brief snatches of the Christmas story he had been able to scribble down on a piece of paper earlier when they were given a Bible for only a few minutes.

"An angel said to them," John read out, "Fear not: for, behold, I bring you good tidings... "

Yet tears were rolling down their unshaven faces as memories were refreshed of the time – almost a year before – when North Vietnamese guards burst in on a church service some of them were attending.

The guards beat the three prisoners leading the prayers. The rest were locked away for the next eleven months in cells not quite one metre by two metres in size. But now they could sing their favourite carol: "Silent Night".

Some years later John McCain recalled, "We had forgotten our wounds, our hunger, our pain... There was an absolute exquisite feeling that all our burdens had been lifted... The Vietnamese guards did not disturb us. But, as I looked up at the barred windows, I wished they had been looking in. I *wanted* them to see us, joyful and, yes, triumphant."

*Themes: Enemies – love for, Fear, Gifts, Joy, Peace, Persecution, Prison, Suffering, Triumphant, War.*

**Scriptures:** Leviticus 19:18; Deuteronomy 32:35; Psalms 27:14; 34:14; Proverbs 20:22, Isaiah 9:6; Daniel 3:16–18; Matthew 5:22–24, 43–48; Luke 2:10, 14; 6:27–36; 10:20, 27; 23:34; John 14:1–4; 15:11; 16:33; Acts

7:60; Romans 5:1–5; 12:9–21; 1 Corinthians 7:15; 13; 2 Corinthians 11:30; 12:9; Galatians 6:2; Ephesians 1:9; Philippians 4:6–7, 13; 1 Thessalonians 5:13; 2 Timothy 2:22; Hebrews 10:30, 36; James 1:2; 1 Peter 3:9, 11.

## 30 CHURCH – PROBLEMS

A minister in London once said that he sometimes has a dream of the Perfect Church.

> The worship is perfect, the problems non-existent, the personnel vibrant. Barry Tone is the superb Director of Music, ably assisted by his associate, Benny Dicktus and a super band, the Magnifi-Cats. Neil Down is the Director of Pastoring, Percy Vere co-ordinates the evangelism, and exercising a strict rule over the training is Ben Dover. Sally Forth maintains the missionary interest, Benny Factor handles the money, while Dina Mite is a Church Co-ordinator, and Sue Preem is Rector's Assistant – the Rector being a firm no-nonsense individual by the name of Dick Tate.

However, he recognises that the reality of church life is very different. A more nightmarish, yet often more true to life team, he said, might include Mark Time, Peter Out, Molly Coddell, and the gossip Di Vulge.

**Themes:** *Church problems, Following, Gifts of the Spirit, Leadership, Music, Pastoral care.*

**Scriptures:** Romans 12:4–8; 1 Corinthians 12:12–31; Ephesians 4:11.

## 31 COMFORT

A mother sent her daughter to the corner shop to buy some milk. It was to be the little girl's first such trip on her own. The mother made it plain her little girl should go straight to the shop and then come straight home. However, the girl was away two hours. Her mother was almost beside herself with worry. When her daughter arrived home she tore strips off her. "Where have you been?"

The girl was quick to answer, "I'm so sorry Mum. I know I am late. But Jane broke her doll and I had to stop and help her fix it."

But the mother replied, "And how could you help her fix that broken doll?"

The girl's response was innocent. "I couldn't really, but I sat down with her and helped her cry."

*Themes:* *Burden, Compassion, Encouragement, Funerals, Grief, Love – of neighbour, Parenting, Suffering, Sympathy.*

**Scriptures:** John 11:19; Acts 11:22– 26; 15:41; Romans 14:19; 15:1; 1 Corinthians 10:23; 2 Corinthians 1:3– 7; Galatians 6:2; Ephesians 4:29; 6:2; Colossians 4:8; 1 Thessalonians 3:2; 4:18; 5:11, 14; 2 Thessalonians 2:16– 17; James 2:8.

## 32 COMMITMENT

A Christian in Nepal, from near the city of Kathmandu, had spent much time in gaol for his change to Christianity.

After he had been released a series of unfortunate events happened in his family, culminating in the death of a daughter in a fall from a tree. (In Nepal women cut leaves for animal fodder.) The local villagers threatened that if he gave his daughter a Christian burial he would be charged with the murder of his daughter!

The dear man went ahead with the Christian funeral service so he was returned to gaol to await trial for murder.

*Themes:* *Discipleship – cost of, Faithfulness, Loyalty, Parenting, Persecution.*

**Scriptures:** Matthew 25:14– 30; Mark 8:34– 38; 11:22– 24; Luke 7:1– 10; Acts 4:1– 22; 6:8 – 8:3; 9:23– 25; 14:5– 6, 19; 16:19– 24; 21:30– 36; 1 Corinthians 4:11– 13; 13:3; 2 Corinthians 6:4– 5; 11:23– 28; 1 Thessalonians 2:9; 2 Thessalonians 3:8.

---

32 Adapted from "Do We Know the Cost of Discipleship?" *Go* (Box Hill, Victoria: Interserve) June 1989, p. 10.

## 33 COMMITMENT

For many years Admiral Hyman Rickover was the head of the United States Nuclear Navy. His admirers and his critics held strongly opposing views about the stern and demanding Admiral. For many years every officer aboard a nuclear submarine was personally interviewed and approved by Rickover. Those who went through those interviews usually came out shaking in fear, anger or total intimidation. Among them was ex-President Jimmy Carter, who, years ago, applied for service under Rickover. This is his account of a Rickover interview:

I had applied for the Nuclear Submarine Program, and Admiral Rickover was interviewing me for the job. It was the first time I met Admiral Rickover, and we sat in a large room by ourselves for more than two hours, and he let me choose any subjects I wished to discuss. Very carefully, I chose those about which I knew most at the time – current events, seamanship, music, literature, naval tactics, electronics, gunnery – and he began to ask me a series of questions of increasing difficulty. In each instance, he soon proved that I knew relatively little about the subject I had chosen.

He always looked right into my eyes, and he never smiled. I was saturated with cold sweat.

Finally, he asked a question and I thought I could redeem myself. He said, "How did you stand in your class at the Naval Academy?" Since I had completed my Sophomore year at Georgia Tech before entering Annapolis as a Pleb, I had done very well and I swelled my chest with pride and answered "Sir, I stood fifty-ninth in a class of 820!" I sat back to wait for the congratulations – which never came. Instead the question: "Did you do your best?" I started to say, "Yes, sir", but I remembered who this was and recalled several of the many times at the Academy when I could have learned more about our allies, our enemies, weapons, strategy, and so forth. I was just human. I finally gulped and said, "No, sir, I didn't always do my best."

He looked at me for a long time, and then turned his chair around to end the interview. He asked one final question, which I have never been able to forget – or to answer. He said, "Why not?" I sat there for a while, shaken, and then slowly left the room.

**Themes:** *Achievement, Commitment, Ethics, Following, Leadership, Parable – of the talents, Perseverance, Work, Zeal.*

**Scriptures:** Matthew 16:27; 25:14–30; Acts 22:3; Romans 12:11; 13:13; 14:7–8; 1 Corinthians 4:1–2; 14:12; Galatians 4:18; 5:13; 6:9; Ephesians 4:28; 6:5–9; Colossians 1:10; 3:23–24; 1 Thessalonians 4:11; 2 Thessalonians 2:16–17; 3:10; 1 Timothy 4:11–13; 2 Timothy 2:21; Titus 2:14; 1 Peter 4:10.

# 34 **CROSS**

Christ did not carry the whole cross, only the cross-piece or *patibulum*. This was made of cypress wood and weighed 75–125 lbs, about as heavy as a bag of cement. Being forced to carry this the 700 yards of narrow, winding streets from Pilate's praetorium to the execution ground at Golgotha was an extra torture for an already flogged – almost flayed – man.

The nails securing Christ's arms to the cross were driven through the wrists, not his palms. The palms could not withstand the weight of the body: the hands would tear through longways. Instead, the eight-inch nails were driven precisely into the space between the wrist bones. These were dislocated, but not shattered.

An important nerve, the median, crosses the wrist joint. The square-edged nails almost always came into contact with the nerve, stretching it over the sharp sides of the nail like the strings over the bridge of a musical instrument. This caused such severe cramp in the thumb that it bent across the palm so violently that the thumb-nail embedded itself in the flesh.

The next step was to hoist the victim and slot the cross-piece on to the vertical stem, or *stipes*. The knees were bent until the sole of one foot could be pressed flat against the *stipes*, and an eight-inch nail was driven through it, precisely in the middle between the second and third metatarsal bones. As soon as the nail emerged through the sole, the other leg was bent into position so that the same nail could be hammered through the second foot and into the wood. The victim was then left to hang from the three nails.

A body suspended by the wrists will sag downwards, pulled by gravity. This produces enormous tension in the muscles of the arms, shoulders and chest wall. The ribs are drawn upwards so that the chest is fixed in position as if the victim has just drawn a large breath – but cannot breathe out. The condemned man begins to stifle.

The severely strained arms, shoulders and chest mus-cles develop agonising cramp. The metabolic rate is raised, but the oxygen supply is reduced.

One result is the production of large amounts of lactic acid in the bloodstream, leading to what is known as "metabolic acidosis", often seen in athletes driven to exhaustion and severe cramp. This is aggravated by the difficulty in breathing and in ridding the body of carbon dioxide, leading to "respiratory acidosis". Unrelieved, the victim finally dies of suffocation. This can occur within half an hour.

So swift a death did not satisfy the Romans. This is why they nailed the feet too. The condemned man could buy time by pushing himself up on the nails in his feet, stretching his legs and so raising the body to relieve the chest and arms. This allowed him to breathe better – for a while. But perching with the full weight of the body on a square nail driven through the middle bones of the feet brings intolerable pain. The victim soon lets his knees sag until once more he is hanging from the wrists, the median nerves again strung over the nail shafts. The cycle is repeated to the limit of endurance.

There were endless "refinements". The torture could be prolonged by using ropes instead of nails, reducing the pain but lengthening the struggle. A sort of seat could be fixed to the vertical stem of the cross, allowing further temporary respite. When this was used, the death throes could be made to spin out for two or even three days.

The executioners could shorten the ordeal too, smashing the legs, thus making it impossible for the dying man to push himself up to breathe.

Excessive sweating brought severe thirst. Blood loss and oedema caused by flogging reduced the circulation volume, blood pressure fell and the heart pounded faster. The severely acidotic condition of the blood, combined with the excessive loss of salt through sweat, was barely compatible with life. The heart began to fail and the lungs filled with fluid. The beginning of the death rattle croaked in each failing, painful breath as the heart began to give out.

*Themes: Crucifixion, Easter, Execution, Jesus – death of, Suffering.*
**Scriptures:** Mark 10:45; 15:21–37; Philippians 3:10; Hebrews 5:8; 13:12; 1 Peter 2:21; 3:18; 4:1.

## 35 CROSS

It was 21 May 1946. The place was Los Alamos. A young and daring scientist was carrying out a necessary experiment in preparation for the atomic test to be conducted in the waters of the South Pacific atoll at Bikini.

He had successfully performed such an experiment many times before. In his effort to determine the amount of U-235 necessary for a chain reaction – scientists call it the critical mass – he would push two hemispheres of uranium together. Then, just as the mass became critical, he would push them apart with his screwdriver, thus instantly stopping the chain reaction.

But that day, just as the material became critical, the screwdriver slipped! The hemispheres of uranium came too close together. Instantly the room was filled with a dazzling bluish haze. Young Louis Slotin, instead of ducking and thereby possibly saving himself, tore the two hemispheres apart with his hands and thus interrupted the chain reaction.

By this instant, self-forgetful daring, he saved the lives of the seven other persons in the room. As he waited for the car that was to take them to the hospital, he said quietly to his companion, "You'll come through all right. But I haven't the faintest chance myself." It was only too true. Nine days later he died in agony.

*Themes:* Courage, Easter, Expiation, Jesus – death of, Jesus – work of, Ransom, Representative man, Sacrifice, Substitution, Suffering.

**Scriptures:** Mark 10:45; 15:21–37; Luke 24:21; John 1:29; 1 Corinthians 1:30; 5:7; Galatians 3:13; Ephesians 1:7; Titus 2:14; Hebrews 5:8–10, 13:12; 1 Peter 1:18–19; 2:21; 3:18; 4:1.

## 36 DEATH *

John Wimber writes:

Margie Morton was a woman of wonderful faith. Over the years I had watched her exercise that faith in many different situations...

Margie suffered from brain tumours for a number of

years. She had surgery that was somewhat successful, but continued on the long, long journey of this condition.

I was praying for her one day when I sensed the Lord speaking to me. It wasn't an audible voice. Rather, I felt that he gave me some guidelines for ministering to Margie while I sat before him quietly. He said, "You taught Margie how to live. Now you must teach her how to die."

I started sweating immediately. I was not happy to hear those words. I loved Margie greatly and did not want to see her life come to an end.

At the time, her doctors wanted to send her to a hospital in Los Angeles with no real prospect of being healed. They recommended a treatment that might prolong Margie's life but without much quality. She would suffer tremendously, even with the treatment. I shared with her that I thought her remaining weeks could be better spent at home with her children, husband and loved ones. I told her to share her heart and life with them, and that I thought she would know when it was time to go be with the Lord. I didn't think that Margie would agree, because she was not one to give up without a fight.

However, the next eight weeks, she chose to stay home, sharing her life with her family and friends while conscious of her impending death. She did not spend her energies simply fighting cancer.

When it was time, she told her husband that she needed to go to the hospital. When she was in the hospital, her children and husband gathered around the bed and prayed for her. As they left they said, "Well, we'll see you tomorrow, Mum." She responded by saying, "You won't find much."

As soon as they left, she took a shower, and put on her brand new nightgown. The nurse happened to come in just as she was getting back in bed, and said, "My, how pretty you

36 John Wimber, "Signs, Wonders and Cancer", *Christianity Today*, Inc/CHRISTIANITY TODAY. 7 October 1996, Vol. 40, No. II, p. 49.

look! You're all dressed up to go some place. Where are you going?"

"I'm going to meet my King," Margie replied. Then she died, and did meet her King. That's victory! That's death that has no sting!

**Themes:** *Confidence – in God, Faith, Fallen creation, Gift of knowledge, God – speaking, Healing, Heaven, Hope, Love – for God, Love – God's, Prayer, Prayer – unanswered.*

**Scriptures:** Job; Daniel 3:16–18; Matthew 5:12, 22–24; John 14:6; Romans 4:18; 5:1–5; 8:9–25; 12:12; 15:13; 1 Corinthians 13; 15:19–28, 54–57; 2 Corinthians 1:10; 4:17; 11:30; 12:9; Galatians 5:5–6; Colossians 1:5, 27; 3:4; Philippians 4:13; 1 Thessalonians 1:2–3; 4:13; 5:3; Hebrews 3:6; 6:10–12; 10:36; 13:14; 1 Peter 1:3–9, 13, 21; 2 Peter 1:3–21; 1 John 2:28; 3:2.

## 37 DISCOURAGEMENT

In Zundert, Holland in 1853, a Lutheran pastor became the proud father of a baby boy. At 16 the boy went to work for a firm of art dealers in The Hague. A few years later he took the opportunity to travel to England. There he fell in love with his landlady's daughter, but she rejected him. In his grief he turned to Christ. He began helping a Methodist minister in Turnham Green and Petersham. The conviction grew that he should become a full-time evangelist, and in his mid-twenties he returned to Holland. He soon found great success in preaching to the poor, dressed like a peasant and living in their company. He washed their clothes, cared for their sick, consoled their dying and he led them to Christ.

However, the church leaders of the day would have nothing to do with him and forced him to give up his ministry. Eventually he gave up following Christ. He went back to the world of art and tried his hand at painting. His name was Vincent van Gogh. If he had not been discouraged, van Gogh might have been able to express his commitment to Christ through his art.

*Themes:* *Backsliding, Church – leaders, Conversion, Encouragement, Love.*
**Scriptures:** Psalms 23; 42:6–11; 55:22; Matthew 5:11–12; Luke 10:27; Romans 8:28; 14:19; 1 Corinthians 10:23; 13; 2 Corinthians 4:8–18; Ephesians 4:29; Philippians 4:4–7; 1 Thessalonians 5:11.

## 38 DISCOVERIES

In 1847 Sir James Simpson was a doctor in Edinburgh when he discovered chloroform, one of the most significant discoveries in modern medicine. Some years later after a lecture a student asked him, "What do you consider to be the most valuable discovery of your lifetime?" He answered, "My most valuable discovery was when I discovered myself a sinner and that Jesus Christ was my Saviour."

*Themes:* *Forgiveness, Parable – Pearl of Great Price, Sin.*
**Scriptures:** Matthew 13:14, Luke 14:33; Philippians 3:7–9; 2 Peter 1:3.

## 39 DISTRACTIONS

An Eastern Air Lines jumbo jet took off from New York's John F. Kennedy Airport. It was 9:20 pm, 29 December 1972. The plane was headed for Miami in Florida. On board were 163 passengers and thirteen crew members. Like almost every other plane flight the journey was uneventful. That is, until the approach to Miami Airport. The landing gear handle was placed in the "down" position. But the green light, which would have indicated that the nose landing gear was fully extended, failed to illuminate.

At 11:31 pm the captain called the control tower to report his problem. The control tower advised the captain to climb back to 2,000 feet. The plane then circled over the desolate, marshy, Florida Everglades. The captain instructed the first officer to engage the automatic pilot. The first officer was then free to repair the nose gear light. He successfully removed the light lens assembly. But it jammed when he attempted to replace it. He continued to have difficulty.

The captain asked the second officer to go down below to see if the landing gear had gone into place. But it was too dark down there. The second officer climbed back into the cockpit and said he could not tell whether or not the nose wheel was up or down. So the crew continued its attempt to free the nose gear light lens from its retainer.

In the midst of all this, a half-second musical C-chord sounded in the cockpit. This was indicating a deviation of 250 feet from the selected altitude. No crew member commented on the chime.

The controller in the tower noticed his radar showing the jumbo at only 900 feet. So he asked how things were coming along. The cockpit voice recorder recorded that the reply was, "Okay, we'd like to turn around and come back in." At 11:42 pm the plane was turned with its left wing lowered.

Suddenly the captain said, "Hey, what's happened here?" At 11:42 and 10 seconds the altimeter warning beeps persistently sounded in the cockpit. The captain and the first officer frantically tried to pour on the power. They pulled back on the controls. Unfortunately, it takes from one to six seconds for jet engines to develop thrust.

Two seconds later, with the aircraft in the left bank, Flight 401 ploughed into the desolate Everglades. The plane disintegrated. One hundred and one people had been killed because high-priced pilots fiddled with a 75-cent light bulb. Miraculously, 75 people survived.

*Themes:*  *Commitment, Discipleship, False leaders, Guidance, Leadership, Priorities, Tragedy.*

*Scriptures:*  Mark 13:22; 1 Corinthians 7:35; Galatians 6:9; 2 Peter 2:1; 1 John 4:1.

## 40 **EASTER**

During the days of Communism in Russia, Easter Sunrise Services were replaced by Sunrise Communist Rallies.

One such meeting was particularly large: 10,000 people were present. At the close of the meeting, the Communist leader asked if there was anything anybody wanted to say. Nobody moved. Eventually, a teenage boy came forward. As he stepped onto the platform and approached the podium, the leader warned the boy, "You must tell only the truth. If you do not you will be shot." The truth the Communist leader required was a denial of Christ and applause for Communism.

All eyes were fixed on the lad as he stood there about to speak. He was flanked by soldiers, rifles pointed at his head. For several brief moments he remained silent. Then, standing tall and taking a deep breath, he called into the microphone, "Christ is risen!"

At the same time that the crack of the rifles rang out, 10,000 voices filled the morning air: "Christ has risen indeed!"

*Themes:*  *Communism, Courage, Persecution, Resurrection, Suffering.*

*Scriptures:*  Psalms 27:14; Matthew 28:1–10; Mark 8:34–38; 16:6; Luke 24:1–12; John 20:1–8; Acts 7:54–8:1; 1 Corinthians 15:1–58.

---

40 Adapted from Dick Innes, "The Day that Changed the World", leaflet (Norwood, South Australia: ACTS, 1992).

## 41 ENCOURAGEMENT

Professor Margaret Kuhn is a research scientist working on the migratory habits of wild geese. These birds fly thousands of kilometres across whole continents in their migratory flights. Professor Kuhn discovered some interesting facts about the birds' ability to fly such long distances. One of these is that they rotate the leaders. Another factor is that they always choose the leaders – the up front birds – from the ones who can handle turbulence. And here is the important point. The other birds just honk along! This honking is not the agony of being out of breath. The birds behind the leader birds are honking encouragement to their leader.

*Themes:* *Barnabas, Humour, Leadership.*

**Scriptures:** Acts 11:22–26; 15:41; Romans 14:19; 1 Corinthians 10:23; Galatians 6:2; Ephesians 4:29; 1 Thessalonians 5:11.

## 42 ENCOURAGEMENT

Nicholas Young was not even a teenager when he joined Captain James Cook's boat *Endeavour* in 1768 as "the surgeon's boy".

On 26 August he was one of nearly a hundred men on the ship when it sailed quietly out of Plymouth Harbour. They were heading for Tahiti to observe the transit of Venus on 3 June the following year.

With that task completed Cook left Tahiti. He sailed south looking for the unknown continent. He found no sign of it. He gave up and turned west in search of New Zealand.

After much patience, by mid-September there were signs of land: seaweed floating by and one or two pieces of barnacle-covered wood and a seal asleep in the water (seals don't venture far from land). Expectations were rising.

To encourage the vigilance of his crew, Cook promised a gallon of rum to the first person to sight land, with the further promise that his name should be given to some part of the coast.

It was Saturday 7 October. The twelve-year-old Nicholas was up the mast in the gentle easterly breezes carrying the ship along. At 2:00 pm young Nick, as he was called, sighted land and gave the excited cry.

True to his promise, as a way of encouraging his crew, Cook named the south-west point of Poverty Bay, "Young Nick's Head".

**Themes:** *Barnabas, Leadership.*
**Scriptures:** Acts 11:22–26; 15:41; Romans 14:19; 1 Corinthians 10:23; Ephesians 4:29; 1 Thessalonians 5:11.

## 4 3 ENCOURAGEMENT *

Derek Redman represented England in the 1992 Barcelona Olympics. He provided one of the incredible moments in the track and field events. He had a life-long dream of a gold for the 400 metres.

In the semi-finals his dream was in sight. The starting gun went off. He began the race of his life. He rounded the turn into the backstretch.

Suddenly, his world came crashing down. He felt a sharp and searing pain go up the back of his leg. He slammed face first onto the track. He had torn his right hamstring.

As the medical attendants approached, Redman fought

43 Adapted from Wayne Rice, *Hot Illustrations for Youth Talks* (El Cajon, CA: Youth Specialities, 1994), pp. 93–94.

to his feet. Later he said it was animal instinct. He set out hopping in a crazed attempt to finish the race.

When he reached the home stretch, a large man in a T-shirt came out of the stands. The man hurled aside the security guard and ran to Redman. He embraced him. It was Jim Redman, Derek's father.

"You don't have to do this," he told his weeping son.

"Yes I do," said Derek.

"Well, then, we're going to finish this together."

And they did. They fought off security men. Sometimes Derek's head was buried in his father's shoulder. They stayed in Derek's lane all the way to the end. The crowd gaped, the crowd rose and howled and wept.

Derek didn't walk away with the gold medal. But he did walk away with the incredible memory of that expression of his father's love for him.

**Themes:** *Barnabas, Battle, Endurance, Fathers, Goals, God – with us, Incarnation, Love, Persistence, Vision.*

**Scriptures:** Exodus 3 – 4; Matthew 28:20; Acts 11:22–26; 15:41; Romans 14:19; 1 Corinthians 10:23; Ephesians 4:29; 1 Thessalonians 5:11.

## 44 ENCOURAGEMENT *

A young father had two daughters: one five and the other two. For several years he had taken his oldest girl out for a "date". Then it was the turn of the two-year-old.

One their first "date" he took her to breakfast at a fast-food restaurant. They had just sat down with their pancakes when he decided it would be a good time to tell her how much he loved and appreciated her.

"Jenny," he said, "I want you to know how much I love

---

44 Adapted from Gary Smalley and John Trent, "The Promises You Make to Worship and Fellowship", in Bill McCartney, (ed.), *What Makes a Man* (Colorado Springs, CO: Navpress, 1992), pp. 141–42.

you and how special you are to Mum and me. We prayed for you for years, and now that you're here and growing up to be such a wonderful girl, we couldn't be more proud of you."

Once he had said all this, he stopped talking and reached over for his fork to begin eating. But he never got the fork into his mouth.

Jenny reached out and laid her little hand on her father's. His eyes went to hers, and in a soft, pleading voice she said, "Longer, Daddy, longer."

He put his fork down and told her even more reasons why he and her mother loved her. "You're very kind, nice to your sister, full of energy... " Then, he again reached for his fork only to hear the same words again. A second time... and a third... and a fourth... Each time he heard the words, "Longer, Daddy, longer."

The father never did get much to eat that morning. But his words made such an impression on little Jenny that a few days later she spontaneously ran up to her mother, jumped in her arms, and said, "I'm a really awesome daughter, Mummy. Daddy told me so!"

*Themes:* Barnabas, Children, Fathers, Incarnation, Love, Parenting, Tongue.

**Scriptures:** Genesis 18:19; Exodus 3 – 4; Deuteronomy 5:16; 6:4–9; Matthew 28:20; Acts 11:22–26; 15:41; Romans 14:19; 1 Corinthians 10:23; Ephesians 4:29; 6:1, 4; Philippians 4:8; Colossians 3:5–17, 20–21; 1 Thessalonians 5:11; James 3:1–18.

## 45 ENCOURAGEMENT *

A teacher in New York decided to honour each of her seniors in high school by telling them the difference they each made. Using a process developed by Helice Bridges of Del Mar, California, she called each student to the front of the class, one at a time. First she told them how the student made a difference to her and the class. Then she presented each of them with a blue ribbon imprinted with gold letters which read, "Who I Am Makes a Difference".

Afterwards the teacher decided to do a class project to see what kind of impact recognition would have on a community. She gave each of the students three more ribbons and instructed them to go out and spread this acknowledgement ceremony. Then they were to follow up on the results, see who honoured whom, and report back to the class in about a week.

One of the boys in the class went to a junior executive in a nearby company and honoured him for helping him with his career planning. He gave him a blue ribbon and put it on his shirt. Then he gave him two extra ribbons, and said, "We're doing a class project on recognition, and we'd like you to go out, find somebody to honour, give them a blue ribbon, then give them the extra blue ribbon so they can acknowledge a third person to keep this acknowledgement ceremony going. Then, please report back to me and tell me what happened."

Later that day the junior executive went in to see his boss, who had been noted, by the way, as being kind of a grouchy fellow. He sat his boss down and told him that he deeply admired him for being a creative genius.

The boss seemed very surprised. The junior executive asked him if he would accept the gift of the blue ribbon and would he give him permission to put it on him. His surprised boss said, "Well, sure." The junior executive took the blue ribbon and placed it on his boss's jacket above his heart.

As he gave him the last extra ribbon, he said, "Would you do me a favour? Would you take this extra ribbon and pass it on by honouring somebody else? The young boy who first gave me the ribbons is doing a project in school and we want to keep this recognition ceremony going and find out how it affects people."

That night the boss came home to his fourteen-year-old son and sat him down. He said, "The most incredible thing happened to me today. I was in my office and one of the junior executives came in and told me he admired me and gave me a blue ribbon for being a creative genius. Imagine, he thinks I'm a creative genius. Then, on my jacket above my heart,  he put this blue ribbon that says, 'Who I Am Makes A Difference'. He gave me an extra ribbon and asked me to find somebody else to honour. As I was driving home tonight, I started thinking about whom I would honour with this ribbon and I thought about you. I want to honour you. My days are really hectic and when I come home I don't pay a lot of attention to you. Sometimes I scream at you for not getting good enough grades in school and for your bedroom being a mess, but somehow tonight, I just wanted to sit here and, well, just let you know that you do make a difference to me. Besides your mother, you are the most important person in my life. You're a great kid and I love you!"

The startled boy began to sob and sob, and he couldn't stop crying. His whole body shook. He looked up at his father and said through his tears, "I was planning on 'running away' tomorrow, Dad, because I didn't think you loved me. Now I don't need to."

*Themes:*  *Barnabas, Fathers, Incarnation, Love, Persistence, Tongue, Vision.*

**Scriptures:** Exodus 3 – 4; Matthew 28:20; Acts 11:22–26; 15:41; Romans 14:19; 1 Corinthians 10:23; Ephesians 4:29; Philippians 4:8; Colossians 3:5–17; 1 Thessalonians 5:11; James 3:1–18.

## 46 ENDURANCE

Shun Fujimoto is a gymnast and physical education teacher from Japan. He was 26 when he competed in the 1976 Summer Olympics' team gymnastics in Montreal. *Newsweek* carried this story.

> During his floor exercise, Fujimoto fractured his right leg. But with the Japanese in contention for a team gold medal, he refused to give up. Fitted with a plaster cast from hip to toe, he somehow competed in the ring exercises – and achieved the highest score of his life. He finished with a triple somersault and twist that doomed him to excruciating pain when he landed. But he executed it flawlessly and fearlessly and maintained his balance long enough to clinch the gold for his team – before his leg crumpled grotesquely beneath him.
>
> "It is beyond my comprehension," said an Olympic doctor who treated Fujimoto, "how he could land without collapsing in screams. What a man."
>
> "Yes, the pain shot through me like a knife," said Fujimoto. "It brought tears to my eyes. But now I have a gold medal, and the pain is gone."

**Themes:** *Courage, Future glory, Pain, Perseverance, Self-control, Sport, Suffering.*

**Scriptures:** Psalms 27:14; Luke 21:9–19; Romans 8:18; 1 Corinthians 9:24; 1 Timothy 2:9, 15; 3:2; 2 Timothy 1:7; 2:3; Titus 1:8; 2:1–6, 12; Hebrews 12:1.

## 47 EVANGELISM

In a meeting of pastors in Australia Ed Silvoso told the following story. The mayor of the city of Resistencia in Argentina invited Ed to his office. The mayor, a colonel in the army, had heard about Ed through his radio station

---

and Christian newspaper. He asked if Ed's organisation could help build water tanks for 21 neighbourhoods that had no running water. During the discussion the mayor brought in the engineer and the drawings. Eventually, as they were parting, Ed asked if he could pray for him. The big macho mayor said, "Sure, go for it!" So Ed prayed. The power of God came over him. He was so moved that tears came to the rim of his eyes.

The next day the mayor turned up unannounced at a pastors' luncheon. He said, "Silvoso, whatever I got yesterday, I love it and I came here for seconds." Ed invited him to sit down next to him and began to share the good news of Jesus with him. Then he said, "Can I pray for you?"

"*Please*! Go for it." Ed said he does not have this kind of gift, but he had to hold up the mayor as he prayed. He was ready to hit the floor.

Eventually, Ed's organisation finished erecting the first two water tanks. The mayor rang and asked if Ed could bless them.

"You provide the microphone and I will bring a Bible. That's all I need and I will bless the water tanks," Ed replied. In passing, Ed asked if a little plaque could be put by the tap on the tank. On the plaque he asked for the words from John's gospel where Jesus says, "Whoever drinks of this water shall thirst again, but if they drink of the water I give them, they will never thirst again."

On the day of the blessing, when the car was about 100 metres away the quotation could be read with ease. Rather than a plaque, the mayor had hired a professional painter. With the colours of the Argentine flag, the entire face of the water tank was covered with the Bible verse. The politicians and other officials made their speeches. At the end they said, "Okay Reverend, would you bless the water tank?" Ed stood up and said, "Would you turn with

me to the water tank and read?" And they all read from
the water tank. Ed spoke briefly on the text on the tank.
Then Ed gave an invitation and many people received
Christ, including the mayor.

**Themes:** *Conversion, Power encounter, Prayer, Preaching, Servant
evangelism, Witnessing.*

**Scriptures:** John 4:13–14; Acts 17:22–33; Romans 14:19; 1 Thessalonians
1:5.

## 48 EVANGELISM

In one of his conferences, Ed Silvoso told the story of
Olmos Prison in the city of La Plata, south-east of Buenos
Aires. A few years ago, this prison of 2,700 inmates,
Argentina's largest maximum security prison, was totally
out of control. There was not a single Christian on the
premises. There was male prostitution, extortion, murder
and rioting. Mafia bosses, drug dealers and gangsters had
the run of the place. There was so much evil that there was
even a church of Satan operating daily. There were animal
sacrifices on a weekly basis. Some people reported that
even demons materialised and walked around.

In the city nearby, a pastor committed a crime and was
sentenced to serve time in the gaol. The pastor repented
and cried out to God, "O God, would you give me a second
chance and fill me with your Holy Spirit?" The Lord forgave him and filled him with the Spirit. Now the pastor
had nothing to lose. He became a "spiritual kamikaze". He
began to drive himself into the church of Satan and into
the Mafia circles and among the gangsters to share the
good news of Jesus with tremendous boldness.

At the same time as this was happening, another pastor
applied for a job in the prison. But the place was so evil
that all three officials who interviewed him each told him

basically the same thing: "We don't want you here. We hate you, and if you get this job we will kill you." But he got the job.

Now, with one Christian in the cells and one Christian in the administration, they began to pray. One of the first things they prayed for was time on the prison radio. Eventually they got an hour and a half a week. That may not sound like much. But this radio station broadcasts to a captive audience. You cannot move the dial, you cannot turn down the volume, you cannot throw out the speakers. As these two men prayed, and as the gospel was pumped in, men came to the Lord.

Then persecution of the Christians began. However, the Christians discovered they could apply for protection under the constitution. The gaol has five storeys and is organised into cell blocks of 42 inmates each. The Christians said, "We need a cell block of our own so that all we Christians can be together." They were given the very worst cell block on the fourth floor. The church of Satan, the Mafia, the gangsters and the drug dealers lived there. Nevertheless, the Christians moved in and formed a church. They recognised a pastor and set aside elders. Then they divided themselves into seven teams of six men. One team was to be on duty each night from 11:00 pm to 5:00 am. Two read the Bible, two prayed, and the other two went from bed to bed, laying hands on their fellow inmates, and interceding before God to bless them and their relations on the outside. After two hours the pairs would switch roles. They did such an excellent job that, today, over 1,500 of the inmates are born-again Christians.

**Themes:** *Church growth, Demons, Elders, Evil, Forgiveness, Guidance, Holy Spirit – filled with, Intercession, Leadership, Persecution, Prayer, Prayer vigils, Principalities and powers, Spiritual warfare, Witnessing.*

**Scriptures:** Genesis 37:22–24; 39:19–23; 40:1–8; 42:16–19; 50:19–20; Exodus 18; Judges 16:21–25; 1 Kings 22:27; 2 Chronicles 16:10; 18:26; Isaiah 42:7; Jeremiah 32:2, 8, 12; 33:1; 37:16, 20, 21; 38:6, 13, 28; Acts 14:23; 16:23–40; 21:27 – 22:29; 28:30; Romans 8:28, 38; 1 Corinthians 15:24; 2 Corinthians 6:5; 11:23; Ephesians 1:20–21; 2:10; 3:8–10; 4:11–12; 6:20; Philippians 1:7, 13, 14, 16, 17; Colossians 2:9–10, 15; 4:3, 18; 2 Timothy 1:16; 2:9; Philemon 10, 13.

## 49 EVANGELISM

On Saturday morning, 21 April 1855, Edward Kimball decided to speak to one of his Sunday School pupils about becoming a Christian. The young man worked in a shoe factory and Kimball was, at first, unsure about calling on him during working hours. But he decided to go in and see him. He found him in the back of the factory wrapping up shoes in paper and stacking them on shelves. Kimball went up to the lad and put his hand on the lad's shoulder. There were tears in Kimball's eyes as he encouraged him to respond to Christ's love.

Kimball said that the young man was ready for the conversation so that, there and then, he gave himself and his life to Christ.

The lad decided that he would gather some derelict young people together. He asked a leading Church to send over some Sunday School teachers to tell the gathering about Christ. By his own efforts and hard work of inviting folk, he gathered 1,200 young people to come each week and hear the stories of Jesus.

His name was D. L. Moody, the great American evangelist of the nineteenth century, who eventually held cru-

---

49 From John Pollock, *Moody: The Biography* (Chicago: Moody Press, 1983), pp. 27, 39.

sades around the world. Because an ordinary Christian told a lad about Jesus, thousands ended up knowing about him.

*Themes:* D.L. Moody, Obedience, Witnessing.

**Scriptures:** Mark 6:7–13; Luke 10:1–20; John 1:35–51; 4:1–42; 14:15–24; Acts 1:8; 5:29; 10:1–48; 1 Peter 3:15.

## 50 EVANGELISM

Scene: 6:00 pm on the London Underground, Bakerloo Line. It is a hot Friday evening. The carriage is crowded with tired commuters. Those lucky enough to be sitting are doing their best not to catch the eyes of those standing.

I noticed a tall, impressive young man entering the train. As the doors closed and the train moved out towards Piccadilly Circus, he cleared his throat and started to speak.

"My friends, please listen to me for a few minutes. I am here to tell you Jesus loves you. If you do not follow Jesus you will go to hell. But Jesus loves you and asks you to follow him."

As he went on people studiously read their evening papers and fidgeted – anything but look at him. But he continued. He had clearly worked out the timing of his script, which ended just as the train pulled into Oxford Circus.

"Thank you my friends for listening. Remember, Jesus loves you, and I love you too."

He left the carriage without looking back. But the passengers had been surprised out of their Friday evening apathy. Some laughed. Quite a few applauded. And then people began to talk to one another.

50 Deirdre Martin, "Preaching to a Captive Audience", *Church of England Newspaper* (London, 12 June 1992), p. 13.

*Themes:* Courage, Preaching, Witnessing.

**Scriptures:** Psalms 27:14; Mark 6:7–13; Luke 10:1–20; John 1:35–51; 4:1–42; Acts 1:8; 8:26–40; 17:22–34; 1 Peter 3:15.

## 51 EVANGELISM *

The preacher John Harper and his much-beloved six-year-old daughter, Nana, were on board the RMS *Titanic* on the fateful night of 14 April 1912.

At 11:40 pm, an iceberg scraped the ship's starboard side, showering the decks with ice and ripping open six watertight compartments.

As soon as it was apparent that the ship was going to sink, Harper took his daughter to a lifeboat. He bent down and kissed his precious little girl; looking into her eyes he told her that she would see him some day.

As the rear of the huge ship began to lurch upwards, Harper was seen making his way up the deck yelling, "Women, children, and unsaved into the lifeboats!" Many people jumped off the decks and into the icy, dark waters below. Harper was one of them.

He was seen swimming frantically to people in the water, leading them to Jesus before the hypothermia became fatal. He swam to one young man who had climbed up on a piece of debris. Harper asked him between breaths, "Are you saved?" The young man replied that he was not. Harper then tried to lead him to Christ, only to have the young man, who was near shock, reply "No!" Harper then took off his life jacket and said, "Here then, you need this more than I do." And he swam away to other people. A few minutes later Harper swam back to the young man and succeeded in leading him to salvation.

Of the 1,528 people who went into the water that night, six were rescued by the lifeboats. One of them was the young man on the debris.

Four years later, at a survivors' meeting, the young man stood up and in tears recounted how, after John Harper had led him to Christ, Harper had tried to swim back to help other people, yet because of the intense cold had grown too weak to swim. His last words before going under in the frigid waters were, "Believe on the name of the Lord Jesus and you will be saved."

*Themes:* *Lost, Love, Personal evangelism, Salvation, Witnessing.*

**Scriptures:** Mark 6:7–13; Luke 10:1–20, 27; John 1:35–51; 4:1–42; Acts 1:8; 8:26–40, 16:31; 17:22–34; 1 Corinthians 1:18–29; 13; 1 Peter 3:15.

## 52 EVANGELISM

An evangelist in Central America was at a university trying to win students to Christ. They showed him a great deal of hostility. After a particular meeting a girl, who was working on her doctorate, came to him and said, "I don't believe any of that hogwash."

He said, "Well, I don't think I agree; but do you mind if I pray for you?"

She said, "No one ever prayed for me before. I don't guess it will do any harm."

He bowed his head, but she looked straight ahead and was defiant when he started to pray. As he prayed for the conversion of that girl, the tears began to flow down his cheeks. When he opened his eyes, she was broken up with tears and said, "No one in my whole life has loved me enough to shed a tear for me."

They sat down on a bench, and she accepted the Lord as her Saviour.

---

52 Adapted from Billy Graham, "The Evangelist and His Preaching: We Set Forth the Truth Plainly", in J. D. Douglas (ed.), *The Work of an Evangelist* (Minneapolis: World Wide, 1984), p. 99.

**Themes:** *Compassion, Conversion, Love, Opposition, Personal evangelism, Prayer, Witnessing.*

**Scriptures:** Mark 6:7–13; Luke 10:1–20, 27; John 1:35–51; 4:1–42; Acts 1:8; 8:26–40; 17:22–34; 1 Corinthians 1:18–29; 13; 1 Peter 3:15.

## 53 EVANGELISM

In Algeria a woman Christian worker, who spoke Arabic well, would often engage a certain man in conversation about the divinity of Jesus, his mission to save us and our need to submit to him.

One particular day, after a lively dialogue, the woman was unable to respond further to his arguments. Smiling, he seemed pleased to think that no one could persuade him to accept Christ. Then, quietly, the woman began to cry.

Concerned, he asked, "Aren't you well? What is the matter?"

"Nothing," she replied. "It's because of your reluctance to recognise God's love for you."

He was deeply moved by her reaction. After a moment of silence he said, "A religion which moves someone to tears over someone else's spiritual welfare must be authentic." He was converted.

**Themes:** *Compassion, Conversion, Empathy, Love, Personal evangelism, Witnessing.*

**Scriptures:** Mark 6:7–13; Luke 10:1–20, 27; John 1:35–51; 4:1–42; Acts 1:8; 8:26–40; 17:22–34; 1 Corinthians 1:18–29; 13; 1 Peter 3:15.

## 54 EVANGELISM – URGENCY

Hudson Taylor was one of the greatest missionaries of modern times. He spent much of his life in China, introducing people to Jesus.

Once he was travelling by a small boat from Shanghai to Ningpo. In his cabin, Taylor was preparing to go ashore.

He was startled by a sudden splash and a cry. Springing quickly up on deck he discovered that Peter, a Chinese friend, had fallen overboard. Taylor begged some men with a dragnet to pull in the drowning man. They refused because it was not, as they said, convenient. He offered them $5 to stop fishing and try to save Peter. They said they would do it for no less than $30. Taylor only had $14 – which they eventually accepted.

But it was too late. Even though Peter was brought on deck with the first sweep of the net, all attempts to revive him failed. Taylor's comment on this sad event is interesting.

"We condemn those heathen fishermen. We say they were guilty of a man's death because they could easily have saved him, and did not do it. But what of the millions whom we leave to perish, and that eternally?"

*Themes: Love for others, Life – price of, Mission – urgency, Missionary work, Missionaries, Salvation, Tragedy.*

*Scriptures:* Psalms 91; 118:5–6; Matthew 9:37 – 10:15; 28:16–20; Mark 6:7–13; Luke 8:22–25; 10:27; Acts 1:8; 1 Corinthians 13.

## 55 EVANGELISM – POWER

John Wimber says that it was at the end of a long day of ministry. He was exhausted and was looking forward to relaxing on the plane journey home. Shortly after take-off he pushed back the seat. As he glanced around he saw something that startled him. Across the aisle was a middle-aged businessman. What Wimber could see written across his face was the word "adultery". He blinked and rubbed his eyes. He was still seeing the word "adultery". It was not with his natural eyes but in his mind's eye that he

---

54 Adapted from Dr and Mrs Howard Taylor, *Biography of James Hudson Taylor* (London: Hodder and Stoughton, 1973).

could see the word. By now the man had become aware that John was looking at him.

"What do you want?" he snapped. As the man spoke, a woman's name came clearly to John's mind.

Somewhat nervously, John leaned across the aisle and asked, "Does the name Jane [not her real name] mean anything to you?"

The poor fellow's face turned ashen. "We've got to talk," he stammered.

They went off to the upstairs lounge of the plane. As John followed him up the stairs he sensed the Spirit speaking to him again. "Tell him if he doesn't turn from his adultery, I'm going to take him." Terrific! All John wanted was a nice quiet plane ride. But, here was John sitting in an aeroplane cocktail lounge with a man he had never seen before, whose name he didn't even know, about to tell him God was going to take his life if he didn't stop his affair with some woman.

They sat down in strained silence. The man looked at John suspiciously for a moment. Then he asked, "Who told you that name?"

"God told me," John blurted out. He was too rattled to think of a better way to put it.

"*God* told you?" he almost shouted back.

"Yes. He also told me to tell you... that unless you turn from this adulterous relationship, he is going to take your life."

John braced himself for the angry defence. But instead the man crumbled and his heart melted. In a choked desperate voice he asked John, "What should I do?"

John explained what it meant to repent or turn away from what is wrong in our lives and to trust Christ with our lives. Then John began to lead the man in a quiet prayer. But the man exploded.

Bursting into tears he cried out, "O *God*, I'm so *sorry...*" And the man launched into the most heart-rending repentance John had ever heard.

It was impossible to hide what was happening. Before long everyone in the tiny cocktail lounge was intimately acquainted with this man's past and now with his contrition. Even the stewardess was weeping along with him.

When things had calmed down the man explained why he was so upset by the mention of the name Jane. His wife was sitting right next to him.

And then John said, "You're going to have to tell her."

"I am? When?" he responded weakly.

"Better do it right now," was John's suggestion.

So off they went downstairs. John couldn't hear the conversation over the noise of the plane. But he could see the stunned look on the wife's face. Her eyes were wide. She stared first at her husband and then at John and then back again. In the end the man led his wife to Christ, there and then.

The plane landed and there was little time to talk. They didn't have a Bible. John gave them his and they went their separate ways.

*Themes:* *Adultery, Confession, Conversion, Forgiveness, Gift – of knowledge, Guilt, Knowledge – gift of, Repentance, Sin, Witnessing.*

**Scriptures:** Exodus 20:14; 32:14; Numbers 5:5–7; Deuteronomy 5:18; 22:22–24; 32:36; 1 Kings 8:33–34; 1 Chronicles 21:16; 2 Chronicles 7:14; Nehemiah 1:6; 9:2, 17; Psalms 32:5; 51; 106:45; 135:14; Proverbs 28:13; Jeremiah 18:8; 26:3, 13, 19; 42:10; Daniel 9:9, 20; Joel 2:13–14; Jonah 4:2; Matthew 3:6; 18:21–35; Mark 1:15; 2:1–12; 10:11; 11:25; Luke 3:7–14; John 8:1–11, 31–36; Acts 2:38; 17:30; 19:18; 26:20; Romans 3:23; 6:23; 12:6; 13:9; 1 Corinthians 12:10; Galatians 5:19; Ephesians 4:32; Colossians 2:13; Hebrews 1; James 2:11; 5:16; 1 John 1:9; 2:12.

## 56 EVANGELISM – PRESENCE

A Christian went to China and saw the pastor of a fast-growing Baptist church. The man from the west asked how he went about evangelism. The answer was a surprise. The Chinese Christian said this quite naturally, "I don't do much searching out of people. They come to me!" The reason became obvious. During the Cultural Revolution (1966–68) this man had been conscripted to work in a soul-destroying factory. He was making parts for radios. He was not allowed to speak about Christ at all. But he whistled while he worked. That was significant for nobody else in that factory could summon up the joy to whistle.

When the days of the Cultural Revolution were over, the man returned to his work as a pastor. Now there was a steady trickle of people from the factory knocking at his office door. They wanted to find out what was the secret of his joy. If it could carry him serenely through such unpleasant circumstances, it must be worth hearing about.

**Themes:** *Fruit of the Spirit, Joy, Persecution, Suffering, Witnessing, Work.*
**Scriptures:** Nehemiah 8:10; Matthew 25:14–30; Luke 2:10; 6:20–22; 19:11–27; John 17:13; Acts 2:46; 27:22, 25; Romans 12:11; 13:13; 1 Corinthians 4:2; 2 Corinthians 4:7–18; 6:4–10, 11:23–28; Galatians 4:18; 5:22; 6:9; Ephesians 4:28; 6:5–9; Colossians 1:10; 3:23–4; 1 Thessalonians 4:11; 1 Timothy 4:12; Titus 2:14; James 1:25; 1 Peter 3:14; 4:13–14; 1 John 1:4; Revelation 22:14.

## 57 EVIL

Up until 1973, London's fruit and vegetable market occupied the square at Covent Garden. In times past they used to sell caged nightingales. Nightingales were known for their beautiful song. Sadly, the birds were captured and blinded by inserting hot needles into their eyes. Because nightingales sing in the dark, a liquid song bubbled almost endlessly from the caged and blinded birds. People had enslaved and blinded the birds to gratify their own desires. More than this, the birds had been enslaved in such a way they could never enjoy freedom. No one could set them free.

**Themes:** *Blindness, Eschatology, Freedom, Joy, Slavery, Suffering.*

**Scriptures:** Nehemiah 8:10; Job; Isaiah 61:1; Luke 2:10; 4:18; 6:20–22; John 17:13; Acts 2:46; 27:22, 25; Romans 1:1; 8:21; 1 Corinthians 7:22; 9:19, 22–23; 2 Corinthians 3:17; Galatians 3:24; 5:1, 22; James 1:2–4, 25; 1 Peter 2:16; 3:14; 4:13–14; 1 John 1:4; Revelation 22:14.

## 58 EVIL – PROBLEM OF

Elie Wiesel was a survivor of Auschwitz. "One day," he says, "when we came back from work, we saw three gallows in the assembly place. There were SS all round us, and machine guns were trained. There were three victims including a child in chains. All eyes were on the child. He was lividly pale, almost calm, biting his lips. The three victims mounted the chairs together. The three necks were placed at the same moment within the nooses.

'Long live liberty!' cried the two adults.

But the child was silent.

'Where is God? Where is he?' someone behind me asked.

At a sign from the head of the camp, the three chairs tipped over. Total silence throughout the camp. On the horizon the sun was setting.

'Bare your heads!' yelled the head of the camp. His voice was raucous. We were weeping.

'Cover your heads!'

58 Adapted from Kenneth Surin, *Theology and the Problem of Evil* (Oxford: Blackwell, 1986), p. 116.

Then the march past began. The two adults were no longer alive. Their tongues hung swollen, blue-tinged. But the third rope was still moving; being so light, the child was still alive... For more than half an hour he stayed there struggling between life and death, dying in slow agony under our eyes. And we had to look him full in the face. He was still alive when I passed in front of him. His tongue was still red, his eyes were not yet glazed. Behind me, I heard the same man asking:

'Where is God now?'

And I heard a voice within me answer him:

'Where is he? Here he is – he is hanging here on this gallows...'"

*Themes:* *Cross, Crucifixion, Holocaust, Incarnation, Suffering.*
**Scriptures:** Job; Mark 15:21–39; Romans 5:6–11; 1 Corinthians 15:3; 2 Corinthians 5:14; 1 Peter 3:18.

## 59 **EVIL – PROBLEM OF**

The Salvation Army preacher Commander Booth-Tucker was in Chicago trying to lead a sceptic to Christ. With a cold, glittering eye and a sarcastic voice the man said, "It is all very well. You mean well, but I lost my faith in God when my wife was taken out of my home. It is all very well; but if that beautiful woman at your side lay dead and cold by you, how would you believe in God?"

Within one month Mrs Booth-Tucker was killed in a terrible train accident. The Commander went back to Chicago, and in the hearing of a large crowd of people said, "Here in the midst of the crowd, standing by the side of my dead wife as I take her to burial, I want to say that I still believe in God, and love him, and know him."

59 Adapted from Aquilla Webb, *1001 Illustrations for Pulpit and Platform* (New York and London: Harper & Brothers, 1926), #123.

*Themes:* *Faith, God – belief in, God – love for, Grief, Suffering, Testing,*
*Tragedy, Witnessing.*

*Scriptures:* Job; Psalms 91; 118:5–6; Matthew 5:4; Mark 11:22–24; Luke
7:1–10; 8:22–25; 10:27; 1 Corinthians 13; 2 Corinthians 1:3–11; James
1:2.

## 60 EXAMINATIONS

A student was to sit for his final exams in logic. He was
doing philosophy at college. The exam was particularly
difficult. It was not an open book exam but the lecturer
had said they could bring as much information into the
exam room as they could fit on an A4 sheet of paper.

On the day of the examination students came with their
crammed pieces of paper. But one student came with a
completely blank sheet of paper. Seating himself for the
examination, the student put his piece of paper on the
floor. He had also brought with him a friend who was an
advanced student in logic. He got his friend to stand on
the piece of paper. The advanced student told him all he
needed to know for the exam. He was the only student to
receive an "A".

*Themes:* *College, Gifts, Grace, Humour, Students, Works of the law.*
*Scriptures:* Romans 3:19–31; Galatians 2:16; Ephesians 2:1–10; Titus
3:1–11.

## 61 EXORCISM

A 32-year-old, twice-married woman was brought in
because of falling "spells" which had been treated with all
kinds of anticonvulsant medication. She was examined by
the neurosurgical service and, after all examinations,
including EEG, brain scan, and pneumoencephalogram

---

61  William P. Wilson, "Hysteria and Demons, Depression and Oppression, Good and Evil",
in John W. Montogmery (ed.), *Demon Possession* (Minneapolis: Bethel House, 1976), pp.
225–26, his emphasis.

were negative, she was transferred to the psychiatric service. Her mental status examination was unremarkable and all of the staff commented that she seemed normal until she had her first "spell".

While standing at the door of the day room she was violently thrown to the floor, bruising her arm severely. She was picked up and carried to her room, all the while resisting violently. Eight persons restrained her as she thrashed about on the bed. *Her facial expression was one of anger and hate.* Sedation resulted in sleep. During the ensuing weeks the patient was treated psychotherapeutically and it was learned that there had been considerable turmoil in her childhood home, but because she was "pretty" she was spoiled. She married the type of individual described by Jackson Smith as the first husband of a hysterical female. She was a "high liver" and, after her separation and divorce, she was threatened with rejection by her parents. She remarried and her second husband was a "nice" but unexciting man. She continued to associate with her "high living" friends. When her husband demanded that she give up her friends and her parties, she started having her "spells".

The usual psychotherapeutic treatment for hysteria including interviews under sodium amytol only aggravated her spells. Seclusion in the closed section brought her assaultive and combative behaviour to an end but she would have spells in which she became mute, especially when religious matters were discussed. More dramatically, when the names of Jesus or Christ were mentioned she would immediately go into a trance. On one occasion, while in a coma, in desperation, a demon was exorcised and her spells ceased. She subsequently accepted Christ as her saviour and has been well ever since.

**Themes:** *Conversion, Deliverance, Demonic, Demons, Evil spirits, God –
power of, Healing, Jesus – name of, Medicine, Psychiatry, Satan, Spirits,
Suffering.*

**Scriptures:** Psalms 34; 91; Mark 1:21–28; 5:1–20; 7:24–30; 9:14–29; Acts
16:16–18; 19:11–20.

## 62 EXORCISM

One day John Tunstall, a minister, received an emergency
phone call from a woman in his new church. The woman
was in a panic and John could hear strange voices in the
background. When he arrived at her house, the woman
was slouched in a chair staring at him. In a masculine
voice she said, "You are the man of God? I have been waiting for you. Show me your power!"

John had come to expect that God could work powerfully. So he snapped back at the spirit, "Show me your
power!"

Instantly, a flowerpot on a shelf exploded into pieces
with a loud noise. But John was ready for it. He said, "My
power is the blood of the Lord Jesus Christ. In Jesus' name
I command you to leave that woman." The evil spirit
struggled. The woman slithered onto the floor like a
snake, then writhed around. But the power of Jesus pre-
vailed, the demon left, and the woman was completely
well.

**Themes:** *Deliverance, Demonic, Demons, Evil spirits, God – his power,
Healing, Jesus – name of, Spirits, Suffering.*

**Scriptures:** Psalms 34; 91; Mark 1:21–28; 5:1–20; 7:24–30; 9:14–29; Acts
16:16–18; 19:11–20.

## 63 **FAITH**

A small plane was flying near Cleveland, Ohio.

"Cleveland Centre, this is 346 Alpha Charley. I'm at 10,500. I'm in the clouds... not instrument rated. Would like radar vectors. Out."

"Six Alpha Charley, Cleveland. Roger. Understand you are not instrument rated. Set transponder code 4582 for radar identification. What is your heading now, sir?"

"Six Alpha Charley is heading 250 degrees. Say again code. It's rough. I'm getting disorientated... I can't see the ground!"

"Six Alpha Charley, Cleveland. Set code 4582. Concentrate on your altitude indicator, sir. Keep wings level and reduce power to start slow descent. We have you on radar contact."

"I'm losing control... losing it... turning... I'm going to spin!... I'm spinning!... which way!! Help! Help!"

"Six Alpha Charley, release your controls, sir! Look at your attitude indicator. Opposite rudder, opposite rudder... "

"Help! Help! I can't stop... "

"Six Alpha Charley, Six Alpha Charley, do you read?" (Silence)

"Radar contact is lost."

The above was based on a recorded conversation between a control tower and a small plane which crashed, killing the pilot. The investigation of this crash revealed that nothing was wrong with the flight instruments in N346 Alpha Charley.

*Themes: Belief, Fear, God – in control, Guidance, Obedience, Trust.*

---

63 Adapted from Loren Cunningham, *Daring to Live on the Edge* (Seattle: YWAM, 1991), pp. 68–69.

**Scriptures:** Exodus 13:21–22; Deuteronomy 31:6, 8; Psalms 23:4; 25:9; 32:8; 34:4; 37:3–5; 48:14; 66:12; 138:7; Proverbs 3:5–6; Isaiah 43:2; Daniel 3:25, 28; Matthew 10:28; Mark 11:22–24; Luke 7:1–10; 12:5; John 20:24–29; 2 Timothy 1:7; Hebrews 11:1–3; 13:5–6.

## 64 FAITH

In 1859 Charles Blondin, the French acrobat, walked across a tightrope suspended across Niagara Falls.

One day, thousands watched him as he pushed a bag of cement in a wheelbarrow along the wire, 50 metres above the raging waters. There was a great cheer when he reached the other side.

Then Blondin challenged a nearby reporter: "Do you believe I can do anything on a tightrope?"

"Oh yes, Mr. Blondin," said the reporter. "After what I've seen today, I believe it. You can do anything." However, the reporter melted into the crowd when he was invited to put his trust to the test and get in the wheelbarrow.

But there was a person there who did trust Blondin with his life. He got into the wheelbarrow and was pushed across the wire. As Blondin made his way high above the falls, people quickly placed bets on the outcome. It looked like any other easy conquest. But, when they were halfway across the 500-metre journey of trust, a man with a heavy bet against Blondin's success crept across and cut one of the guy ropes.

Suddenly, the tightrope pitched crazily back and forth. Blondin fought for his balance, only seconds away from death. For, when the rim of the wheelbarrow came off the wire, they could both be pitched into the churning water. Blondin spoke, cutting through the terror of his passenger. "Stand up!" he ordered. "Stand up and grab my shoulders."

64 Adapted from Loren Cunningham, *Daring to Live on the Edge* (Seattle: YWAM, 1991), p. 191.

The man sat there paralysed.

"Let go and stand up! Let go of the wheelbarrow! Do it or die!"

Somehow the man managed to stand up and step out of the swaying wheelbarrow.

"Your arms... put them round my neck! Now, your legs... round my waist!" said Blondin.

Again the man obeyed, clinging to Blondin. The wheelbarrow fell, disappearing into the frothy turmoil far below. The aerialist stood there, using all his years of experience and every trained muscle to stay on the wire until the pitching subsided a little. Then, inch by inch, he made his way across, carrying the man like a child. Finally, he deposited him safely on the other side.

**Themes:** *Belief, Courage, Fear, God – in control, Guidance, Obedience, Trust.*

**Scriptures:** 2 Kings 18:5, 19–25; Psalms 2:12; 7:1; 9:10; 13:4–5; 16:1; 25:2, 20; 27:14; 31:1; 32:8; 34:4; 37:3–5; 38:15–16; 44:4–8; 56; 62; 73:28; 84:8–12; 91; 94:16–23; 112; 115:9–11; 146:3; Proverbs 3:5–6, 21–27; 4:10–19; 11:28; 28:26–28; 29:25; Isaiah 12:2; 26:3–4; 36:1–10; 63:10–14; Jeremiah 17:7–8; Matthew 10:28; Mark 11:22–24; Luke 7:1–10; 12:5; John 20:24–29; 1 Timothy 4:10; 5:5; 2 Timothy 1:7; Hebrews 11:1–3; 13:5–6.

## 65 FAITH

Sarah is now 17. When she was thirteen she got something like the flu. But then her eyesight began to degenerate. Her memory started to go. Tests were done at the hospital. But they could find nothing wrong.

As the months passed, Sarah lost more and more muscle control as well as mental ability. At the beginning of 1994 she was transferred to a special hospital for chronic care.

On 27 February 1994, Sarah's friend Rachel went to

church. She was prayed for in the ministry time. She had a vision and sensed God saying that she needed to go to the hospital to pray for Sarah.

The next day, Rachel and her dad went to the hospital to pray for Sarah. Sarah was in a special wheelchair that looked more like a bed. Saliva was dribbling out of her mouth. She could hear voices but could not see or comprehend what was going on. Rachel and Simon wheeled Sarah to a quiet spot in the hospital.

They began to pray for her. As they prayed over the next two-and-a-half hours, Sarah began to cry and then to shake. Her sight began to come back. Her legs started to move. Slowly she began to sit up on her own. The dribbling stopped. Eventually she was able to say, "I'm getting stronger."

Before coming into the hospital Rachel was so convinced Jesus was going to heal Sarah that she had brought some crisps for her to eat. Over the next few days, Sarah began walking and eating those crisps. Her sight began to improve. News of what was happening spread quickly through the hospital.

On 22 April 1994, Sarah returned home from the chronic care hospital.

**Themes:** *Gift – of knowledge, Guidance, Healing, Knowledge – gift of, Miracles, Prayer, Trust, Visions.*

**Scriptures:** Deuteronomy 32:20; Psalms 18:2; 26:1; 37:3–6; Proverbs 3:5; Mark 2:1–12; 5:21–43, 36; 9:14–29; 10:45–52; 11:20–24; Luke 17:6; John 4:48; 5:1–9; 10:38; 20:30–31; Acts 4:30; 14:9; 1 Corinthians 12:8, 9, 28, 30; 13:2, 8; 14:6, 30; Hebrews 2:4.

## 66 FAITHFULNESS

During the conflict with the Koreans, Communist soldiers moved into a peaceful village. One day the soldiers made all the people gather in the church. The soldiers jerked a picture of Christ from the wall and ordered each person to come to the front and spit on the picture. The first man to walk down the aisle was a deacon. He looked at the picture for a few seconds, quickly spat, and walked to one side. Three others did the same. The fifth person to walk forward was a young teenage girl. She looked at the picture of Christ and then bent down and wiped the spit off with her skirt. She hugged the picture of Jesus to her heart and said, "Shoot me, I am ready to die." The soldiers couldn't shoot. They ordered everyone to get out. The people overheard the Communist soldiers say to the girl, "You are not fit to live. If you had a chance to renounce Communism, you would do the same thing." Shortly after the people heard four shots. Because of the strong faith of one girl, the rest of the village was saved.

*Themes:* *Martyrs, Persecution, Sacrifice, Substitution, Suffering.*

**Scriptures:** Daniel 3:16–18; Matthew 25:14–30; Mark 8:34–38; 11:22–24; Luke 7:1–10; Acts 4:1–22; 6:8 – 8:3; 7:54 – 8:8; 9:23–25; 14:5–6, 19; 16:19–24; 21:30–36; 1 Corinthians 4:11–13; 13:3; 2 Corinthians 6:4–5; 11:23–28; 1 Thessalonians 2:9; 2 Thessalonians 3:8.

## 67 FAITHFULNESS

A minister and two girls were sentenced to death by the Chinese Communists. The minister was promised release if he would shoot the girls. He accepted. On the day of the execution in the courtyard the girls whispered to each

---

66 Adapted from Billy Kim, "God at Work in Times of Persecution (Acts 7:54 – 8:8)", in J. D. Douglas (ed.), *Let the Earth Hear His Voice* (Minneapolis: World Wide, 1975), p. 58.

67 David Watson, *I Believe in the Church* (London: Hodder and Stoughton, 1978), p. 137.

other, then bowed respectfully before the minister. One of them said:

> Before being shot by you, we wish to thank you heartily for what you have meant to us. You baptised us, you taught us the way of eternal life, you gave us Holy Communion with the same hand in which you now have the gun. May God reward you for all the good you have done us. You also taught us that Christians are sometimes weak and commit terrible sins, but they can be forgiven again. When you regret what you are about to do to us, do not despair like Judas, but repent like Peter. God bless you, and remember that our last thought was not one of indignation against your failure. Everyone passes through hours of darkness. We die with gratitude.

The minister then shot the girls. Afterwards he was shot by the Communists.

***Themes:*** *Betrayal, Forgiveness, Judas Iscariot, Enemies – love for, Martyrdom, Persecution, Revenge, Suffering.*

**Scriptures:** Matthew 5:43–48; 25:14–30; 27:3–10; Mark 8:34–38; 11:22–25; 14:10–11, 43–50; Luke 7:1–10; Acts 7:54 – 8:8; Romans 12:12, 14; Galatians 6:2, 9.

## 68 FAMILY

Diane's father was a well-respected lawyer in the community. But he was a terror to live with. Verbally and sometimes physically abusive, he was always critical and unreachable.

When she was nine, her mother caught her father in the midst of an affair. In a fit of anger, she threatened to expose her husband and ruin his reputation in their small town. But like a wounded lion he turned on her and suc-

---

68 Adapted from Gary Smalley with John Trent, *Love is a Decision* (Milton Keynes: Word, 1989), pp. 189–190.

cessfully sued her for divorce first. He thoroughly slandered her name in the process.

Their "soap opera" courtroom theatrics became so bad that other parents forbade their children to play with or even talk to Diane or her older brother at school. Then, one day, circumstances turned from bad to far worse. When Diane and her brother came home from school, the removal firm were in the house packing all their things and getting ready to cart them away. Their father had won the divorce decree and had even obtained a court order evicting his former wife from the house.

As the mother wept, Diane's older brother became furious. He stormed into the house and up to his father's room, grabbing a gun he knew his father always hid in his bedside drawer. When he came out of the house, his grandmother was walking up to the porch and saw him with the gun. In a burst of anger he told her he was on the way to kill his father. She grabbed at him, trying to wrestle the gun away. But, in the struggle, the gun went off. In a terrible accident Diane's brother had killed his own grandmother.

Tragedy would follow tragedy that day. When the police came to the house they tracked down the boy, who was hiding in a neighbour's garage. A gun battle broke out. An officer was critically wounded and Diane's brother was killed.

Only nine years old, Diane had lived through the trauma of her parent's hostile divorce. She had lost her grandmother and brother in a single day. There was nothing good about what happened to Diane or her family. The pain caused by her father and brother will always be with her. What a terrible marriage partner she would make with such a background.

Yet, she says, "It has taken many years, but I can actually say that God has used my terrible childhood to make me a much better person, especially with my own family. I have had to work through a lot, but I know God has made me a more loving wife and mother because of what I have been through."

*Themes: Adultery, Anger, Divorce, Families, Healing – inner, Marriage, Murder, Parenting, Trauma, Violence – domestic.*

**Scriptures:** Deuteronomy 6:20–25; Psalms 91; 118:5–6; Matthew 5:21–26; Mark 10:2–12; Luke 8:22–25; Romans 12:10, 16, 17–18; 2 Corinthians 1:3–7; Ephesians 6:1–4; Colossians 3:18–21.

## 69 FAMILIES

A 32-year-old woman rang a Christian psychiatrist's office. When she was told that she could not be seen for two months she began to scream and cry. The secretary handed the phone to the psychiatrist. The woman said she did not think she could survive any longer as she was. It turned out she could be seen. At the appointment the woman said that she was raised in a religious home. But her mother had used love-withdrawal as a way of disciplining her. Mum would refuse to speak to her and turn her back on her for up to two weeks at a time.

To get away from the verbal abuse of this so-called "Christian" mother, she married in her second year at college. Her husband was a successful man. But he was also a bore, as she put it. After their first child she had an affair. The same thing happened after the second child. A few months later she moved in with another man. Then she began dating a biker. He introduced her to shop lifting, drugs and Satan worship. At this very first visit the psychiatrist introduced her to Christ. After accepting Christ, the woman announced, "I'm free, I feel as though a burden has been lifted."

She went home and within a few days again felt

oppressed. But then she burnt her books on witchcraft and Satan and was relieved. She then planned to return to her husband.

*Themes:* *Abuse, Children, Conversion, Discipline, Healing – inner, Love, Parenting, Religion.*

**Scriptures:** Deuteronomy 6:20–25; Matthew 5:21–26; Acts 19:11–20; Romans 12:10, 16–18; Ephesians 6:1–4; Colossians 3:18–21.

## 70 FATHERS

Phillip Adams is an Australian journalist and radio announcer. There was a day in his school life that sums up what he knows about fathers.

To the outside world his dad was all charm and decency; to him and his mum he was nothing but a sadist. His parents' marriage flew apart and he ended up with a stepdad.

Phillip says that the most horrific day of his childhood was when he set out to see his dad and meet his new wife. She was supposed to look like a film star. But, just before Phillip left home for the railway station, there was a huge fight between his mum and his stepfather. He knocked his stepfather over to save his mum. In fact he sent him flying across the room, pounding into the venetian blinds and leaving them buckled forever.

Phillip ran from the house in fear. His stepdad charged after him in his big black car and tried to run him down. He only saved himself by hurling himself into the grass by the side of the road and hiding until he went away. However, to his horror, at the next train station on the way to his dad's, there was that lunatic face in the window and his hand on the door. It was peak period and it seemed as if there were thousands of people milling around watching. He dragged Phillip out of the carriage,

70 Adapted from Terry Lane, *As The Twig is Bent* (Melbourne: Dove, 1979), pp. 105–110.

threw out his suitcase, scattered everything, screamed to everyone that Phillip was a thief. Then he switched, with his usual skill, to being sweetly reasonable. He apologised to the crowd, which was becoming a bit menacing. He got a bit tearful; said that he would take Phillip to his father in the car. The train had long gone. Phillip begged people not to let him put him in the car. But into the car he went. As they were going past a police station Phillip flung himself out of the car.

Somehow Phillip got to his father's that night. His "film star" stepmother turned out to be more like the witch from *The Wizard of Oz*.

He will never forget walking down the path to the little house his father had. Through the window he could see this extraordinary woman trying to stab his dad with a pair of scissors. His father was screaming in terror like a stuck pig. As he ran out of the door in horror Phillip ran in and knocked her unconscious. That was his first meeting with his stepmother. He and his father went and sat in the car. He remembers shaking and crying, with the accumulated horror of the day. That day summed up Phillip's experience of a father.

*Themes:* *Adultery, Anger, Divorce, Families, Family relationships, Marriage, Murder, Parenting, Trauma, Violence – domestic.*

**Scriptures:** Deuteronomy 6:20–25; Matthew 5:21–32; Mark 10:2–12; Romans 12:10, 16, 17–18; Ephesians 6:1–4; Colossians 3:18–21.

## 7 1 **FATHERS**

A father was waiting for his son to go to gaol. A friend said to the man, "I hear that lad of yours has been in trouble again."

"I am afraid he has," said the father.

"Ah!" said the other fellow, "I know it is not the first

time by any means. I know all you've tried to do for him in the past. But I gather the offence is worse than ever this time. Do you know what I would do if he was my son? I'd put him smartly out the door, shut it, and then turn the key once and for all."

"Aye," said the father, "do you know, if he were a lad of yours I would do exactly the same thing. But you see, he is my son and I will not."

*Themes: Acceptance, Children, Families, Forgiveness, Love, Parable – Prodigal Son, Parenting, Prison, Rejection, Sin.*

**Scriptures:** Deuteronomy 6:20–25; Matthew 5:21–26; Luke 15:11–32; Romans 12:10, 16–18; 15:11–32; Ephesians 6:1–4; Colossians 3:18–21.

## 72 FATHERS *

Jay Carter is from Missouri, which he says is a state known for the stubbornness of its people.

One of the greatest days in his life came when he returned from school depressed again. The kids had been talking about what their dads did for a living. Jay's dad was a "bookmaker", and made his living bookin' horses and running a poker parlour.

When his father asked him what was wrong, he told of his embarrassment regarding what he did. It was a Friday.

Jay's dad was an honest gambler. So honest, in fact, his poker chips were legal tender at most of the markets and restaurants in their little town. Dad would make his rounds every Wednesday to redeem his chips.

But on this particular Friday he gave his notice. On Monday he collected all his chips, settled up, and began a legitimate business from which he would retire ten years later.

---

72 Jay Carter, "The Love of a Father", in Bill McCartney, (ed.), *What Makes a Man* (Colorado Springs, CO: Navpress, 1992), pp. 100–101.

Jay never had to ask if his dad loved him or not. He gave up thousands of dollars a week, back when a thousand dollars was a lot of money. And he did it for the respect of his son and out of his love for him. He didn't just tell Jay he loved him, he showed it.

**Themes:** *Career, Children, Families, Family relationships, Grace, Integrity, Love, Parable – Prodigal Son, Parenting.*

**Scriptures:** Deuteronomy 6:20–25; Matthew 5:21–26; Romans 12:10, 16–18; 15:11–32; Ephesians 6:1–4; Colossians 3:18–21.

## 73 FORGIVEN

It had been the custom of a kindly doctor to go through his books from time to time noting those who had not paid. When he realised that the debts remained because the patients could not pay he put a red line through the debt and wrote by the side of it, "Forgiven, unable to pay."

After his death, his wife was looking through his books and saw all the marks and said to herself, "My husband was owed a lot of money. I could do with that money now." She took the matter to the local court to sue the debtors for the money. The judge, however, looked at the doctor's account book and said, "No court in the world will give you a verdict against those people when your husband, with his own pen, has written, 'Forgiven, unable to pay.'"

**Themes:** *Debt, Doctors, Grace, Mercy, Parable – Unforgiving Servant, Pardon, Release.*

**Scriptures:** Exodus 34:9; Numbers 14:19–20; Nehemiah 9:17; Psalms 25:11; 51; Isaiah 40:2; 55:7; Matthew 18:21–35; Mark 2:1–12; 1 John 1:8–9.

73 Aquilla Webb, *1001 Illustrations for Pulpit and Platform* (New York and London: Harper and Brothers, 1926), #161.

## 74 FORGIVENESS

It was when leaving Greenwich in her barge to set out on her progress on 17 July 1579 that Elizabeth nearly lost her life. She was heading, Stow records in his *Annals*, with Lord Lincoln and the French ambassador, for Deptford. "It chanced that one Thomas Appletree, with two or three children of her Majesty's Chapel", was rowing up and down this reach with a caliver [gun], "shooting at random, very rashly". He must have been unbelievably careless in his aim, for one of his random shots passed within six feet of the Queen, piercing one of her watermen clean through both his arms and knocking him out of his seat. This not unnaturally "forced him to cry out and screech out piteously, supposing himself to be slain". Elizabeth showed herself equal to the occasion, and, seeing him maimed, "she never bashed thereat, but bid him be of good cheer, and said he would want of nothing that might be for his ease". Young Appletree, however, was given a terrible lesson. He was condemned to death and, four days later, brought to the gallows which had been set up by the waterside near the scene of his crime. But "when the hangman had put the rope about his neck, he was, by the Queen's most gracious pardon, delivered from execution".

*Themes:* *Capital punishment, Debt, Grace, Mercy, Pardon, Release, Sin.*

**Scriptures:** Exodus 34:9; Numbers 14:19–20; 1 Kings 8:22–53; 2 Chronicles 6:12–42; Nehemiah 9:17; Psalms 25:11; 51; 103:3; Isaiah 40:2; 55:7; Jeremiah 31:34; 36:3; Daniel 9:19; Amos 7:2; Matthew 6:12, 14, 15; 18:21–35; Mark 2:1–12; 11:25; John 8:34–36; Romans 5; Ephesians 2:8; 1 John 1:9.

---

74 Ian Dunlop, *Palaces and Progresses of Elizabeth I* (London: Jonathan Cape, 1962), p. 27.

## 75 FORGIVENESS

In ancient times, if a person became bankrupt, the list of his debts was written on a parchment and nailed up in a public place. There was a nail at the top and another at the bottom of the parchment. A rich friend seeing this humiliating document could take out the bottom nail, double up the parchment, write his name across the folded document and drive the bottom nail in to secure the folded parchment. The signature across the document meant that the person would take responsibility for his friend's debt.

*Themes:* *Freedom, Grace, Mercy, Pardon, Release, Sin.*

**Scriptures:** Exodus 34:9; Numbers 14:19–20; 1 Kings 8:22–53; 2 Chronicles 6:12–42; Nehemiah 9:17; Psalms 25:11; 51; 103:3; Isaiah 40:2; 55:7; Jeremiah 31:34; 36:3; Daniel 9:19; Amos 7:2; Matthew 6:12, 14, 15; 18:21–35; 26:28; Mark 1:4; 2:1–12; 11:25; Luke 1:77; 3:3; 4:18; 24:47; John 8:31–36; Acts 2:38; 5:31; 10:43; 13:38; 26:18; Romans 5; Ephesians 2:8; Colossians 1:14; 1 John 1:9.

## 76 FORGIVENESS

Some years ago, God began dealing with the attitude that the Korean, Paul Cho, had towards Japan, the long-standing enemy of Korea.

Paul Cho was invited to speak to a group of ministers in Japan. When he got up to speak, he tried to say nice things about Japan but could not. He began to weep. A deep silence filled the audience of ministers. He looked up and confessed how he felt.

"I must confess that I hate you all. I don't hate you personally, but I hate the fact that you are Japanese. I know that this is wrong, but this is the way I honestly feel. Won't

76 Adapted from Paul Y. Cho, *More Than Numbers* (Milton Keynes: Word, 1986), p. 118.

you please forgive me? I am repenting of my sin and ask you to pray for me."

With these words spoken, he simply bowed his head and began to cry aloud. When he looked up he saw that all of the ministers were crying also. After a few minutes, one of the Japanese ministers stood and said,

"Dr. Cho, we as Japanese take full responsibility for the sins of our fathers. Will you please forgive us?"

Paul Cho came down from the platform and threw his arms around the man who had just spoken.

"Yes I forgive you and I commit myself to pray for you and Japan."

Cho says that he instantly felt healed of the bitterness that he had felt since he was a child. He was free.

*Themes:* Bitterness, Confession, Enemies, Freedom, Hate, Inner healing, Lord's Prayer, Love, Reconciliation, Repentance, Sin.

*Scriptures:* 1 Samuel 12:1–15; Psalms 51; Proverbs 28:13; Matthew 5:43–48; 6:5–15; 18:21–35; Mark 2:1–12; 11:25; Luke 10:27; John 8:31–36; Romans 12:14; 1 Corinthians 13; Galatians 5:1; James 5:16.

## ~~77~~ FORGIVENESS

The Australian actor Barry Humphries tells of his student days.

> I started to read Fine Arts, which I enjoyed, but I found myself drifting more and more into the amateur theatrical life of the campus. The Union Theatre was small but well equipped and I spent most of my time there. We were rehearsing, I think, a production of Hecht's *The Front Page* when a strange cathartic event occurred. Standing at the stage door and looking across an expanse of lawn towards the medical school, I saw a vaguely familiar figure sitting stu-

77 Barry Humphries, *More Please: An Autobiography* (London: Viking, 1992), pp. 126–127.

diously beneath a gum tree reading. I experienced a painful flashback to Grade One at Camberwell Grammar. It was John Bromley, the boy with the soft slug-like skin who delighted in giving me "Chinese Burns" and "Rabbit Choppers", the archetypal bully of my childhood.

How quiet and peaceful he seemed now, poring over his book in the feathery shadow of the foliage! Immediately I descended to that room beneath the stage used for storing scene-painting equipment. Looking quickly around, I saw a large sack of white powder and, seizing this, I lugged it upstairs and out the stage door. Bromley still sat there in deep shadow. He hadn't moved. Very quickly, with my heart pounding, I crept stealthily towards him until I was directly behind him, and then raised and tilted the heavy sack. A twig cracked sharply under my foot and Bromley looked around and up. By then the bag was evacuating a dense cascade of pigment over the seated student. Just when I thought the whole torrent was petering out, it seemed to renew itself. When the bag was finally empty, I turned and cravenly bolted, only once glancing over my shoulder. Standing now, though seemingly rooted to the spot, stood a totally white figure under a tree. Back in my dressing-room, slightly puffed, I experienced the voluptuous satisfaction of vengeance. I remembered, with intense pleasure also, the victim's face as it turned towards me in that instant before the clown-white avalanche struck. It was not Bromley. Not, in fact, much like Bromley at all. But thereafter Bromley was forgiven. That blanched and bewildered figure on the Union lawn had unwittingly performed a noble act of expiation.

**Themes:** *Cross, Easter, Expiation, Revenge, Substitution.*

**Scriptures:** Isaiah 53; Matthew 5:43–48; Mark 10:45; 11:25; John 11:50; Romans 3:21–25; Galatians 3:13; 1 Timothy 2:6; Hebrews 9:28; 1 Peter 2:24.

## 78 FORGIVENESS

Corrie Ten Boom's family hid Jews above their family watchmaker's shop until she and her sister Betsie were arrested by the Nazis and put in Ravensbruck concentration camp. There Betsie died.

After the war Corrie was speaking in a church in Munich. Then, as she shook hands with people, she found herself confronted by a man she recognised as having been a guard in the camp. She heard him saying, "You mentioned Ravensbruck in your talk. I was a guard there. But since that time I have become a Christian. I know that God has forgiven me for the cruel things I did there, but I would like to hear it from your lips as well. Fraulein, will you forgive me?"

Corrie says that she could not. Betsie had died in that place. Could he erase her slow terrible death simply for the asking? Corrie says that it could not have been many seconds that he stood there, hand held out. But to her it seemed hours as she wrestled with the most difficult decision she had ever had to make. She stood there with the coldness clutching her heart. But she knew that forgiveness is not an emotion, it is an act of the will to hand on the forgiveness she knew.

"Jesus help me," she prayed silently. "I can lift my hand. I can do that much. You supply the feeling."

So woodenly, mechanically, she thrust her hand into the one outstretched to her and offered the forgiveness God had given her. As she did, an incredible thing took place. She says that the current started in her shoulder, raced down her arm, sprang into their joined hands. And then

78 Adapted from "I'm Still Learning to Forgive", #7No1 Good News Publishers 9825 W. Roosevelt Road, Westchester IL 60153.

this healing warmth seemed to flood her whole being, bringing tears to her eyes.

"I forgive you, brother!" she cried. "With all my heart!"

For a long moment they grasped each other's hands, the former guard and the former prisoner. Corrie had never known God's love so intensely as she did then. She was able to forgive as she had been forgiven.

*Themes:* *Forgiveness – handed on, God – his love, Lord's Prayer, Reconciliation.*

**Scriptures:** Psalms 51; Matthew 6:5–15; 18:21–35; Mark 11:25; Romans 12:14; 1 Thessalonians 5:13.

## 79 FORGIVENESS

Erich Honecker was the Head of Government in former East Germany. In the downfall of the Communist regime (1989–90), Honecker and Margot, his wife, were evicted from their luxurious palace in Vandlitz and made homeless.

For 26 years Mrs Honecker had been responsible for education policy. Anyone who refused to take an oath of atheistic allegiance to the State was refused higher education for their children.

Uwe Holmer, a Lutheran evangelical pastor, and his wife had ten children, nine of whom had been refused higher education. Yet they took the Honeckers into their home for two months, sharing their lives and meals with them.

As a result, the pastor and his wife were ostracised for harbouring a man who was so wicked, an "enemy of the people".

*Themes:* *Acceptance, Enemies – love for, Grace, Martyrs, Parable – Unforgiving Servant, Rejection, Sacrifice, Shame.*

**Scriptures:** 2 Samuel 11; Psalms 32; 51; Matthew 18:21–35; Mark 2:1–12; 11:25; Luke 6:27–38; 11:4; 17:3; Romans 12:14; 1 Corinthians 13; Galatians 6:2, 9.

## 80 FORGIVENESS

A minister's wife was having an affair. She wandered into the woods to think and pray through her broken and crumbling life. She poured out her bitterness to God and described her disastrous life to him. As she stood silent and still before the Lord she had a vision. She saw a broken vessel representing her life. Into the picture came Jesus. Tenderly he stooped and sensitively picked up the broken pieces, as if every one was precious. With skill Jesus put the vessel together. In her vision the woman saw Jesus hold the flawless vessel up to her. That vision was a promise to the woman of the forgiveness and healing of Jesus that enabled her to turn her back on the sin in her life and begin again in her marriage.

**Themes:** *Adultery, Brokenness, Grace, Healing – inner, Inner healing, Leadership, Pastors, Recreation, Visions.*

**Scriptures:** Exodus 34:6; 2 Samuel 11; Nehemiah 9:17; Psalms 32, 51; 103:12; Isaiah 38:17; 43:25; 61:1; Jeremiah 31:34; Daniel 9:9; Micah 7:19; Mark 2:1–12; Luke 4:18; John 8:1–11; Romans 3:25; 2 Corinthians 1:3–7; 1 John 1:9.

## 81 FORGIVENESS

Stephen first learned about forgiveness from Miss Roberts, his first-grade teacher. Each day after lunch she allowed her class to purchase an "orangesicle" – a frozen orange juice on a stick – for dessert. It was the highlight of Stephen's school day.

One day he forgot his money. It just so happened, however, that Miss Roberts had found a dime on the classroom floor that day and offered to return it to its owner. As he raced forward to claim the money, he was challenged by a red-haired girl who insisted that it was hers. Two people claiming the same dime – a problem for most people, but not for Miss Roberts. She settled the dispute quickly, suggesting that each of them bring a note from their mother stating that they had been sent to school that day with a dime.

Miss Roberts must have seen the horror on Stephen's face, as he realised that everyone would soon discover that he was both a thief and a liar. He was already dreading the spanking his mother would give him for his dishonesty. Just as the consequences of his "crime" were about to overwhelm him, Miss Roberts came and knelt beside his desk.

"Stevie, I found another dime," she said. She looked him right in the eye and handed the dime to him. "Here, it must be yours."

Immediately, Stephen broke down in tears and confessed what Miss Roberts already knew. "That's OK," she said, patting him on the head. "We all make mistakes." After apologising to the red-haired girl, he enjoyed the best-tasting orangesicle he had ever eaten.

*Themes:* Atonement, Confession, Cross, Jesus – work of, Lord's Prayer, Sin, Solomon – wisdom of, Wisdom.

**Scriptures:** Exodus 34:6; 2 Samuel 11 – 12; 1 Kings 3:16–28; Nehemiah 9:17; Psalms 32; 52; 103:12; Isaiah 38:17; 43:25; 61:1; Jeremiah 31:34; Daniel 9:9; Micah 7:19; Matthew 6:14–15; Mark 2:1–12; Luke 4:18; 11:1–4; John 8:1–11; Romans 3:25; Ephesians 5:2; 1 Peter 2:24; 1 John 1:8–9.

## 82 FORGIVENESS

In one of his prayer letters, Ed Silvoso says that,

Ruth and I ministered to a group of approximately 150 Chinese women. Ruth spoke first, and then I began to share about intimacy in marriage from a biblical perspective. As I did so, all of a sudden I began to feel the pain that many of those women felt due to the abuse inflicted by the men in their lives. I was able literally to feel that pain. Nothing in that audience of Chinese women – who normally are neither expressive nor emotional – could have given me a clue as to what was going on inside their souls. I know it had to be God, and I had no choice but to respond.

I told the women that I felt many of them had been abused – verbally, physically, and sexually, by men. I went on to give them specific examples. Some of them had been called "idiot" or "useless" by their fathers or brothers or husbands. Others had been taken advantage of sexually. As I did this, I could see tears rimming the eyes of many of them.

At that point I told them, "I want to take the place of that man that has hurt you, who never asked your forgiveness, and I want to ask your forgiveness so that you can be healed." I had not inflicted those hurts, but the gender to which I belonged had. As a man, I was in a position to repent on behalf of my peers.

I asked the women that wished to receive my plea and extend forgiveness stand up. Close to 60 per cent of the audience did so. Many began to weep. Others cried out loud. A few were trembling. As I knelt down and asked for forgiveness, something came upon the group. It was a sublime moment. I believe that not only God, but angels were there ministering to those women.

I told them, "Many of you are feeling pain, deep pain, pain that you have chosen to ignore because it has been so unbearable. Do not be afraid of it. The pain you are feeling now is pain on the way out, not on the way in. Let it come up so that Jesus can take it... " When I said this, the dam holding all that misery broke and this assembly of supposedly unemotional Chinese women simply broke before the Lord.

There I was on my knees, like Nehemiah, asking forgiveness for the sins of my ancestors and the sins of my own generation. Like the early Christians in Acts 2:43 I was enveloped by a divine sense of awe. I no longer had a message. I no longer was the feature speaker. God had manifested himself in our midst and his people were being set free. I literally watched inner healing take place. That evening, testimonies would be heard from every corner of the assembly of how God had set his people free.

Finally, I stood up. As I wiped the tears from my eyes and I embraced Ruth, a song of joy flooded my soul and burst through my lips.

*Themes:* *Abuse, Family, Freedom, Grace, Grief, Healing – inner, Inner healing, Intimacy, Joy, Marriage, Men, Sex, Shame.*

**Scriptures:** Exodus 34:6; Nehemiah 9:17; Psalms 103:12; Isaiah 38:17; 43:25; 61:1; Jeremiah 31:34; Daniel 9:1–27; Micah 7:19; Mark 2:1–12; Luke 4:18; Acts 2:43; James 5:16; 1 John 1:9.

## 83 FORGIVENESS

An elderly woman came into contact with Christians. She was a bitter person. Over a number of weeks she heard the Good News. Though no one had told her what to do, it turned out to be life-changing.

On the top of her wardrobe was a small portable typewriter which she had not thought about for a long time. But now, each time she went in the room she could not get it out of her mind. Then she had the strange urge to write a letter to her sister whom she had not contacted for years and ask her forgiveness for the rift between them. Eventually she got the machine down and typed a letter. Even before she posted it, as she was folding up the letter, she said her body felt as if it was being washed all over and she had a sense of being forgiven.

The two sisters have been restored to each other.

*Themes:* *Bitterness, Good Works, Grace, Healing – inner, Inner healing, Lord's Prayer, Parable – Unforgiving Servant, Reconciliation.*

*Scriptures:* Psalms 32; 51; Matthew 18:21–35; Mark 11:25; Luke 11:1–4; Romans 12:14; 1 Corinthians 11:29–32; 1 Thessalonians 5:13.

## 84 FORGIVENESS – NECESSARY

Some years ago, John Wimber was asked to pray for healing for a woman in her late forties. She suffered from chronic stomach disorders and arthritis. When John started to pray over her he received insight that she was bitter. So he asked her if she was feeling hostility, anger or bitterness towards someone, and he felt led to ask specifically if she had felt that way towards her sister.

She stiffened up, then said, "No. I haven't seen my sister for 16 years."

John enquired further: "Are you sure?"

Then she told John how years ago her sister had married a man she loved, then later divorced him. "I cannot forgive my sister for that," she admitted.

"If you don't forgive her," John told her, "your bones will waste away, just as David complained his did when he kept silent about his sin of adultery with Bathsheba."

When she heard his words she relented. "What should I do?" she asked.

John Wimber told her to write her sister a letter, forgiving her and asking to renew their relationship. She wrote the letter immediately, but she did not post it for several weeks. During that time she became more ill, until

---

84 Adapted from John Wimber, *Power Healing* (London: Hodder and Stoughton, 1986), p. 86.

she thought she was going to die. Then she remembered the letter. Somehow she summoned the strength to drive to the post office and post it. The very *moment* she dropped the letter in the box, she experienced relief, and she was completely healed by the time she reached home.

*Themes:* Anger, Bitterness, Grace, Healing, Hostility, Reconciliation, Relationships, Resentment, Sickness.

*Scriptures:* 2 Samuel 11; Psalms 32; 51; Matthew 5:22–24; 6:5–15; 18:21–35; Mark 2:1–12; 11:25; Romans 12:14; 1 Corinthians 11:29–32; 13; 1 Thessalonians 5:13.

## 85 FORGIVENESS – REFUSED

During the presidency of Andrew Jackson, George Wilson, a postal clerk, robbed a federal payroll from a train and in the process killed a guard. The court convicted Wilson and sentenced him to hang. Because of public sentiment against capital punishment, however, a movement began to secure a presidential pardon for Wilson (first offence), and eventually President Jackson intervened with a pardon. Amazingly Wilson refused it.

Since this had never happened before, the Supreme Court was asked to rule on whether a person could refuse a presidential pardon. Chief Justice John Marshall handed down the court's decision: "A pardon is a parchment whose only value must be determined by the receiver of the pardon. It has no value apart from that which the receiver gives to it. George Wilson has refused to accept the pardon. We cannot conceive why he would do so, but he has. Therefore, George Wilson must die."

George Wilson, as punishment for his crime, was hanged.

85 George Maronge, Jr. in *Leadership* 12 (3, 1991) p. 49.

Pardon, declared the Supreme Court, must not only be granted, it must be accepted.

*Themes: Capital punishment, Forgiveness – received, Grace – refused, Pardon, Rejection, Sin.*

**Scriptures:** 1 Kings 8:22–53; 2 Chronicles 6:12–42; Psalms 103:3; Jeremiah 31:34; 36:3; Daniel 9:19; Amos 7:2; Mark 10:17–22; 11:25; John 8:34–36; Romans 5; Ephesians 2:8.

## 86 FORGIVENESS – TRANSFORMS

The musical *Les Misérables* follows Victor Hugo's sprawling novel. It recounts the story of Jean Valjean, a French prisoner hounded and eventually transformed.

Jean served a 19-year gaol term of hard labour for stealing a loaf of bread to feed his hungry family. He entered the French penal system as an impressionable young man. He emerged tough, hardened and embittered by the experience. No one could beat Jean in a fist fight. No one could break his will.

After serving his term, at last, he was set free. But convicts in those days had to carry identity cards. No innkeeper would let a dangerous felon like Jean spend the night in his establishment. For four days he wandered the village roads seeking shelter. Finally, a kindly bishop had mercy on him.

That night Jean lay still in a comfortable bed until the bishop and his sister had drifted off to sleep. Then he rose, rummaged through the cupboards for the family silver, and crept off in the darkness with six silver plates and a silver soup ladle – the bishop's pride and joy.

The next morning, three policemen knocked on the bishop's door. Jean was with them. They had found the convict running away, with the stolen silver in his bag. Jean's unlikely story was that the bishop had given him the silver. The police were ready to put the scoundrel in chains for life. Jean had failed to live up to the new life he was offered.

However, the bishop did the very opposite to what the police, or Jean, expected. The bishop greeted Jean like a worthy friend.

"So here you are! I'm delighted to see you. Have you forgotten that I gave you the candlesticks as well? They're silver like the rest, and worth a good 200 francs. Did you forget to take them?" Jean's eyes widened in disbelief. He was now staring at the old bishop with an expression for which there were no words.

The bishop turned to assure the police. "This silver was my gift to him." Satisfied, the police withdrew.

The bishop did not change when he was alone with Jean. Indeed, he gave the candlesticks to his guest who was now speechless and trembling. He said to Jean, "Do not forget, do not ever forget, that you have promised me to use the money to make yourself an honest man."

The next day, Jean's knees buckled under him as if an invisible power overwhelmed him as a blow, with the weight of his bad conscience. He fell exhausted on a large stone, his hands clenched in his hair, and his face on his knees. "What a wretch I am!" he cried.

Then his heart swelled and he burst into tears. It was the first time he had cried in 19 years. He wept long and bitterly; with more weakness than a woman and with more tenderness than a child. At first there were tears of remorse and guilt. Then, as he cried, the light grew brighter and brighter in his mind – an extraordinary light, a light transporting and terrible.

A revengeful detective stalked Jean for the next 20 years in an attempt to catch him out. But, repentance and forgiveness had transformed Jean. He became the dignified and respected mayor of a town. The detective could find nothing and eventually threw himself off a bridge into the Seine.

**Themes:** *Confession, Conversion, Debt, Grace, Guilt, Mercy, Pardon, Release, Remorse, Repentance, Revenge, Theft, Transformed.*

**Scriptures:** Exodus 34:9; Numbers 14:19–20; 1 Kings 8:22–53; 2 Chronicles 6:12–42; Nehemiah 9:17; Psalms 25:11; 51; 103:3; Isaiah 40:2; 55:7; Jeremiah 31:34; 36:3; Daniel 9:19; Amos 7:2; Matthew 5:43–48; 6:12, 14, 15; 18:21–35; Mark 2:1–12; 11:25; Romans 5; Ephesians 2:8; 1 John 1:9.

## 87 FREED

In the time of the Napoleonic wars a man was ballotted as a conscript who did not want to go. But he had a friend who wanted to go to war and so the friend went in his place. The friend was killed in battle. He was buried on the battlefield. Some time later there was another ballot to obtain conscripts. By some mistake the first man was ballotted a second time. He refused to go.

"You cannot take me," he said.

"Why not?" they asked.

"I am dead," was his reply.

"You are not dead you are alive and well."

"But I am dead," he insisted.

"Why, man, you are mad. Where did you die?"

"At the battlefield. And you left me buried on the field."

"You talk like a mad man," they cried.

But the man stuck to his point; that he had been dead and buried several months.

"You look up your records," he said, "and see if it is not so."

They looked and found that he was right. They found the man's name entered as drafted and sent to war and

---

87 Adapted from Aquilla Webb, *1001 Illustrations for Pulpit and Platform* (New York and London: Harper and Brothers, 1926), #946.

marked off as killed.

"Look here," they said, "you did not die. You must have got someone to go for you. It must have been your substitute."

"I know that," he said. "He died in my place. You cannot touch me. I can go free. The law has no claim against me."

The authorities would not accept this. And the case was actually taken to Napoleon. He ruled that the man was right. Legally, even though through a substitute, he had died and was buried on a battlefield. France had no claim on him.

**Themes:** *Atonement, Christ – our ransom, Christ – our representative, Christ – our substitute, Forgiveness.*

**Scriptures:** Isaiah 53; Mark 10:45; 11:25; Luke 1:68; 2:38; John 11:50; Romans 3:21–25; Galatians 3:13; 1 Timothy 2:6; Hebrews 9:11–14, 28; 1 Peter 2:24.

## 88 FREEDOM *

An Englishman went to California. Gold had been discovered and he struck it rich. On his way home he saw a public auction in New Orleans of a beautiful slave girl. Within a minute, bids surpassed what most slave owners would pay for a black girl. The auctioneer called out, "Going once! Going twice!"

In a moment the Englishman yelled out a figure. It was exactly twice the previous bid. The crowd laughed. They thought the Englishman was joking. The auctioneer motioned for him to come forward. He wanted to see his money. The Englishman opened up his bag of gold. The auctioneer's eyes widened and he shook his head in disbelief. The auctioneer was paid and the girl walked down the

88 Adapted from Wayne Rice, *Hot Illustrations for Youth Talks* (El Cajon, CA: Youth Specialties, 1994), pp. 52–55.

platform. She spat straight into her new owner's face saying, "I hate you!"

The girl couldn't make out what was happening. Her new owner seemed to be looking for something or someone as they walked down the street. Finally they stopped outside a shop. The girl waited outside as the new owner went inside. She couldn't make out what was going on inside. Someone was saying loudly, "It's the law! It's the law!" When she looked through the window she saw her owner pour gold out from his bag. She saw the store owner pick up the gold and leave the room. He came back with some papers. Both men signed them.

When the Englishman came out of the store he handed the papers to the girl. He said, "Here are your manumission papers. You are free."

But the girl quickly yelled back, "I hate you! Why do make fun of me?"

"No! Listen! These are your freedom papers. You are a free person."

The girl looked at the papers. She couldn't read them. But they looked important.

"You bought me," she said, "and now, you're setting me free?"

The Englishman assured her that he had bought her to set her free. Tears began to run down her face. Then she started to sob and fell to the ground. "You bought me to set me free! You bought me to set me free!" she kept repeating. Then the girl put her arms around his legs. As she rocked to and fro she looked up and said this, "All I want to do is to serve you – because you bought me to set me free!"

**Themes:** *Atonement, Cross, Expiation, Freedom, Jesus – work of, Redeemed, Rescue, Slavery.*

**Scriptures:** Exodus 6:6; Psalms 77:14–15; Mark 10:45; Luke 24:21; John 1:29; 8:31–36; 1 Corinthians 1:30; 5:7; 6:19–20; 7:22–23; Galatians 3:13; 4:4–5; 5:1; Ephesians 1:7; 5:2; Titus 2:14; Hebrews 9:15; 1 Peter 1:18–19; 1 John 2:2.

## 8⁹ FREEDOM

The story is told of an Arab called Bark who was kidnapped into slavery. He learned to tremble at a handclap and to come running on command. One day a kind friend purchased his freedom. The friend provided him with money, and sent him on his way.

At first Bark tried to act out all the dreams of freedom he had harboured and dreamed of as a slave. He went to a restaurant and paid a waiter to wait on him. He bought a woman and bid her please him. But his dreams were soon used up, and freedom became a fearful burden. Then he met a tearful child. With the child he searched the city to secure some consoling toy. This was it. For the rest of his life Bark gave his freedom as a willing slave to the ragtaggle children of the street.

**Themes:** *Atonement, Cross, Expiation, Good works, Materialism, Money, Redeemed, Rescued, Sacrifice, Service, Slavery, Wealth.*

**Scriptures:** Exodus 6:6; Psalms 77:14–15; Mark 10:45; Luke 24:21; John 1:29; 8:31–36; 1 Corinthians 1:30; 5:7; 6:19–20; 7:22–23; Galatians 3:13; 4:4–5; 5:1; Ephesians 1:7; 2:10; 5:2; 1 Timothy 2:6; Titus 2:14; Hebrews 9:15; 1 Peter 1:18–19; 1 John 2:2.

## 90 GENEROSITY *

Paul received an automobile from his brother as a Christmas present. On Christmas Eve when Paul came out of his office, a street urchin was walking around the shiny new car, admiring it.

"Is this your car, Mister?" he asked.

Paul nodded. "My brother gave it to me for Christmas." The boy was astounded.

"You mean your brother gave it to you and it didn't cost you nothing? Boy, I wish..." He hesitated. Of course Paul knew what he was going to wish for. He was going to wish he had a brother like that. But what the lad said jarred Paul all the way down to his heels.

"I wish," the boy went on, "that I could be a brother like that."

Paul looked at the boy in astonishment, then impulsively he added, "Would you like to take a ride in my car?"

"Oh yes, I'd love that."

After a short ride, the boy turned and, with his eyes aglow, said, "Mister, would you mind driving in front of my house?" Paul smiled a little. He thought he knew what the lad wanted. He wanted to show his neighbours that he could ride home in a big car. But Paul was wrong again.

"Will you stop where those two steps are?" the boy asked. He ran up the steps. Then in a little while Paul heard him coming back, but he was not coming fast. He was carrying his little crippled brother. He sat him down on the bottom step, then sort of squeezed up against him and pointed to the car.

"There she is, Buddy, just like I told you upstairs. His brother gave it to him for Christmas and it didn't cost him a thing. And some day I'm gonna give you one just like

90 Adapted from http://www.geocities.com/Heartland/Flats/4610/snow.html

it... then you can see for yourself all the pretty things in the Christmas windows that I've been trying to tell you about."

Paul got out and lifted the lad to the front seat of his car. The shining-eyed older brother climbed in beside him and the three of them began a memorable holiday ride.

*Themes:* *Brotherly love, Giving, God – his provision, Materialism, Money, Offerings, Sacrificial giving, Tithing, Wealth.*

**Scriptures:** Psalms 112:9; Isaiah 55:10–11; Mark 10:17–31; 12:41–44; Luke 19:1–10; 2 Corinthians 8 and 9; 1 Timothy 6:17–19; Hebrews 13:5.

## 91 GENEROSITY

A woman was invited to a Zulu church. She went, and was conspicuous as the only white person there. They welcomed her, translated for her, and made her thoroughly at home. They had a collection to build a new Zulu church down the road. Later in the service, they had another collection for Zulu Christians who had no shoes. By this time, she had put in all the money she had with her. Imagine how staggered she was when they had a third collection. She had nothing left. But the collection was announced "for petrol for our white sister". That woman came out with an entirely new perspective on Christian giving.

*Themes:* *Giving, God – his provision, Grace, Materialism, Money, Offerings, Sacrificial giving, Tithing, Wealth.*

**Scriptures:** Psalms 112:9; Isaiah 55:10–11; Malachi 3:8–12, Mark 10:17–31; 12:41–44; Luke 19:1–10; 2 Corinthians 8 and 9; 1 Timothy 6:17–19; Hebrews 13:5.

91 Adapted from Michael Green, *To Corinth With Love* (London: Hodder and Stoughton, 1982), p. 104.

## 92 GIFTS OF THE SPIRIT – USING

On 27 May 1840, Niccolo Paganini, perhaps the greatest violinist of all time, lay dying. He reached slowly from his bed to hold just once more the instrument he loved best. But as his fingers lightly brushed over the vibrant strings Paganini died. He was 58.

A few days later, on 1 June, his will was opened and read. It disposed of a fortune of roughly two million lire (c. £80,000), a valuable collection of jewellery, instruments, and a large amount of property and securities across several European countries. After providing generously for his sisters, everything else was to go to his son, Baron Achille Paganini. However, the will directed that Paganini's favourite Guarneri violin be preserved in the Municipal Museum of Genoa.

His son fought hard to retain his favourite instrument, the last thing touched by the great master. But the city fathers of Genoa refused to waive the right given them by the will. Achille offered the city the fine marble bust Varni had made, in place of the violin; the mayor refused.

To this day the violin is very rarely played, standing in a glass case surrounded by other relics of the great man.

***Themes:*** *Body, Hidden talents.*

**Scriptures:** Matthew 25:14–30; Romans 12:3–6; 1 Corinthians 12:12–27; Ephesians 4:12–16; 1 Peter 4:7–11.

## 93 GIFTS OF THE SPIRIT – USING

Antonio Stradivari has not been surpassed in the making of violins, even though he died in 1737.

In 1716 he built an instrument which became his

---

92 Adapted from Jeffrey Pulver, *Paganini: The Romantic Virtuoso* (London: Herbert Joseph, 1936), pp. 304–305.

favourite and it never left him. When he died it passed into the hands of his sons Francesco and Paola. Then it was sold to Count Cozio di Salabue in 1775, and valued at about £100.

In 1827, Luigi Tarisio, the famous collector, purchased it. But then it was not seen for decades.

It received that name *La Messie*, for those hearing the raptures of Tarisio became sceptical of there being such an instrument, as no one had ever set eyes upon it.

One morning in 1854 Luigi Tarisio was found dead. There were 246 exquisite violins found in the place. Some were crammed in the attic. One – the best one – was in the bottom drawer of an old rickety bureau.

When the greatest Stradivarius, *La Messie*, was brought out and played it had been cruelly silent for 147 years. But again the silence continues. In 1931 the instrument was purchased by W. E. Hill and Sons for £2,000 and, in 1938, presented by them to the Ashmolean Museum in Oxford to be kept in perpetuity in a room specially prepared for it. Luigi Tarisio and other collectors have robbed the world of the sound of this violin.

*Themes:* Body, Evangelism – failure, Hidden talents.

**Scriptures:** Matthew 25:14–30; Romans 12:3–6; 1 Corinthians 12:12–27; Ephesians 4:12–16; 1 Peter 4:7–11.

## 94 GIVING

The late R. G. LeTourneau, the great Texas industrialist, had the gift of giving. The key question in relation to the gift of giving is described in his autobiography. In it he said, "The question is not how much of my money I give to

---

93 Adapted from W. Henley, *Antonio Stradivari: Master Luthier Cremona, Italy, 1644–1737* (Brighton: Amarti, 1961), p. 62 and *Cyclopedia of Bible Illustrations*, Paul E. Holdcroft, p. 109. Copyright renewal Oct. 1974 by Lola G. Holdcraft.

God, but rather how much of God's money I keep." He answered it in his life by turning 90 per cent of the assets of the company over to his Christian foundation, and then he and his wife gave in cash 90 per cent of the income that was realised from the share of the business that he kept. He and his wife never lacked.

*Themes:*  *Giving, God – his provision, Materialism, Money, Offerings,*
*Sacrificial giving, Tithing, Wealth.*

**Scriptures:** Psalms 112:9; Isaiah 55:10–11; Malachi 3:8–12; Mark 10:17–31; 12:41–44; Luke 19:1–10; 2 Corinthians 8 and 9; 1 Timothy 6:17–19; Hebrews 13:5.

## 95 GIVING

Graham and Treena Kerr were wealthy and famous when they came to know the Lord. You probably remember Graham from his TV show, *The Galloping Gourmet*. When they were converted, God told them to give away everything, and they did. Millions of dollars. They were rich young rulers who obeyed.

What was surprising was the criticism they received from Christians because of their obedience. Some charged them with not being good stewards. They said they should have invested it so they could continue giving more and more.

Such responses show where people's real values lie. Like the disciples when the woman broke the expensive alabaster vial of perfume over Jesus' head, they say, "This money could have been better spent!"

*Themes:*  *Giving, God – his provision, Money, Offerings.*

**Scriptures:** Psalms 112:9; Isaiah 55:10; Malachi 3:8–12, Mark 10:17–31; 11:22–24; 12:41–44; Luke 7:1–10; 19:1–10; 2 Corinthians 8 and 9; 1 Timothy 6:17–19; Hebrews 13:5.

95 Loren Cunningham, *Daring to Live on the Edge* (Seattle: YWAM, 1991), p. 165.

## 96 GIVING

George Carey tells of a church rebuilding programme. In relation to the principle of going beyond our means he tells the story of a thirteen-year-old boy who had about $800 (£500) in his savings, and after talking with his parents came to see Carey because he wanted to loan it to the church free of interest, and for as long as they liked! It was times like these that showed Carey that sacrificial giving was running very deep in the congregation. People were diverting money into the building project from savings, holidays, life insurances and so on. George Carey said, "All this indicated that our giving had passed from generosity to surrender of our possessions."

*Themes:* *Generosity, Giving, God – his provision, Materialism, Money, Offerings, Sacrificial giving, Tithing, Wealth.*

**Scriptures:** Psalms 112:9; Isaiah 55:10–11; Malachi 3:8–12; Mark 10:17–31; 12:41–44; Luke 19:1–10; 2 Corinthians 8 and 9; 1 Timothy 6:17–19; Hebrews 13:5.

## 97 GOD – ACCESS TO

During the American Civil War, as a result of family tragedy, a soldier had been granted permission to seek a hearing from the president. He wanted to request exemption from military service. However, when he arrived at the White House he was refused entry and sent away. He went and sat in a nearby park.

A young boy came across him and remarked how unhappy he looked. The soldier found himself telling the young lad everything. Eventually the boy said, "Come with me." He led the dejected soldier back to the White House. They went around the back, none of the guards stopping them. Even the generals and high-ranking government officials stood to attention and let them pass through. The soldier was amazed.

Finally, they came to the presidential office. Without knocking, the young boy opened the door and walked straight in. Abraham Lincoln, standing there, turned from his conversation with the Secretary of State and said, "What can I do for you, Todd?"

"Dad," Todd said, "this soldier needs to talk to you."

*Themes:* *Access, Holy of Holies – entrance to, Jesus – the High Priest, Prayer.*
**Scriptures:** Romans 5:1–2; Ephesians 2:18; Hebrews 4:14 – 5:10.

## 98 GOD – HIS CARE *

The story is told of a boy travelling alone in a railway compartment in England. At one of the stations an elderly gentleman engaged the boy in conversation:

"Are you travelling all alone, Sonny?"

"Yes, sir."

"How far are you travelling?"

"To the terminus."

"Are you not afraid taking such a long journey all by yourself?"

"No, I'm not."

"Why not?"

"Because my father is the engine driver."

*Themes:* *Afraid, Fear, God – faithful, Peace, Trust.*
**Scriptures:** Exodus 15:2; Psalms 27:1; 34:4; 37:3–5; 46; 62:2; Proverbs 3:5–6; Isaiah 60:19; Matthew 6:19–34; 10:28; Luke 12:5; John 14:1–4; 16:33; Romans 5:1–5; Philippians 4:6–7; 2 Timothy 1:7; Hebrews 13:5–6; 1 Peter 5:5–6.

98 Billy Graham, *World Aflame* (Kingswood: World's Work, 1966), p. 187.

## 99 GOD – HIS CARE

Hudson Taylor was a missionary statesman in China in the nineteenth century. Part of the entry from his journal dated 18 November 1857 reads as follows: "On Saturday, the 4th... we supplied, as usual, a breakfast to the destitute poor, who came to the number of seventy... On that Saturday we paid all expenses, and provided for the morrow, after which we had not a single dollar left between us. How the Lord was going to provide for Monday we knew not..." But he goes on to say, "That very day the mail came in, a week sooner than was expected, and Mr Jones received a bill for two hundred and fourteen dollars. We thanked God and took courage." A note in the journal says, "On Monday the poor had their breakfast as usual."

*Themes:* *Generosity, Giving, God – his provision, Missionaries, the Poor, Worry.*

**Scriptures:** Genesis 15:1; 50:20; 1 Kings 17; Job 38:41; Psalms 37:5, 23–24; 55:22; 56:4–5; 91; 118:6; Proverbs 3:5–6; Isaiah 49:15; Malachi 3:8–12; Luke 12:4–7, 22–24; Romans 8:28; 2 Corinthians 8 and 9; Hebrews 13:5; 1 Peter 5:7.

## 100 GOD – DISCOVERING

Irina lived in Odessa, on the north coast of the Black Sea, in the Khrushchev years. At school she often wondered why the teachers bothered with the truckloads of words against God. She used to think "[God] must exist – and he must be very powerful for them to fear him so greatly."

It didn't often snow in Odessa. But this particular day, it did. Irina was looking out of the window, ignoring what the teacher was saying. But she said in her mind, "Okay, God... If you're so powerful, make it keep snowing." That was Irina's first prayer. It was the largest snowfall for 60 years. Irina began to think about the God the teachers denied. She began to talk to him secretly, late at night. She had no idea what God wanted from her. Yet, the moment she thought this, an answer seemed to echo from within. "Don't worry, you will find out what you need to know when the time comes." She began to devour the great Russian books on her parents' shelves: Dostoevsky, Pushkin, Turgenev and Tolstoy. In these she found a reflection of the God whom she sensed was kind and all-powerful. Then came the confusion of adolescence. Suddenly, her parents' beloved books offered no help. She realised she knew so little about Christ. All she had were a few quotes picked from various books. Irina began to write poetry to express her struggle to find God. One night, as she penned some lines, she felt a benevolent eye looking over her shoulder. She said, "I shivered despite the delicious warmth, for I knew whose glance it was. He had not abandoned me. He was with me... And he didn't mind that I couldn't pray properly."

*Themes: Atheism, God – his existence, God – his nature, God – searching for, God – with us, Prayer – answered, Prayer – difficulties, Prayer – first, Revelation.*

**Scriptures:** Exodus 3 – 4; Psalms 37:3–5; 53:1; 145:10–13; Isaiah 7:14; 40:12–26; Jeremiah 10:1–16; Matthew 1:23; 28:19–20; Luke 11:1–13; John 4:24; Acts 17:23–30; Romans 1:18–20; 8:26; Ephesians 6:18; Hebrews 10:6.

## 101 GOD – HIS EXISTENCE

Isaac Newton was the Professor of Maths at Cambridge University from 1669 to 1701. He is said to be one of the greatest scientists of all time. He did much of his brilliant original work in his parents' home in Lincolnshire immediately after he graduated from university; the university being closed for a couple of years during the great plague.

His most far-reaching achievement was the formulation of the universal law of gravitation, explaining the motion and behaviour of the planets. Newton was also a fine Christian.

It is said that one day he was sitting at his desk working. One of his atheist friends came to see him. In his room, to one side, there was a beautifully made orrery – a clockwork model used to demonstrate the movement of the planets around the sun. During the conversation the atheist was admiring this complicated and beautifully crafted machine. Eventually he asked Newton, "Who made the orrery?"

"Oh, no one," said Newton. "It just happened!"

*Themes:* Atheists, God – Creator.
**Scriptures:** Psalms 53:1; Isaiah 40:12–26; Jeremiah 10:11–16; Acts 17:24–29; Romans 1:19–20.

## 102 GOD – HIS EXISTENCE

A young Communist was showing a Christian around Moscow. After a time the Communist chided the Christian for his belief in God. "I'm astonished," he said, "that an intelligent person like you can possibly believe in a foolish myth like that!"

The Christian said nothing, paused for a moment, and then grabbed the Communist by his wrist. "Look at your watch!" he said. "See its precision and accuracy. Think of the incredibly delicate nature of its mechanism. But according to your reasoning it just happened. It all fell into place by chance. There was no maker or designer behind it!"

The Communist appeared startled. He said nothing. "Now look at your hand," continued the Christian. "Look

---

102 Adapted from David Watson, "What Can We Know About God?" (London: Falcon audio tape).

at the fantastic mechanism of your hand. It is a thousand times – a million times – more wonderful than your watch. Yet, according to your reasoning, it just happened! It all fell into place by chance. There was no maker or designer behind it. Now I am astonished that an intelligent person like you can believe that your watch was created, but that your hand was not. And that's just your hand, let alone the rest of your body, or the rest of creation!"

**Themes:** *Atheists, Communism, God – Creator, God – his existence.*

**Scriptures:** Psalms 53:1; Isaiah 40:12–26; Jeremiah 10:11–16; Acts 17:24–29; Romans 1:19–20.

## ∧03 GOD – HIS EXISTENCE

The story is told of a man who walked too near the edge of a cliff. He fell off, and as he plunged down he put out his hand and hung onto a thorn bush growing from the cliff face. He looked up: the cliff was too high to climb. He looked down: it was too far to fall!

In desperation he looked up again and shouted, "Is anyone there?" To his delight, there was an answering voice. "Yes, I – the Lord your God – am here."

"What shall I do?" called the man.

After a pause, the voice replied, "Let go."

The man looked down at the rocks 100 metres below. Then he looked up, and called out again, "Is there anyone else there?"

**Themes:** *Atheists, Faith, God – his care, Humour, Trust.*

**Scriptures:** Psalms 37:3–5; 53:1; 145:14–21; Proverbs 3:5–6; Isaiah 40:12–26; Jeremiah 10:11–16; Matthew 6:25–34; Mark 11:22–24; Luke 7:1–10; Acts 17:24–29; Romans 1:19–20.

---

[103] Adapted from John Young, *The Case Against Christ* (London: Hodder and Stoughton, 1986), reprinted in *The Church of England Newspaper* (London) 19 December 1986, p. 9.

## ⨪104 GOD – HIS EXISTENCE

William Paley was a lecturer in Oxford and then a priest in Carlisle in the eighteenth century. He is virtually forgotten now except for his famous example of the argument from design for God's existence. He begins his book, *Natural Theology*, with a parable.

Suppose a man is walking across a moor and he happens to hit his foot against a watch. He picks it up; he has never seen a watch before; he examines it. He sees that the hands are moving round the dial in what is clearly an orderly way. He opens it up and he finds inside a host of wheels and cogs and levers and springs and jewels. He discovers that by winding up the watch, you can set it going, and that the whole complicated machinery is moving in what is obviously a predetermined pattern. What then does he say? Does he say: "By chance all these wheels and levers and jewels and springs came together and formed themselves into this thing I have in my hand. By chance they set themselves going. By chance they move in an orderly way. By chance this watch became an instrument which counts the hours and minutes and seconds"? No. If he applies his mind to this problem at all, he says: "I have found a watch. *Somewhere there must be a watch-maker.*" So then when we discover a world where there is an order more accurate than any watch, where tides ebb and flow according to schedule, where spring, summer, autumn and winter come back in unvarying succession, where the planets never leave their courses, where the same cause always produces the same effect, we are bound to say: "I have found a world. *Somewhere there must be a world-maker.*"

104 As in William Barclay, *The Plain Man Looks at the Apostles' Creed* (London and Glasgow: Collins/Fontana, 1967), pp. 27–28. *See also* William Paley, *Natural Theology; or, Evidence of the Existence and Attributes of the Deity* (Edinburgh: John Fairburn, et al., 1822).

**Themes:** *Atheists, God – Creator.*

**Scriptures:** Psalms 53:1; Isaiah 40:12–26; Jeremiah 10:11–16; Acts 17:24–29; Romans 1:19–20.

## ⋀0⋀5 GOD – IMAGE OF *

A well known speaker started his seminar by holding up a $20 note. In the room of 200 people he asked, "Who would like this $20 note?" Hands started going up. He said, "I am going to give this $20 to one of you but first, let me do this." He proceeded to crumple the note. Then he asked, "Who still wants it?" The hands remained in the air.

"Well," he replied, "What if I do this?" And he dropped it on the ground and started to grind it into the floor with his shoe. He picked it up, all crumpled and dirty. "Now who still wants it?" Still the hands stayed in the air.

"My friends, you have all learned a very valuable lesson. No matter what I did to this money, you still want it because it does not decrease in value. It is still worth $20. Many times in our lives, we are dropped, crumpled, and ground into the dirt by the decisions we make and the circumstances that come our way. We feel as though we are worthless. But no matter what has happened or what will happen, you will never lose your value in God's eyes. To him, dirty or clean, crumpled or finely creased, you are still priceless to him."

**Themes:** *God – his love, Humankind – value of, Sin.*

**Scriptures:** Genesis 1:26–27; 5:1–3; 9:6; Psalms 8; 1 Corinthians 11:7; James 3:9; 1 John 1:9.

## ⤳06 GOD'S LOVE – FREE

A mother gave her son a ticket to the football match. However, instead of enjoying the game, he spent the entire time walking around the ground collecting cans and bottles to pay her back for the price of the ticket.

"We didn't want him to work during the game," the mother said sadly. "We wanted him to enjoy it."

She said, "I'll never forget his sweaty little face as he told me he lacked only two bottles before he could pay us back. His father and I had thought all the time that he was enjoying the ballgame with his friends."

*Themes:* *Earning God's favour, Forgiveness, God – his favour, God – his love, Grace, Works.*

**Scriptures:** Psalm 143:2; Mark 11:25; Luke 10:27; Acts 10:43; Romans 1:17; 3:20; 1 Corinthians 13; Galatians 2:16; Ephesians 2:1–10.

## ⤳07 GOD – HIS SOVEREIGNTY

Some years ago, Ray Steadman and his wife were part-way through a long car trip. In the motel the night before, Susan, their little daughter, had developed a fever. But it didn't seem serious. As they drove along, suddenly Susan went into convulsions. Her eyes turned up, her body began to jerk. She was obviously in considerable danger. Ray's heart seemed to miss a beat. He stopped the car there and then. He grabbed Susan, and stumbled across the road to a farmhouse that happened to be visible nearby. It was just becoming light when he frantically kicked on the door as he held Susan. A cautious woman opened the door a little. "My daughter is very sick. She's having convulsions. Do you have a bath where we can put

---

106 Adapted from *The Upper Room* (12 November 1983).

107 Adapted from Michael P. Green (ed.), *Illustrations for Biblical Preaching* (Grand Rapids, MI: Baker, 1989), #891.

her in cool water?" The lady was so taken aback she did not really speak. She just opened the door a little more and mumbled and pointed. Ray pushed the door right open, strode down the passage to the back of the house and ran a bath to cool off his treasured girl. Then he rang a local doctor to make an appointment.

The incredible thing is that there was not another house for many miles around. And, of all the homes in the area, Ray and his wife found out that this was the only one with a bath and a telephone.

*Themes:* *Coincidence, Fear, God – his care, God – his provision, Healing, Miracles, Worry.*

**Scriptures:** Genesis 15:1; 50:19–20;1 Kings 17; Job 38:41; Psalms 27:1; 37:5, 23–24; 55:22; 56:4–5; 91; 118:6; Proverb 3:5–6; Isaiah 49:15; Luke 12:4–7, 22–34; Romans 8:28; 1 Peter 5:7.

## ⅂08 GOD – WITH US

During the First World War a soldier in the trenches saw his friend out in no-man's-land (the ground between our trenches and those of the enemy) stumble and fall in a hail of bullets. He said to his officer, "May I go, sir, and bring him in?" But the officer refused. "No one can live out there," he said. "I should only lose you as well." Disobeying the order, the man went to try to save his friend, for they had been like David and Jonathan throughout the whole war. Somehow he got his friend on to his shoulder and staggered back to the trenches, but he himself lay mortally wounded and his friend was dead.

The officer was angry. "I told you not to go," he said. "Now I have lost both of you. It was not worth it."

---

[108] L. D. Weatherhead, *Prescription for Anxiety* (London: Hodder and Stoughton, 1956), p. 120.

With his dying breath the man said, "But it was worth it, sir."

"Worth it!" said the officer. "How could it be? Your friend is dead and you are mortally wounded."

The boy shrank from the reproach, but, looking up into his officer's face, he said, "It was worth it, sir, because when I got to him, he said, 'Jim, I knew you'd come.'"

**Themes:** *Atonement, Compassion, Friendship, Incarnation, Ransom, Redemption, Rescue, War.*

**Scriptures:** Exodus 3 – 4; 15:2; Psalms 27:1; 34:4; 46; 62:2; Isaiah 42:13–53:12; 60:19; Matthew 1:23; 6:19–34; 10:28; 28:19–20; Mark 10:45; John 11:50; Romans 3:21–25; Galatians 3:13; Philippians 4:6; 1 Timothy 2:6; 2 Timothy 1:7; Hebrews 9:28; 13:5–6; 1 Peter 2:21–25; 5:5–6.

## 109 GOD – WITH US *

I was walking down a dimly-lit street late one evening when I heard muffled screams coming from behind a clump of bushes. Alarmed, I slowed down to listen, and panicked when I realised that what I was hearing were the unmistakable sounds of a struggle: heavy grunting, frantic scuffling, and tearing of fabric.

Only yards from where I stood, a woman was being attacked. Should I get involved? I was frightened for my own safety, and cursed myself for having suddenly decided to take a new route home that night. What if I became another statistic? Shouldn't I just run to the nearest phone and call the police?

Although it seemed an eternity, the deliberations in my head had taken only seconds, but already the girl's cries were growing weaker.

I knew I had to act fast. How could I walk away from

109 From Bill Champion, Tidbits Daily Devotional. To subscribe to the free Tidbits Daily Devotional, send an email to: <tidbits-request@mlists.net> and put SUBSCRIBE in the body of the email.

this? No, I finally resolved, I could not turn my back on the fate of this unknown woman, even if it meant risking my own life.

I am not a brave man, nor am I athletic. I don't know where I found the moral courage and physical strength. But once I had finally resolved to help the girl, I became strangely transformed.

I ran behind the bushes and pulled the assailant off the woman. Grappling, we fell to the ground, where we wrestled for a few minutes until the attacker jumped up and escaped. Panting hard, I scrambled upright and approached the girl, who was crouched behind a tree, sobbing. In the darkness, I could barely see her outline, but I could certainly sense her trembling shock.

Not wanting to frighten her further, I at first spoke to her from a distance. "It's OK," I said soothingly. "The man ran away. You're safe now."

There was a long pause and then I heard the words, uttered in wonder, in amazement. "Dad, is that you?" And then, from behind the tree, stepped my youngest daughter, Katherine.

*Themes:* Compassion, God – his care, God – his love, Love, Redemption, Rescue.

**Scriptures:** Exodus 3 – 4; 15:2; Psalms 27:1; 34:4; 46; 62:2; Isaiah 42:13–53:12; 60:19; Matthew 1:23; 6:19–34; 10:28; 28:19–20; Mark 10:45; John 11:50; Romans 3:21–25; Galatians 3:13; Philippians 4:6; 1 Timothy 2:6; 2 Timothy 1:7; Hebrews 9:28; 13:5–6; 1 Peter 2:21–25; 5:5–6.

## ⌒⌒⃝ GOOD NEWS – EAGER TO HEAR

Early in January 1940 two men found their way to a mission hospital in India. They said they had come on behalf of their village to ask for someone to be sent to tell them about Christianity. Lesslie Newbigin continues the story:

Two or three days later three of us set off... for the village... In the middle of the village was a small, well-built temple. To our surprise, the temple was immediately opened, a lamp brought, and ourselves invited to sit down inside. In a few minutes a large crowd was gathered round the porch of the temple, and the leading man,... spoke to us... "We have invited you to come, and we are glad that you have come. Now here we are, and we know nothing about Christianity, but we want you to tell us all about it from the beginning."

One of those with Newbigin began from the idol in whose temple they were sitting and went on to announce the good news of Jesus. A church had begun.

*Themes:* *Evangelism, Idols, India, Missionaries, Witnessing.*

**Scriptures:** Matthew 28:16–20; Mark 3:13–19; 6:7–13; Luke 9:1–6; 10:1–20; Acts 10:1–48; 17:16–23.

## ↑↑↑ GRACE – SUFFICIENT

Three-year-old Mandy was born into the home of Marshall and Susan Shelley. Mandy was severely and profoundly disabled due to microcephaly.

Marshall and Susan desperately prayed that Mandy would develop some skills. But, eventually, they had to accept that Mandy would never talk, nor walk, nor sit up, nor use her hands. She suffered frequent seizures. She stopped swallowing so they learned to administer medication and formula through a tube surgically implanted in her stomach. The parents never knew if she could see or hear. On the outside Mandy may not have appeared valuable. Yet, as they and other folk loved and cared for Mandy, something happened to them.

---

[110] Lesslie Newbigin, *Unfinished Agenda* (Grand Rapids, MI: William B. Eerdmans, 1985), pp. 63–64.

[111] Adapted from "Editorial", *Leadership* 13 (3, 1992), p. 3.

When the Shelleys arrived at church several sets of arms would reach out to take her. People you would not expect – teenage boys, a woman recently widowed, men who didn't usually exhibit much interest in babies – would take turns in cuddling her. After church they would have to hunt for her as she had been passed from lap to lap.

The Shelleys and those near them had many questions: Why was such a child born? What is her future? There were no easy answers. But in loving and caring for Mandy people were set free.

For example, after observing Mandy, one hospital employee said she decided "to get God in my life", as she put it.

In February 1992, Mandy contracted viral pneumonia. Her body did not have the strength to shake it off. One Thursday, Marshall and Susan sat in Mandy's room, taking turns holding her. A procession of people came to visit. A hospital volunteer came to comfort the family. She poured out her story of divorce, remarriage, and a feeling of estrangement from God. But, she added, she now had a desire to renew her relationship with God.

Another health-care professional, who was caring for Mandy, uncharacteristically broke into tears. She told of growing up in a boarding school, away from her missionary parents, and never being openly angry at them but never feeling close to them or to God. Now, after caring for Mandy, she longed to regain intimacy with her earthly and heavenly father. Mandy died that evening at seven o'clock.

**Themes:** *Grief, Hospitals, Love – of others, Parents, Relationships, Sickness, Suffering.*

**Scriptures:** Matthew 5:4; Luke 10:27; 1 Corinthians 13; 2 Corinthians 1:3–11; 11:30; 12:9; Philippians 4:13; 1 Peter 4:13.

## 112 GRATITUDE

Mother Teresa told a moving story about a six-year-old orphan boy. The Sisters had rescued him from the streets of Calcutta where he was dying of fever and nursed him back to health. On the day that he was to leave for another home they gave him a small packet of sugar – a highly-prized commodity amongst the poor. A quarter of a kilo of sugar equals a day's wages. As the little boy walked through the gates he saw the Sisters carrying in another child, obviously in great need. He walked straight over to them and handed the sugar to the Sisters, saying that he wanted the sick boy to have it. Mother Teresa asked him why he had done it. "I think that is what Jesus would have done," he replied.

*Themes:* *Generosity, Gifts, Offerings, Sacrifice.*

**Scriptures:** Psalm 112:9; Isaiah 55:10–11; Mark 10:17–31; 12:41–44; Luke 19:1–10; 2 Corinthians 8 and 9; 1 Timothy 6:17–19; Hebrews 13:5.

## 113 GRATITUDE

Mother Teresa tells of a man who had been beaten up and was picked up on the streets of Melbourne. He was an alcoholic who had been in that state for years and the Sisters took him to their Home of Compassion. From the way they touched him and the way they took care of him, suddenly it was clear to him "God loves me!" He left the Home and never touched alcohol again, but went back to his family, his children and his job. Afterwards, when he got his first salary, he came to the Sisters and gave them the money, saying, "I want you to be for others the love of God, as you have been to me."

---

[112] Barry Kissell, *Walking on Water* (London: Hodder and Stoughton, 1986), p. 149.

*Themes:* *Alcoholism, Generosity, God – his love, Love – changed by, Reformed.*

***Scriptures:*** Psalms 112:9; Isaiah 55:10–11; Mark 10:17–31; 12:41–44; Luke 10:27; 19:1–10; 1 Corinthians 13; 2 Corinthians 8 and 9; 1 Timothy 6:17–19; Hebrews 13:5.

## 114 GREED

In the movie *Wall Street*, Gordon Gekko is played by Michael Douglas. He is a cunning, unprincipled, multimillionaire corporate raider. One day he speaks to a meeting of spellbound shareholders who are worried about a takeover bid. He declares,

> "... ladies and gentlemen,... greed – for lack of a better word – is good. Greed is right. Greed works. Greed clarifies, cuts through and captures the essence of the evolutionary spirit. Greed, in all of its forms – greed for life, for money, for love, for knowledge – has marked the upward surge of mankind..."

Later in the film, Gordon's friend Bud asks, "Tell me, Gordon, when does it all end?.... How many yachts can you water-ski behind? How much is enough?"

*Themes:* *Generosity, Giving, God – his provision, Materialism, Money, Offerings, Sacrificial giving, Tithing, Wealth.*

***Scriptures:*** Psalm 112:9; Isaiah 55:10–11; Matthew 6:19–21; Mark 10:17–31; 12:41–44; Luke 19:1–10; 2 Corinthians 8 and 9; 1 Timothy 6:17–19; Hebrews 13:5.

## 115 GRIEF

In the very early hours of Sunday morning, 6 January 1985, a couple learned the shocking news that their younger son of 18 had put a gun under his chin and shot himself. When the minister went to the house there was a profound sadness over the people gathered there. In some of the rooms, and outside as well, there were friends and members of the extended family sitting or standing in disbelief. Some were openly and uncontrollably crying. The only place the minister could talk with the parents was in their bedroom. They embraced each other and shared the grief as much as they could. Then they sat on the bed. The minister prayed for them. Then he invited them to ask God to take control of their lives in the midst of tragedy and fill them with his Spirit.

Here is how the father related the event exactly six months later. "I... asked God to refill my life with the Holy Spirit and almost instantly I felt a warm peaceful feeling throughout my whole body, it was like being defrosted, only from the inside out. Since that time I have been at peace with God and the world... Don't get me wrong, Christians do cry, and I still cry for my family and my son, but I am peaceful when I do."

*Themes:* Comfort, Conversion, Death, God – his peace, Holy Spirit – filled with, Peace, Suicide.

**Scriptures:** 2 Samuel 12; Psalms 6:5–7; 23:4; 46; 55:22; 119:28; Isaiah 25:8; 53:3–4; Hosea 13:14; Matthew 5:4; John 11; Romans 5:1–5; 1 Corinthians 15:54–57; 2 Corinthians 1:3–7; 1 Thessalonians 4:13–18; James 1:2–4; 1 Peter 5:6–7.

## ⋀⋀6 GUIDANCE

Hannah Whitall Smith, the Quaker lady, tells of a woman who, each morning, having consecrated the day to the Lord as soon as she woke, "would then ask Him whether she was to get up or not", and would not stir until "the voice" told her to dress. As she put on each article she asked the Lord whether she was to put it on. Very often the Lord would tell her to put on the right shoe and leave

---

[116] Adapted from Group Movements of the Past and Experiments in Guidance in J. I. Packer, *Knowing God* (London: Hodder and Stoughton, 1973), pp. 213–214.

off the other. Sometimes she was to put on both stockings and no shoes; and sometimes both shoes and no stockings; it was the same with all the articles of dress.

*Themes:* *Faith, God – in control, Neurosis, Responsibility, Trust.*

**Scriptures:** Exodus 13:21–22; Deuteronomy 31:6, 8; Psalms 23:4; 25:9; 32:8; 37:3–5; 48:14; 66:12; 138:7; Proverb 3:5–6; Isaiah 43:2; Daniel 3:25, 28; Mark 11:22–24; Luke 7:1–10; John 20:24–29; Hebrews 11:1–3.

## 117 GUIDANCE

Kenneth McAll, in his pre-war days as a missionary doctor in China, was walking towards a desert village. He had already had one narrow escape when arrested and tried by the invading Japanese. As he walked, a man joined him and asked him to change direction and go to a different village. He turned and accompanied the man to their destination. When they arrived, the villagers were delighted and said they needed plenty of help. "But why did you change direction?" they asked. "You were walking towards a village which we think is occupied by the Japanese." They said they had watched him walking in the desert, but had seen no man stop and talk to him. When Kenneth looked around there was no trace of the man. It was then that he realised that his guide had spoken to him in English!

*Themes:* *Angels, Miracles, Visions.*

**Scriptures:** Exodus 13:21–22; Deuteronomy 31:6, 8; Psalms 23:4; 25:9; 32:8; 48:14; 66:12; 138:7; Proverb 3:5–6; Isaiah 43:2; Daniel 3:25, 28.

## 118 GUIDANCE

Two men were walking down a noisy and busy street. One of them was a scientist, an entomologist – a bug catcher.

---

117 John Woolmer, *Growing Up to Salvation* (London: Triangle, 1983), p. 84.

Suddenly he stopped and asked his friend, "Can you hear that?"

"All I can hear is the noise of passing people and the roar of traffic," said the friend.

"Yes, and I can also hear a cricket," put in the scientist.

Going over to the wall of a tall office block he moved a small loose stone in the footpath. Under it was the cricket which had been making its shrill music. As they continued along the friend asked how on earth he could hear the cricket above all the noise. To show how easy it was the scientist took out a 20 cent piece and dropped it on the ground in the middle of the rushing crowd. You can guess what happened. A number of people instantly stopped and looked around for the coin, which made the barely audible yet recognisable tinkling sound of a coin.

*Themes: Listening to God, Obedience, Prayer.*

**Scriptures:** Exodus 13:21–22; 33:14; Deuteronomy 4:30; 31:6, 8; 1 Kings 19:11–12; Psalms 23:4; 25:1–4, 9; 32:8; 48:14; 66:12; 138:7; Proverbs 3:5–6; Isaiah 43:2; Daniel 3:25, 28; John 10:27; 16:13.

## ११९ GUIDANCE

Smith was in deep trouble. He was sitting on his roof during a terrible flood, and the water was already up to his feet. He was a Christian and began to pray that the Lord would provide a miracle and rescue him.

Before long, a fellow in a boat paddled by and shouted, "Can I give you a lift to higher ground?"

"No, thanks," said Smith. "I have faith in the Lord and he will save me."

Soon the water rose to Smith's waist. At this point, a motorboat pulled up and someone called out,

"Can I give you a lift to higher ground?"

"No, thanks. I have faith in the Lord and he will save me."

Later a helicopter flew by, and Smith was now standing on the roof with water up to his neck.

"Grab the rope," yelled the pilot. "I'll pull you up."

"No, thanks," said Smith. "I have faith in the Lord and he will save me."

But then after hours of treading water, poor, exhausted Smith drowned and went to his reward.

As he arrived at the Pearly Gates, Smith met his maker and complained about this turn of events.

"Tell me, Lord," he said, "I had such faith in you to save me and you let me down. What happened?"

The Lord replied, "What do you want from me? I sent you two boats and a helicopter!"

*Themes:* *Faith, Humour, Listening to God, Obedience.*

**Scriptures:** Exodus 13:21–22; 33:14; Deuteronomy 4:30; 31:6, 8; 1 Kings 19:11–12; Psalms 23:4; 25:1–4, 9; 32:8; 48:14; 66:12; 138:7; Proverbs 3:5–6; Isaiah 43:2; Daniel 3:25, 28; Joel 2:28; John 10:27; 16:13; Acts 2:17; 10:9–16.

## 120 GUILT [120]

A newspaper reported the tragic story of the drowning of eight-year-old Christopher. He had been accompanied by three friends, who said that he had slipped into the pond. They said they thought he was playing a trick on them.

It was almost two years before the secret was uncovered when the fifteen-year-old boy who pushed Chris into the water confessed his guilt to a friend. Soon the police were involved. In those two years one of the three began crying frequently after Chris' death and had to sleep with his mother.

A second, an 18-year-old, was fired from his job because he would stay home from work on days when he felt angry and disgusted about telling a lie to protect a friend. The third boy started hearing voices and seeing visions and barely talked to his parents. He later entered a hospital for emotionally disturbed children.

*Themes:* *Confession, Forgiveness, Healing – of emotions, Justice, Law, Murder, Remorse, Repentance, Sin.*

**Scriptures:** Exodus 20:13; Deuteronomy 5:17; Psalms 31:10; 51; Proverbs 20:9; Mark 11:25; John 8:34–36; 1 John 1:8–9.

## 121 **HEALING**

Francis MacNutt is a former Catholic priest and scholar. His book *Healing* is one of the best on the subject. He also has the gift of healing. MacNutt received a letter from Mrs Sophie Zientarski two weeks after he had prayed for her.

> I am the diabetic over whom you prayed... and it is with great joy I want to tell you that the Lord has healed me... [In two weeks] I have taken no medicine, and I feel great. Never in a million years did I think that this would happen to me...

Seven months later another letter came.

> ... I have the doctor's verification,... and he can't find anything wrong with me... I am able to do my housework, which last year I could not do. My heart has been healed, too;... I could not walk up the stairs, and now stairs do not bother me at all. I feel ten years younger, praise the Lord.

*Themes:* *Diabetes, Miracles, Prayer.*

**Scriptures:** Matthew 8:5–13; 9:27–31; Mark 1:29–31, 40–44; 2:1–12; 3:1–6; 5:24–34; 7:31–37; 8:22–26; 10:46–52; Luke 13:10–17; 14:1–6; John 4:46–54; 9:1–34; James 5:14–15.

121 Taken from Francis MacNutt, *Healing* (Notre Dame: Ave Maria, 1974), pp. 193–194.

## 122 HEALING

John Wimber tells that he received a phone call from a distraught father. The man was sobbing and could hardly talk. "My baby is here in the hospital," he said, "and they have tubes from machines attached all over her body. The doctors say she will not survive the night. What can you do?" John told him he would come to the hospital. After he put the phone down he prayed, "Lord, is this baby supposed to die?" John sensed the Lord saying, "No!" John walked into the hospital with the knowledge that he was a representative of Christ, a messenger who had a gift for that baby girl.

When John entered the baby's room, he sensed death, so he said quietly, "Death, get out of here." It left, and the whole atmosphere of the room changed, as though a weight had been lifted. Then he went over and began praying for the girl. After only a few minutes he knew she was going to be healed, and so did her father. Hope came into his eyes.

"She is going to be okay," he said, "I know it."

Within 20 minutes she improved greatly; several days later she was released, completely healed.

*Themes:* *Death, Deliverance, Demonic, Miracles, Prayer, Sickness.*

**Scriptures:** Matthew 8:5–13; 9:27–31; Mark 1:29–31, 40–44; 2:1–12; 3:1–6; 5:24–34; 7:31–37; 8:22–26; 10:46–52; Luke 13:10–17; 14:1–6; John 4:46–54; 9:1–34; 11:25–26; James 5:14–15; 1 Peter 1:13.

## 123 HEALING

Dr James R. Friend of Bakersfield, California wrote the following letter to John Wimber.

---

122 From John Wimber, *Power Healing* (London: Hodder and Stoughton, 1986), p. 174.
123 Wimber, *Power Healing*, pp. 143–145.

July 6, 1984

Dear Pastor Wimber:

... On Friday night when you were teaching, there was a young mother with her four-and-a-half-year-old baby right down in the front row. This youngster was terribly brain damaged... She... could not feed herself, had never even sucked her thumb, was unable to speak, and her body would go through a constant array of terribly contorted disfiguring, purpose-less movements... Her arms and legs were rigidly spastic, her eyes were usually back in her head and she could not hold her head even for a moment. That night God clearly spoke to me and four other people in that audience that he wanted to heal her. The child's name is Tina. The following Wednesday we gathered with Tina's family... The five of us clearly could wit-ness to the fact that God had unmistakably spoken to us that he was going to heal Tina, and so we just laid claim to that in Jesus' name and to the glory of the Father. That began a whole series of miraculous events. First of all... the purpose-less movements ceased within three weeks. The rigidity of her arms and legs began to diminish... and within four or five weeks she no longer drooled and her eye movement was nearly normal and she was very attentive to those around her. She now sucks her thumb... She goes to a special school for handicapped brain damaged children and the teachers' notes are an accurate chronology of this miracle...

Your brother in Christ,
James R. Friend, MD

**Themes:** *Miracles, Prayer, Sickness.*

**Scriptures:** Matthew 8:5–13; 9:27–31; Mark 1:29–31, 40–44; 2:1–12; 3:1–6; 5:24–34; 7:31–37; 8:22–26; 10:46–52; Luke 13:10–17; 14:1–6; John 4:46–54; 9:1–34; James 5:14–15.

## 124 HEALING

There was quite a stir in Fuller Theological Seminary over healings that took place in some classes.

Sam Sasser had served as a missionary for many years in the South Pacific. One day he was in the back of the class at Fuller. He was sitting in a wheelchair with his right foot wrapped in a thick bandage. He had survived several accidents, including two in a boat, and a plane crash. He also had coral poisoning, which had caused his bones to deteriorate. In the prayer time before the class began Sam asked for prayer. Several students stood around him as someone led in prayer.

The next day Sam said he wanted to give a testimony. "I don't go for theatrics," he said, "but yesterday I didn't mention that I was also legally blind as a result of the coral poisoning. The first day I did not see you as you taught the class. After prayer yesterday, I could see you through the whole class. Not only that, but this morning the nurse came to change the bandage on my foot, and she couldn't believe what she saw. She told me that if whatever had started were to continue, I would be well in a week."

Within another week, Sam Sasser was walking around the Fuller campus, pushing his own wheelchair. He cancelled his enrolment to learn to use a guide dog. When I heard this story Sam was not able to play tennis or to read, and signs of the underlying coral poisoning flare up from time to time. But God has been greatly glorified as the light of Jesus has brought healing to Sam.

*Themes: Blindness, Miracles, Prayer, Sickness.*

124 From C. Peter Wagner, *How to Have a Healing Ministry* (Eastbourne: Monarch, 1988), pp. 104–105.

***Scriptures:*** Matthew 8:5–13; 9:27–31; Mark 1:29–31, 40–44; 2:1–12; 3:1–6; 5:24–34; 7:31–37; 8:22–26; 10:46–52; Luke 13:10–17; 14:1–6; John 4:46–54; 9:1–34; James 5:14–15.

## ⋏∠S **HEALING** *

John Wimber writes:

I was speaking in South Africa at a large conference. A friend, John McClure, was with me, and we were asked to go to the home of a lady of the church. She was dressed beautifully but was very emaciated, weighing only 85 pounds. She had been sent home from the hospital to die. Her body was full of cancer. Her only hope of survival was divine intervention. We prayed for her, but not with great fervency. John had confidence that she would be healed. I felt nothing.

That night she woke up with a vibrant, tingling feeling throughout her body. For the next four hours her body was full of intense heat. She tried to call out to her husband in the next room but couldn't raise her voice loud enough for him to hear.

Alone and frightened, she crawled into the bathroom, her body racked with pain. At the time she thought, "O my God. My body is coming apart and I'm dying." Without knowing it, she eliminated from her body a number of large tumours. Finally, exhausted from the night's events, she fell back asleep. She didn't know if she'd wake up.

But a half an hour later she woke up incredibly refreshed. Later her husband woke up to the smell of freshly brewed coffee. "What are you doing?" he asked, astonished to see his wife on her feet and preparing breakfast.

She replied with sudden understanding: "God has healed me."

Two days later she reported to her doctors, who gave her

---

[125] John Wimber, "Signs, Wonders and Cancer", *Christianity Today*, Inc/CHRISTIANITY TODAY. 7 October 1996, Vol. 40, No. II.

a clean bill of health. They couldn't find a cancer in her body. God had completely delivered her of all of it.

Without much energy to pray on our part and without any desperation or faith on her part, the Lord chose to heal this woman's cancer-infested body through divine means. That's God, and that is sometimes how he does it.

**Themes:** *Faith, Miracles, Prayer, Signs and wonders.*
**Scriptures:** Matthew 8:5–13; 9:27–31; Mark 1:29–31, 40–44; 2:1–12; 3:1–6; 5:24–34; 7:31–37; 8:22–26; 10:46–52; Luke 13:10–17; 14:1–6; John 4:46–54; 9:1–34; 11:25–26; Acts 2:22; 5:12; 8:8; 14:8–18; Romans 15:18–19; 1 Corinthians 12:9, 28, 30; 2 Corinthians 12:12; Galatians 3:5; 1 Thessalonians 1:5; James 5:14–15; 1 Peter 1:13.

## 126 HEALING

In an interview, John Wimber said,

> I remember one time when a team member and I were called to pray for a woman whose left hand had actually died. I mean, it was black to the elbow; her fingers were drawn up and rotting. An amputation was scheduled for the next day. The odor was incredible. I could almost see bones through the skin of the fingers. I stood there swallowing, trying to settle my queasy stomach... when suddenly I knew I had to touch that hand. I *had* to. I put my hand over hers, closed my eyes, and prayed. As soon as I got outside the room, I began crying. *Why in the world did I do that? I probably embarrassed her to death by drawing attention to her blight....* We went home with no sense at all of having won a victory or done any mighty deed. I fully expected to hear the next day that the amputation had been completed. Two weeks later, her brother came up to me with a rather lengthy letter the woman had written – and she was left-handed. It told how overnight her hand had begun to recover just enough to forestall the operation.

126 John Wimber in *Leadership* 6 (2, 1985), p. 127.

The doctors kept postponing it a day at a time, until finally she was well.

**Themes:** *Doubt, Laying on hands, Miracles, Prayer, Sickness, Touch.*

**Scriptures:** Matthew 8:5–13, 26; 9:27–31; 14:28–31; Mark 1:29–31, 40–44; 2:1–12; 3:1–6; 5:24–34; 7:31–37; 8:22–26; 10:46–52; Luke 13:10–17; 14:1–6; John 4:46–54; 9:1–34; Hebrews 11; James 5:14–15.

## 127 HEALING

Kate Semmerling tells of her experience as a student nurse in a clinic in Haiti. A woman brought a small boy with crippled legs. He could not stand or walk. She tried to explain that there was nothing she could do, but she wanted to get rid of the woman so, as she says, "I sighed and offered to pray for her – a God-bless-this-woman-type of prayer that would send her on her way." But there was a grain of faith that told her God could heal, although she expected nothing. She put her hands on the crippled legs and said, "Dear God, please come and do your work here."

That was enough faith in that case. Over the next five minutes the legs pumped up as if they were small balloons, and they filled with new muscle. Kate said, "I thought I was in the Twilight Zone. I had never seen anything like this happen before." The boy's legs became normal, and he stood up and walked around. Kate's response: "Oh my God, look at this!"

**Themes:** *Faith, Miracles, Prayer, Trust.*

**Scriptures:** Psalms 37:3–5; Proverbs 3:5–6; Matthew 8:5–13; 9:27–31; Mark 1:29–31, 40–44; 2:1–12; 3:1–6; 5:24–34; 7:31–37; 8:22–26; 10:46–52; 11:22–24; Luke 7:1–10; 13:10–17; 14:1–6; John 4:46–54; 9:1–34; James 5:14–15.

---

[127] Adapted from Kate Semmerling with Andres Tapia, "Haiti," U Magazine, February 1987, p. 13 in C. Peter Wagner, *How to Have a Healing Ministry* (Eastbourne: Monarch, 1988), pp. 253–254.

## 128 HEALING

Susan Speight was a domestic science teacher in Wetherby. But for four years she had been confined to a wheelchair with a crippling complication of diabetes known as neuropathy. Susan had lost all feeling from her waist downwards. Her specialist had told her that it would not come back.

In June 1977 she went to a festival in the Leeds Town Hall where David Watson was speaking. During David's talk one night she began to feel her feet getting hot, and eventually complete feeling was restored. She realised this meant that she ought to be able to walk.

When the meeting was over, she called to Andrew, one of David Watson's team members. She told him what had happened. Andrew helped her out of the wheelchair and together they walked right round the outside of the Town Hall without using her sticks. Realising that she could now walk perfectly, they went back into the Town Hall to tell David and they spent some time together praising God for his unexpected healing power.

*Themes:* *Miracles, Praise.*

**Scriptures:** Psalms 100; Matthew 8:5–13; 9:27–31; Mark 1:29–31, 40–44; 2:1–12; 3:1–6; 5:24–34; 7:31–37; 8:22–26; 10:46–52; Luke 13:10–17; 14:1–6; John 4:46–54; 9:1–34; 1 Thessalonians 5:16–18; Hebrews 13:15; James 5:14–15.

## 129 HEALING

Tony Campolo was speaking at a small college in the American Midwest. As he was finishing his presentation on the second night a woman came down the aisle of the

---

[128] Adapted from Teddy Saunders and Hugh Sansom, *David Watson: A Biography* (London: Hodder and Stoughton, 1992), p. 168.

[129] Adapted from Tony Campolo, *It's Friday, But Sunday's Comin'* (Berkhamsted: Word, 1985), pp. 76–82.

auditorium carrying her child in her arms. The child was crippled and in calipers. The woman was obviously not a student.

"What do you want?" Campolo asked.

"God told me to come," she answered. "You are supposed to heal my child," she went on.

"Dear lady, I don't have the gift of healing... Teaching is my gift."

The students had picked up what was going on at the front and there was quite a bit of chatting and sniggering. A very "with it" chaplain came to Tony's rescue. Tony explained to the chaplain what the woman wanted. The chaplain spoke to the audience.

"Those who do not believe that this child is going to be healed this evening, please leave the auditorium. If you are not absolutely convinced that this child will have his legs straightened through prayer, I want you to get out of here."

Five Pentecostal young people were left. They were already "into it" with their hands in the air and speaking in tongues, expressing their dependence on God.

The chaplain anointed the child with oil and Campolo prayed. He started with a kind of non-committal, formal prayer. Then he stopped. They all stopped. They felt a strange and awesome presence break loose in their midst. Campolo removed his hand from the child and felt ashamed. They all removed their hands. Tony said that he now expected that the child would be healed then and there. However, it was not. Everyone went home.

Three years later Tony Campolo met the mother in another meeting. Standing next to her was a fine lad standing up straight without any calipers. After the meeting, three years previously, the lad had woken crying. His calipers were tight, so the mother loosened them. This happened a number of times over the succeeding few days until the legs were straight.

*Themes:* *Gifts of the Spirit, Laying on hands, Miracles, Prayer, Tongues – gift of.*

**Scriptures:** Matthew 8:5–13; 9:27–31; Mark 1:29–31, 40–44; 2:1–12; 3:1–6; 5:24–34; 7:31–37; 8:22–26; 10:46–52; Luke 13:10–17; 14:1–6; John 4:46–54; 9:1–34; James 5:14–15.

## 130 HEALING

A dad could hear his wife in the next room trying to comfort their daughter, who was in the throes of a week-long illness. As a man who claimed that God answered prayer for healing he felt he should go in and pray for his daughter. But he had prayed for his children so many times before when they were sick, and never did it seem to make much difference.

"How can I have faith when nothing ever happens?" he said to himself. "Where do you get faith?"

The dad then recalled the passage in Romans 10:17 where Paul talks about faith coming from hearing about Christ. So he picked up his Bible and went in to his wife and his little girl. Sitting on the edge of the bed, he started to read aloud the stories of Jesus healing the sick. Something began to happen inside dad. He grew more and more confident that Jesus *was* able to heal his daughter. He could see the same trust growing in his daughter's eyes. Then, together, they asked Jesus to make her well. From that moment she recovered rapidly.

*Themes:* *Faith, Healing, Illness, Miracles, Prayer, Prayer – unanswered, Sickness, Signs and wonders.*

**Scriptures:** Matthew 8:5–13; 9:27–31; Mark 1:29–31, 40–44; 2:1–12; 3:1–6; 5:24–34; 7:31–37; 8:22–26; 10:45–52; Luke 13:10–17; 14:1–6; John 4:46–54; 9:1–34; 11:25–26; Acts 2:22; 5:12; 14:8–18; Romans

5:18–19; 10:17; 1 Corinthians 12:9, 28, 30; Galatians 3:2, 5; 1
Thessalonians 1:5; James 5:14–15; 1 Peter 1:13.

## 131 HEALING

Pamela Reddy had been told by doctors that she needed
her diseased right kidney removing. She was also recovering from hepatitis. She had been exposed to tuberculosis
at the hospital where she worked. And because of injury to
her shoulder and neck her left arm did not function well
or without pain (she is left-handed). Doctors told her she
would never have full use of her arm or freedom from
pain.

One Sunday she came for special prayers at her church.
A married couple, George and Pam, laid hands on her and
prayed. The pain in Pamela's kidney disappeared, and her
shoulder gained mobility. Over the next few weeks other
prayers were answered. Eventually, she underwent a physical examination for her new job. All the tests came back
negative. There was no kidney disease and no residue of
hepatitis or TB. Her neck has straightened, the bones in
her shoulder are no longer rubbing and she has the full
range of movement in her arm with no pain.

*Themes: Laying on hands, Miracles, Prayer, Signs and wonders.*

**Scriptures:** Matthew 8:5–13; 9:27–31; Mark 1:29–31, 40–44; 2:1–12;
3:1–6; 5:24–34; 7:31–37; 8:22–26; 10:46–52; Luke 13:10–17; 14:1–6;
John 4:46–54; 9:1–34; 11:25–26; Acts 2:22; 5:12; 14:8–18; Romans
15:18–19; 1 Corinthians 12:9, 28, 30; 2 Corinthians 12:12; Galatians 3:5;
1 Thessalonians 1:5; James 5:14–15; 1 Peter 1:13.

## 132 HEALING

John White and his wife were in Malaysia and praying for
a two-year-old child. Her body was completely covered
with raw, weeping eczema sores. She ran around the room

restlessly so that her parents had to catch her to bring her struggling to John and his wife.

They began to pray and extended their hands to lay them on her. The instant their hands touched her she fell into profound and relaxed slumber in her mum's arms. John said, "I shall never forget our sense of exhilaration and excitement as the weeping areas began to dry up, their borders shrinking visibly before our eyes like the shores of lakes in time of drought."

*Themes:* *Joy, Laying on hands, Miracles, Prayer, Signs and wonders.*

**Scriptures:** Matthew 8:5–13; 9:27–31; Mark 1:29–31, 40–44; 2:1–12; 3:1–6; 5:24–34; 7:31–37; 8:22–26; 10:46–52; Luke 13:10–17; 14:1–6; John 4:46–54; 9:1–34; 11:25–26; Acts 2:22; 5:12; 8:8; 14:8–18; Romans 15:18–19; 1 Corinthians 12:9, 28, 30; 2 Corinthians 12:12; Galatians 3:5; 1 Thessalonians 1:5; James 5:14–15; 1 Peter 1:13.

## 133 HEALING

Colin and Caroline Urquhart were staying with Charles and Joyce and their family, while Colin was ministering for a few days in Cornwall. Colin and Caroline were sitting having a leisurely cup of coffee when they heard screams.

One of the boys came rushing into the kitchen: "Dad, there's been an accident." The father didn't wait to hear any more. He ran out of the house and across the yard, closely followed by Joyce, the mother.

On the previous evening Colin had been speaking about the prayer promises of Jesus and what it means to pray with faith or trust, knowing that God is going to answer you. Colin and Caroline were praying when Charles carried ten-year-old Joanna into the room.

In the garage the children had been melting down lead to pour into moulds, to make gifts for Christmas. One of them dropped a cold piece of metal into the container, causing some of the molten mixture to fly into Joanna's face. Some of the lead had gone into both eyes. Can you imagine the effect of molten lead on eyes?

It took her mother nearly 40 minutes to remove all the pieces of metal. During that time they all prayed, silently and aloud, with Joanna and for her. But all the time they thanked the Lord that there would be no damage to the eyes, and praised him for his healing.

Joanna was obviously in considerable distress, so once the metal had been removed from her eyes they asked the Lord to give her a good sleep, so that she would not suffer from shock after such an experience.

She slept, and at 5:00 pm was downstairs having what the British call tea. Joanna's eyes were not even bloodshot! And it was subsequently confirmed that she had suffered no damage to them at all.

*Themes:* *Faith, Miracles, Prayer, Signs and wonders.*

**Scriptures:** Matthew 8:5–13; 9:27–31; Mark 1:29–31, 40–44; 2:1–12; 3:1–6; 5:24–34; 7:31–37; 8:22–26; 10:46–52; Luke 13:10–17; 14:1–6; John 4:46–54; 9:1–34; 11:25–26; Acts 2:22; 5:12; 8:8; 14:8–18; Romans 15:18–19; 1 Corinthians 12:9, 28, 30; 2 Corinthians 12:12; Galatians 3:5; 1 Thessalonians 1:5; James 5:14–15; 1 Peter 1:13.

## 134 **HOLY SPIRIT**

On 12 October 1492, Rodrigo de Triana was aloft in the rigging of the good ship *Pinta*. They were somewhere in the Atlantic. At two in the morning he set up the long awaited cry *"Tierra, tierra!"* ("Land, land!").

Christopher Columbus went ashore and named the island San Salvador in honour of the Saviour for answering their prayers. One of the major reasons why Columbus discovered the New World was his courage. It is an inter-

---

134 Adapted from F. Fernandez-Armesto, *Columbus and the Conquest of the Impossible* (London: Weidenfeld and Nicolson, 1974), pp. 86–93.

esting feature of the history of maritime exploration that most maritime explorers have fought against the wind and sailed into the wind. They did this because, although they wanted to discover new things, they were more fearful of not being able to go back to where they came from. But Christopher Columbus, a man of great courage, sailed with the wind. So keen was he to discover the New World over the horizon that he was prepared to sail with the wind.

*Themes:* *Adventure, Courage, Discovery, Faith, Obedience, Risk, Trust.*

**Scriptures:** Psalms 27:14; 37:3–5; Proverbs 3:5–6; Matthew 28:19; Mark 3:14; 6:7; 11:22–24; Luke 7:1–10; 9:1–6; 10:1–20; John 14:15–24; Acts 5:29; 8:26, 29; 9:10, 15; 10:9–16; 11:1–18; 13:1–4; 15:28; 16:6–10.

## 135 HUMILITY

The eyes of the world have often been on Linford Christie. He is Britain's greatest sprinter. He has won more than 20 medals, including an Olympic gold at Barcelona in 1992. Linford is also one of Britain's richest sportsmen, with appearance money of about £30,000 a race and sponsorship deals. He shops in Paris and New York.

Christie owes much of his success to an unlikely hero, 63-year-old Ron Roddan, who has been his coach for 16 years. Ron is a former geologist who is rarely seen in public. Ron refuses to be paid for his coaching, choosing to live on his pension after being made redundant some years ago. "I don't coach people for money but because I enjoy the sport," says Ron. Rather than accompany Linford to track meetings, Ron prefers to analyse Linford's races on television. "You have to respect Ron's wish to be in the background," says Linford. "He lets my feet do the talking." John Regis, another sprinter, says,

"Linford gets all the acclaim but without Ron he would never have had much success."

*Themes: Apprenticing, Encouragement, Fame, Greatness, Jesus – character, John the Baptist, Leadership, Mentoring, Money, Moses, Parable – Pharisee and the Tax Collector, Purpose, Retirement, Service, Sport, Success, Support, Teaching.*

**Scriptures:** Numbers 12:3; Deuteronomy 18:2; 2 Samuel 22:36; Psalms 18:35; 113:5–6; Proverbs 3:34; 15:33; 18:12; 25:6–7; Daniel 25:22; Matthew 11:29; Mark 1:7; 9:33–37; Luke 1:16, 52; 8:9–14; 9:46–48; 11:43; 14:7–14; 18:9–14; 20:46; John 1:6–9; Romans 12:3; 1 Corinthians 2:16; 13; Ephesians 4:2; Philippians 2:1–11; Colossians 3:12; James 2:2–4; 4:10; 1 Peter 5:5–6.

## 136 IDENTITY

He began his life with all the classic handicaps and disadvantages. His mother was a powerfully built, dominating woman who found it difficult to love anyone. She had been married three times, and her second husband divorced her because she beat him up regularly. The father of the child I'm describing was her third husband; he died of a heart attack a few months before the child's birth. As a consequence, the mother had to work long hours from his earliest childhood.

She gave him no affection, no love, no discipline, and no training during those early years. She even forbade him to call her at work. Other children had little to do with him, so he was alone most of the time. He was absolutely rejected from his earliest childhood. He was ugly and poor and untrained and unlovable. When he was thirteen years old a school psychologist commented that he probably didn't even know the meaning of the word "love". During adolescence, the girls would have nothing to do with him and he fought with the boys.

136 James Dobson, *Hide or Seek* (Old Tappan, NJ: Revell, 1974), pp. 9–10.

Despite a high IQ, he failed academically, and finally dropped out during his third year of high school. He thought he might find a new acceptance in the Marine Corps; they reportedly built men, and he wanted to be one. But his problems went with him. The other marines laughed at him and ridiculed him. He fought back, resisted authority, and was court-martialled and thrown out with an undesirable discharge. So, there he was – a young man in his early twenties – absolutely friendless and shipwrecked. He was small and scrawny in stature. He had an adolescent squeak in his voice. He was balding. He had no talent, no skill, no sense of worthiness. He didn't even have a driving licence.

Once again he thought he could run from his problems so he went to live in a foreign country. But he was rejected there too. Nothing had changed. While there, he married a woman who herself had been an illegitimate child and brought her back to America with him. Soon, she began to develop the same contempt for him that everyone else displayed. She bore him two children, but he never enjoyed the status and respect that a father should have. His marriage continued to crumble. His wife demanded more things than he could provide. Instead of being his ally against the bitter world, as he hoped, she became his most vicious opponent. She could outfight him, and she learned to bully him. On one occasion, she locked him in the bathroom as punishment. Finally, she forced him to leave.

He tried to make it on his own, but he was terribly lonely. After days of solitude, he went home and literally begged her to take him back. He surrendered all pride. He crawled. He accepted humiliation. He came back on her terms. Despite his meagre salary, he brought her $78 as a gift, asking her to take it and spend it any way she wished. But she laughed at him. She belittled his feeble attempts to supply the family's needs. She ridiculed his failure. She made fun of his sexual impotency in front of a friend who was there. At one point, he fell on his knees and wept bitterly, as the greater darkness of his private nightmare enveloped him.

Finally, in silence, he pleaded no more. No one wanted him. No one had ever wanted him. He was perhaps the most rejected man of our time. His ego lay shattered in a fragmented dust! The next day, he was a strangely different man. He arose, went to the garage, and took a rifle he had hidden there. He carried it with him to his newly acquired job at a book-storage building. And, from a window on the third floor of that building, shortly after noon, 22 November 1963, he sent two bullets crashing into the head of President John Fitzgerald Kennedy.

Lee Harvey Oswald, the rejected, unlovable failure, killed the man who, more than any other man on earth, embodied all the success, beauty, wealth, and family affection which he lacked.

**Themes:** *Love, Marriage, Murder, Parenting, Rejection, Security, Violence – domestic.*

**Scriptures:** Luke 10:27; 1 Corinthians 13; Ephesians 6:1–4; Colossians 3:18–21.

## 137 **INCARNATION**

There is a legend concerning a tribe of Indians who lived around Niagara Falls. Each year the men of the tribe would cast lots to choose a young girl to sacrifice as the bride of the falls.

One particular year the lot fell to the youngest and loveliest daughter of a very old chieftain. He received the news without moving, as he sat in his tent smoking his pipe. The fateful celebration drew near. A little boat was cut out of timber and painted white. On the day, the girl was placed in the canoe surrounded by treasured food. Four men pushed the vessel and girl out into the swirling river as far as they dared. Then they returned to the bank.

As all the people watched the canoe head to the deadly falls they saw another canoe come from the other side of the river. As it got closer they saw that it was the old chief. He was rowing as hard as he could straight for the sacrificial canoe. When he reached his daughter he grabbed hold of the little boat. With one last look of love, they went over the falls together.

*Themes:* *Cross, God – love of, Jesus – death of, Love, Sacrifice.*

**Scriptures:** Matthew 11:25–27; Luke 10:27; John 1:1–5; 5:19–23; Romans 8:32; 1 Corinthians 13; 2 Corinthians 5:19; Colossians 1:15–20; Hebrews 1:3.

## 138 INCARNATION

Shah Abbis was a Persian monarch who loved his people very much. To know and understand them better, he would mingle with his subjects in various disguises.

One day he went as a poor man to the public baths, and in a tiny cellar sat beside the fireman who tended the furnace. When it was mealtime the monarch shared his coarse food and talked to his lonely subject as a friend. Again and again he visited and the man grew to love him.

One day the Shah told him he was the monarch, expecting the man to ask for some gift from him. But the fireman sat gazing at his ruler with love and wonder and at last spoke: "You left your palace and your glory to sit with me in this dark place, to eat of my coarse food, to care whether my heart is glad or sorry. On others you may

---

138 Adapted from Michael P. Green (ed.), *Illustrations for Biblical Preaching* (Grand Rapids, MI: Baker, 1989), #130.

bestow rich presents, but to me you have given yourself, and it only remains for me to pray that you never withdraw the gift of your friendship."

*Themes:* *Christmas, Jesus – friend of sinners, God – love of.*

**Scriptures:** Exodus 33:20; Matthew 11:25–27; Luke 10:27; John 1:1–5, 14, 18; 3:16; 5:19–23; 6:38, 46; 7:29; 8:19, 34–36; Romans 5:8; 8:32; 1 Corinthians 13; 2 Corinthians 4:4; 5:19; Galatians 4:4; Philippians 2:6–8; Colossians 1:15–20; Hebrews 1:3; 2:14; 1 John 4:9.

## 139 INCARNATION *

Søren Kierkegaard says that there was a king, who ruled a peaceful land with justice and fairness. It was a happy place and everyone thought the king was happy, with his wealth and position and the adoration of his people. But in fact he was lonely. He wanted a bride, a queen to rule beside him, someone he could love and who would love him for who he was. He pondered long and hard about where to find such a woman, for he knew his courtiers would only promote their relatives to gain privilege and influence.

Then one day, as he drove through the countryside in his carriage, he saw a peasant girl. He fell in love immediately. However, he wondered how he could get her to marry him.

First he thought he would simply issue a royal decree, instructing her to become his wife. But that would only mean that she obeyed him, not that she loved him. Then he thought he would call at her home dressed in his royal robes, and simply sweep her off her feet. But he realised he would never be sure whether she too had married him simply for wealth and power.

Then he decided he would dress in peasant clothes, and have his carriage drop him off outside town and then try to convince her to marry him. But this trick did not appeal at all.

So finally, he decided to go a step further. He shed his royal robes, and he went to live in her village. He became a peasant himself. He lived with her and her people. Eventually they fell in love and were married.

*Themes:* *Christmas, Jesus – friend of sinners, God – love of, Marriage.*

**Scriptures:** Exodus 33:20; Matthew 11:25–27; Luke 10:27; John 1:1–5, 14, 18; 3:16; 5:19–23; 6:38, 46; 7:29; 8:19, 34–36; Romans 5:8; 8:32; 1 Corinthians 13; 2 Corinthians 4:4; 5:19; Galatians 4:4; Philippians 2:6–8; Colossians 1:15–20; Hebrews 1:3; 2:14; 1 John 4:9.

## 140 INCARNATION

One day man came to God on his heavenly throne and said to him, "Which do you think is harder, to be man or to be God?"

"Being God is much harder," God answered. "I have a whole universe to worry about, planets and galaxies. All you have to worry about is your family and your job."

"True enough," said man. "But you have infinite time and infinite power. The hard part in being a man is not doing the job, but doing it within the limits of human strength and the human life span."

God answered, "You don't know what you're talking about. It's much harder to be God."

Man replied, "I don't know how you can say that so confidently when you've never been human and I've never been God. What do you say we change places for just one second, so you can know the feeling of being man and I can know what it feels like to be God. Just for one second, that's all, and then we'll change back."

God didn't want to, but man kept begging and pleading, and so God finally relented. They changed places. Man became God and God became human.

And the story goes on to say that, once man sat on the divine throne, he refused to give God back his place, and ever since then man has ruled the world and God has been in exile.

*Themes:* *Alienation, Fall, Parable – Prodigal Son, Pride, Rebellion.*

**Scriptures:** Genesis 3; Job 38:1–40:2; 40:6–41:34; Luke 15:8–10; Romans 1:18–32; Ephesians 2:1–12; 4:18.

## ᐁᐱᐁ INCARNATION

In March 1993 the Serbian attack on Bosnia besieged the town of Srebrenica. There were mortar attacks on civilians, causing terrible suffering.

General Philippe Morillon was the commander of the United Nations forces. He decided to shield the citizens from attack by making Srebrenica his centre of operations. He refused an offer from the Serbs of safe passage out of the town. The citizens of Srebrenica described the General as "the only way of salvation".

Morillon stayed there for eight days to show his solidarity with the people, and to act as a human shield. Then he left. On 19 March 1993 he led a convoy back into the besieged city. He brought supplies and took out the sick and wounded.

*Themes:* *Adam and Christ, Exodus, God – his love, Jesus – work of, Leadership, Protection, Rescue, Salvation, Victory.*

**Scriptures:** Luke 4:18; John 1:14; Acts 26:18; Romans 5:12–21; Galatians 1:4; 2:20; Colossians 1:13; 2:15.

## ᐁᐱᐁ INCARNATION

One night in 1963, a theatre production was part-way through its performance in the old Birmingham Repertory Theatre, Station Street. One of the actors walked across the stage. He was holding a transistor radio on his shoulder. It was tuned to the local station, playing pop music. It was all part of the play. Then, suddenly, as the actors spoke their lines the music was interrupted. A news flash announced, "President Kennedy has been assassinated." To save interrupting the play the actor quickly snapped off the radio. But it was too late. The audience had heard the news. As much as they tried, the news meant the actors could not carry on as before.

*Themes:* Change, God – voice of, Murder.
**Scriptures:** Genesis 18:1–15; Exodus 3:1–6; 1 Samuel 3:1–4:1; Isaiah 7:14; Matthew 1:23; John 1:1–18.

## 143 INCARNATION

A salesman had been away from home for several days at a regional conference. The closing session had overrun its time and, as soon as it was over, he hurried with his friends to the main-line station. They had barely enough time to catch a train which would get them back early enough to spend some of the evening with their families. If they missed that particular train, there would be a considerable wait before the next, and they would be very late home.

As the group charged through the terminal, the man inadvertently kicked over a small table supporting a vendor's box of fruit. Apples tumbled out and rolled across the floor in all directions, but the men rushed on to the platform with only seconds to spare before the train left. As they boarded the train, the man responsible for the accident stopped in his tracks, almost unable to move. His colleagues urged him to catch the train but, deep inside, he felt desperately unhappy. Should he go on or go back? He noticed a young boy, about ten years old, standing by the table, selling the apples.

More than anything, he longed to be back with his family. However, waving goodbye to his puzzled friends, he briskly made his way back to the main concourse. People were rushing for their trains, dodging the apples. Many had been kicked here and there by hurrying travellers and the man was puzzled that the lad had done nothing whatever to retrieve his apples. As he got closer, he realised why the boy was just standing there, dazed and helpless. He was blind.

Quickly the salesman began to collect the apples. Setting up the table again, he could see that many of them were badly bruised. Opening his wallet, he took out a note and pressed it into the boy's hand, saying, "Here, please take this five pounds for the damage we did. Hope we haven't spoilt your day." Slowly he began to walk away when, above the noise of the station, he heard the loud voice of the boy calling after him, "Sir, are you Jesus?"

*Themes:* *Body of Christ, Fruit of the Spirit, Good works, Humility, Imitating Jesus, Kindness, Servant evangelism, Service.*

**Scriptures:** Exodus 22:1–3; Numbers 12:3; Psalms 113:5–6; Proverbs 15:33; 18:12; Matthew 5:16; Romans 12:5; 1 Corinthians 4:16; 6:20; 11:1; 12:27; Galatians 5:22; Ephesians 2:10; Philippians 2:5; 3:17; 1 Thessalonians 1:6; 2:14; 2 Thessalonians 3:7–9; 2 Timothy 3:17; Hebrews 12:1–3; 1 Peter 2:12, 21; 1 John 2:6; 3:17; 4:7–11.

## ꓥꓤꓤ INHERITANCE

The wealthy English Baron Fitzgerald had only one son. The son had left home and died while away. Fitzgerald never got over the loss of his son, his only heir. As his wealth increased, Fitzgerald continued to invest in paintings by the masters. At his death, his will called for all his

144 Adapted from Kenneth Dodge, "A Packaged Inheritance", *Parables, Etc.* 12 (#6 August 1992), p. 1.

paintings to be sold. Because of the quality of the art in the holdings, a message was sent to collectors and museums. A great crowd gathered for what was to be an amazing auction.

When the day of the auction came and the large crowd assembled, the lawyer read from the will of Fitzgerald. It instructed that the first painting to be sold was the painting "of my beloved son". The painting was by an unknown painter and of poor quality. The only bidder was an old servant who had known the boy and loved him. For a small sum of money he bought it for its sentimental value and the memories it held.

The lawyer again read from the will, "Whoever buys my son gets all. The auction is over."

**Themes:** *God – love of, Incarnation, Jesus – centrality of.*

**Scriptures:** Luke 10:27; John 3:36; Romans 8:32; 1 Corinthians 13; 1 John 2:23; 5:12.

## 145 INJUSTICE

For Robert Hearsch, his job became a nightmare that wouldn't end. For four years Hearsch had been a successful supervisor for Hughes Aircraft. Then General Motors took over the company – and his career took a nose dive. As part of the restructuring, he was put in charge of buying pens and pencils. He found orders backlogged and records in disarray. He spent most of his days appeasing angry secretaries. However, he stayed on, arriving early, leaving late, working through his breaks. But, as Hearsch tells the story, things only got worse. His supervisors hinted that his position might be phased out. They ignored his diligence and recorded small mistakes into his file. They even left him off the guest list for the department office party. The pressure took its toll. Hearsch lost

20 pounds. His marriage ended. He suffered a minor nervous breakdown. Hearsch finally filed a workers' compensation claim, blaming his health and emotional problems on Hughes. He subsequently accepted a $20,000 settlement from the company, which refuses to comment on the case. The money, he says, is small consolation. "I lost my wife, my house and my career."

**Themes:** *Anxiety, Family, Pressure, Stress, Suffering, Unemployment, Work, Worry.*

**Scriptures:** Psalms 34:4; 46; 55:22; Matthew 6:19–34; 10:28; Luke 12:5, 22–31; Romans 12:12; Philippians 4:6; 2 Timothy 1:7; Hebrews 13:5–6; 1 Peter 5:5–6.

## ⫪⪘6 JESUS – CHARACTER

Dostoevsky was a Russian novelist. When he arrived at a Siberian prison camp on Christmas Eve 1849 two women slipped him some money hidden in a copy of the New Testament. While the guard momentarily turned away, they suggested he should search the pages thoroughly.

Later he found a 25-rouble banknote. Although the money was useful it was the New Testament he treasured. He read it from cover to cover, pondering every word and learning much of it by heart. Here is his conclusion on Jesus.

I believe that there is nothing lovelier, deeper, more sympathetic, more rational, more manly and more perfect than the Saviour: I say to myself with jealous love that not only is there no one else like him but there could be no one else.

146 Adapted from Ian Barclay, "Hind Sight", *Church of England Newspaper* (19 December 1986), p. 9.

*Themes:* Bible, Memorisation, Persecution, Servant.

**Scriptures:** Isaiah 52:13–53:12; Matthew 11:29; Mark 10:45; Luke 10:29–37; John 1:1–18; 2 Corinthians 10:1; Philippians 2:1–11; Colossians 1:15–20; 2 Timothy 3:16; 1 Peter 1:18–19; 1 John 1:1–5; 3:17.

## ⟨147⟩ LEADERSHIP

A couple decided to hire a small plane. He had been a pilot for thirteen years. They set off for a small town 100 kilometres away to have a snack and then fly home.

At one point in the flight home the husband remarked that he felt a little faint. And, in an instant, he collapsed in his seat. His face went completely white and his eyes rolled back in his head. The wife did not have the slightest idea how to fly the plane. She pressed the transmitter button on the microphone and cried out, "Help me. Help me. I can't fly this aeroplane." The radio was tuned to a frequency used by many pilots and air traffic controllers. Her frantic message was picked up by dozens of very helpful people. Suddenly there were voices saying, "Follow a highway…" "Fly towards the sun…" "Turn on the landing light…"

Listening to this babble on the airwaves was a flight instructor. He ran to his plane, a small Cessna. He took off to try the impossible: find the voice in the sky asking for help. He waited for a lull in the transmissions. Then he asked all the other transmitters to leave the frequency so he could make radio contact with the endangered woman. "Madam, what is your name?" he asked. She stated her name. He calmly introduced himself and began to establish a rapport with her. All the time he was scanning the skies looking for the little plane.

Then he saw a plane with its landing light on. "Can you turn your landing light off?" The light went off. It was her. He flew his plane in front of her to show the woman he was there. Then he manoeuvred his plane just a little behind and to the side of her. He explained that he was an experienced flying instructor. Calmly and quietly he taught her the basics of flying. As they came to the air field the instructor gave more detailed help. They flew over the strip first and then made the final approach. The woman was able to land the plane and walk away quite unhurt.

*Themes:* *Apprenticing, Courage, Discipleship, Example, Following, Imitating Jesus, Mentoring, Tragedy.*

**Scriptures:** Mark 1:16–20; 2:14; 8:34–36; 10:21; Luke 9:57–62; John 1:43; 10:1–6, 27; 21:22; 1 Corinthians 4:16; 11:1; Philippians 2:5; 3:17; 1 Thessalonians 1:6; 2:14; 2 Thessalonians 3:6, 9; Hebrews 12:1–3; 1 Peter 2:21; 1 John 2:6; 4:7–11.

## 148 LIFE

During the Second World War the island of Crete in the Mediterranean was invaded by the Nazis. As German paratroopers rained out of the sky onto the fields of Crete they were gunned down.

The retribution was terrible. The Germans lined up whole villages of people and gunned them down. In the end hatred was the only weapon the Cretan people had. They vowed never to give up their hate. Never.

Yet now, on the site where the paratroopers landed, there is an institute where people come to learn about Greek culture and political harmony and peace. Why? Because of Dr Alexander Papaderos, whose influence has changed his community. He is an exceptional human being.

During the War he was only a boy. One day, on the road, he found the broken pieces of a mirror. A German motor bike had crashed there. He tried to find all the pieces and reassemble the mirror, but he couldn't. So he kept the largest piece. By scratching it on a stone he made it round. He began to play with it as a toy. It became a game to reflect light into the most inaccessible places. Then Papaderos said this, "I came to understand that this was not just a child's game but... what I might do with my life... I am a fragment of a mirror... I can reflect light into the dark places of this world."

***Themes:*** *Darkness, Hatred, I am – the Light, Light, Reconciliation, Retribution, Salt and light, War.*

***Scriptures:*** Matthew 5:13–16; Mark 9:49–50; John 1:3–9; 3:19–21; 5:31–36; 8:12; 9:5; 11:9–10; 12:35–36; 12:46; Acts 13:47; 26:23; Romans 2:19; 1 Corinthians 4:5; 2 Corinthians 4:4–6; Ephesians 5:8, 13; 1 Thessalonians 5:5; 1 Peter 2:9; 2 Peter 1:19; 1 John 1:5; Revelation 21:23; 22:5.

## 149 LIFE *

A woman was serving a life sentence in prison. Angry and resentful about her situation, she decided she'd rather die than live another year in prison.

Over the years she had become good friends with one of the prison caretakers. One of his jobs was to bury prisoners who died. They were buried in a graveyard outside the prison walls. When a prisoner died the caretaker rang a bell, which was heard by everyone. The caretaker then got the body and put it in a coffin. Next, he entered his office to fill out the death certificate before returning to the coffin to nail down the lid. Finally, he put the coffin on a wagon to take it to the graveyard and bury it.

Knowing the routine, the woman devised an escape plan. She shared it with the caretaker. The next time the bell rang, the woman would leave her cell and sneak into the dark room where the coffins were kept. She would slip into the coffin with the dead body while the caretaker was filling out the death certificate. When the caretaker returned, he would nail down the lid and take the coffin outside the prison with the woman in the coffin along with the dead body. He would then bury the coffin. The woman knew there would be enough air for her to breathe until later in the evening. At that time the caretaker would return to the graveyard under the cover of darkness. He would dig up the coffin, open it, and set her free.

The caretaker was reluctant to go along with this plan. But, since he and the woman had become good friends over the years, he agreed to do it.

The woman waited several weeks before someone in the prison died. She was asleep in her cell when she heard the death bell ring. She got up. She picked the lock of her cell. Slowly she walked down the hallway. She was nearly caught a couple of times. Her heart was racing. She opened the door to the darkened room where the coffins were kept. Quietly in the dark she found the coffin containing the dead body. Carefully she climbed in and pulled the lid down over her.

Soon she heard footsteps. Then there was the pounding of the hammer and nails. Even though she was very uncomfortable with the dead body, she knew that with every nail she was one step nearer to freedom. The coffin was lifted onto the wagon and taken outside to the graveyard. She could feel the coffin being lowered into the ground. She didn't make a sound as the coffin hit the bottom of the grave with a thud. Finally, she heard the dirt dropping on to the top of the wooden coffin. She knew it was only a matter of time until she was free at last.

After several minutes of absolute silence, she began to laugh. She was free! She was free!

Feeling curious, she decided to light a match to find out the identity of the dead prisoner beside her. To her horror, she discovered she was lying next to the dead caretaker.

*Themes:* Death, Humour.

*Scriptures:* Mark 8:34–38; John 8:36; Romans 6:23.

## 150 LIFE – STORMS

Victor Hugo wrote a story called *Ninety-Three*. In it he tells of a ship that was caught in a terrific storm. When the storm was at its height, the frightened crew heard a terrible crashing sound below deck. On investigation the source of the sound was discovered. A cannon they were carrying had broken loose. It was banging into the sides of the ship, tearing gaping holes in it with every smashing blow.

Risking their lives, two men went below. They managed to secure the cannon again. The captain and crew knew the loose cannon was more dangerous than the storm outside. The storm could toss them about, but the loose cannon within could be the means of sinking and destroying them.

*Themes:* Character, Church politics, Gossip, Leadership, Loyalty, Negativity, Old nature, Storms, Temptation.

*Scriptures:* Mark 1:12–13; Luke 4:1–13; Romans 6:12–14; 2 Corinthians 12:1–13; Galatians 5:16–24; Ephesians 4:22; Colossians 3:8; James 1:2–4, 13–15, 21; 1 Peter 2:1.

## 151 LOVE

A young woman in New England counted the days to the end of the Civil War, when her fiancé would return. In the meantime she received letters. But they suddenly stopped. Eventually she received a letter in an unfamiliar hand. It read something like this: "There has been another terrible battle. I have been unfortunate this time; I have lost both my arms. I cannot write myself, but my comrade is writing this letter for me. I write to tell you that you are as dear to me as ever; but I shall now be dependent upon other people for the rest of my days, and I have had this letter written to release you from your engagement." That letter was never answered. The young woman was on the next train and found her way to the hospital and eventually to her fiancé's bed. Like any good love story, she threw her arms around the soldier. "I will never give you up," she said.

*Themes:* *Acceptance, Parable – Prodigal Son, Reconciliation, War.*

**Scriptures:** Proverbs 10:12; Luke 15:11–32; John 3:16; Romans 12:10; 1 Corinthians 13; 1 Thessalonians 4:9; 1 Peter 1:21; 4:8.

## 152 LOVE

John Heinz is a paramedic. On one of his days off he was driving down a motorway near his home.

On the two-way radio he heard a call from someone to attend an emergency. A child had fallen from a tree and needed medical help immediately. John noted the address and saw that it was quite close to where he was. He took the next exit and made his way quickly to the house.

However, a couple of miles from the house he was stopped by some road works. A backhoe had nearly completed a trench right across the road. John jumped out of his car. He hastily explained that he needed to get to a nearby house as there had been an accident. The backhoe driver began quickly filling in the trench, just enough for John to be able to complete his mercy dash and attend to the child.

The next morning John was on his way to work and drove past the same backhoe redigging the trench. John stopped to thank the driver for his cooperation. But, as John got out of his car, the backhoe driver climbed out of his cabin and ran to John.

Before John could speak the man said, "Oh, thank you, it was my child you saved yesterday."

*Themes:* *Atonement, Christmas, Easter, Evangelism, Family, God – his love, Rescue, Salvation.*

*Scriptures:* Mark 10:45; Luke 4:18; 15:1–7, 8–10; 1 Corinthians 6:20; 7:23; 13; Galatians 4:4; Ephesians 2:11–21; 1 Timothy 2:5–6.

## 153 LOVE

A news magazine from America carried the headline: "'I want my son to die,' says mother." The young man was on death row. His mother was so disgusted by the dreadful things he had done that she wrote to the state governor and said, "Don't reprieve him. What he has done is so bad I want my boy to die."

He had completed one sentence for rape but when he was released he raped and murdered a teenage girl. He was arrested again and sentenced to death. His name was Jimmy Lee Davis and he was in his early twenties. He was perverted, twisted, and rejected even by his mother.

A young Pentecostal man in Melbourne read the news article. He thought, "Jesus loves this man! Oh if he could know Jesus like I know Jesus, what a difference it would make." He wrote a letter to Jimmy on death row and told him that Jesus loved him. He sent the letter to America expecting that the chap would tear up the letter and swear.

To his amazement, within a couple of weeks he got a letter back saying, "It's the most wonderful letter I've ever had in my life. I do wish I could meet you. I just wish I could know Jesus in my life like you do. I've made such a mess of it. You have given me hope."

Then the young man in Melbourne got the idea that the Lord wanted him to go to America and visit this young man and lead him to Christ. He prayed about it and shared it with his friends. Before long all sorts of sums of money were coming in and he had his fare to the United States.

He landed in Jackson, Mississippi knowing nobody, hoping to get into the death cell to lead this chap to Christ. By a whole series of coincidences he eventually had permission to go into death row, twice a week for four hours a visit, for a couple of months. He took his guitar in with him. He sat in that cell with Jimmy in death row. He sang choruses. They cracked jokes, they laughed, they behaved like brothers.

He led him to Jesus. There was a couple of months of marvellous Christian fellowship between this young Melbourne Pentecostal and Jimmy. The last visit was Jimmy's baptism. A Christian magazine article carried a picture of the prison chaplain and Jimmy dripping with water, coming up out of the baptistry. The young Australian's visa had expired and he had to leave. He and Jimmy hugged each other as brothers in Christ.

He came back home to Melbourne and for two years Jimmy waited for his fate. In the meantime, they wrote letters to each other. Jimmy was growing as a Christian and in one of his letters said, "There is one thing I'm not going to do. I am not going to dishonour the Gospel by using my conversion to escape the death penalty."

One day the young man in Melbourne was at work when he got a phone call from his wife, who said, "Can you come home at once? Jimmy's just got permission to ring us from prison; he's being executed tonight."

So he got leave from work and tore home and got through to the prison in America two hours before Jimmy was due in the gas chamber. But he said he just broke down and cried on the phone. However, Jimmy at the other end said, "I love you man. Thank you for all that you have done for me. I've got go now. Goodbye. Be seeing you." And Jimmy hung up.

**Themes:** *Conversion, Evangelism, Friendship, Love – of others, Self-sacrifice, Testimony, Witnessing.*

**Scriptures:** Luke 10:27; Romans 12:10; 1 Corinthians 13; 1 Thessalonians 4:9; Hebrews 13:1; 2 Peter 1:7; 1 John 3:11–18.

## 154 LOVE

*The Miracle on the River Kwai* is one of the most remarkable stories of the Second World War. The conditions for Allied prisoners in the Japanese prisoner-of-war camp on the River Kwai were so abysmal, and the mortality so high, that the men became almost bestial in their selfishness. They did not shrink from stealing food from their dying mates in a desperate attempt to survive. Ernest Gordon, who wrote the book, was himself given up as incurable by the MO, but was nursed back to life by the devoted self-sacrifice of a man in his Company, Dusty Miller. But the "miracle" was the transformation of attitudes in that camp as people in it began to understand and respond to the love of Christ. How did that begin to get through to men in such desperate conditions? It all started with a Scotsman, Angus McGilvray, who literally gave his life for his friend. The friend was very ill and about to die. Someone had stolen his blanket. Angus gave him his own. Someone had stolen his food. Angus gave him his own. The result? Angus's friend got better. But Angus collapsed one day from starvation and exhaustion. He pitched on his face and died.

154 Michael Green, *Jesus Spells Freedom* (London: IVP, 1972), p. 80.

**Themes:** *Atonement, Cross, Crucifixion, Easter, Jesus – death of, Love, Self-sacrifice.*

**Scriptures:** Mark 10:45; Luke 10:27; Romans 5:6–8; 1 Corinthians 5:7; 13; 15:3; 1 Timothy 2:6; Hebrews 9:11–12.

## 155 LOVE

In a farming village in the south of France there is an annual mid-summer celebration of the Feast of Saint John.

When the first star can be seen in the night sky, the villagers light a bonfire on the school oval. A folk band begins to play and couples dance in a universal two-step, the great fire their only light. It could be a scene from a novel or a movie.

At the first break in the music the couples do not leave for refreshment. They stand staring into the fire. Suddenly, an athletic couple grab each other by the hand. They run, leap high in the air through the flames, landing safely on the other side. As the crowd applauds the couple embrace, glad they have emerged unscathed to dance again. Then another couple try, then another. This leaping is the key to the festival. It works like this.

If you are in love and want to seal your covenant, you make a wish that you will never part, and then you hold hands and jump through the flames. It is said that the hotter the fire and the higher the flames, the longer and closer will be your relationship. It is also said that if you misjudge the fire or one of you lets go and refuses to jump, then your relationship is doomed. So the youngest and fittest couples jump early on. This is serious business even though there is much laughter and applause.

At the end of the evening a traditional tune signals a

---

155 Adapted from Robert Fulghum, *It was on Fire When I Lay Down on it* (London: Grafton/Collins, 1990), p. 181.

last dance. As the final note on the shepherd's flute fades, the villagers encircle the soft glow of the embers. Then, two old people – the couple married the longest – hold hands and gracefully, solemnly, step over the remaining few coals. They all embrace and walk home in the starry night, all affirming the treasure of marriage.

*Themes:* *Celebration, Commitment, Divorce, Love, Marriage.*
**Scriptures:** Deuteronomy 24:1–5; Matthew 5:27–28, 31–33; Mark 10:2–12; Luke 10:27; 16:18; 1 Corinthians 7:1–16; 13.

## 156 LOVE – CHANGED BY

In the late 1940s a gunman called Ezio Barberi became notorious in Italy as a cold-blooded killer, and leader of a celebrated gang which raided banks and jewellers, shooting down any who came between them and their loot. He was arrested in 1949, sentenced to 57 years of imprisonment, and committed to the maximum security wing of the San Vittore prison in Milan.

Although he was universally execrated, this man was loved by one person, a girl of 17 whom he had never met. Maria Soresina started to keep a scrapbook of Ezio's escapades and crimes. She carried the book around with her and went to church each day to pray for him. She began to write to him regularly in gaol. She understood him when nobody else did. She really cared. She pleaded with him. She loved him although he was not in himself the least bit lovable.

Gradually Barberi changed. Being on the receiving end of love like that began to make a new man of him. He had already been involved in organising one mutiny in the prison, but his attitude changed. His violent ways began

---

[156] Michael Green, *Jesus Spells Freedom* (London: IVP, 1972), pp. 81–82.

to disappear. He exchanged the pin-ups on his wall for a picture of Maria. He replied to her letters with a tenderness that he had never shown to anyone or anything before. Was this the hate-filled gangster of Milan?

The new Barberi became a model prisoner. He took a leading part in arranging and carrying out social and charitable events, and working voluntarily in the prison hospital. Love had challenged him, melted him, won him. And on 18 June 1968, 21 years after Maria had fallen in love with him, they were married in the prison chapel.

**Themes:** *Christ – his love, Commitment, Conversion, God – his love, Love – transforms, Perseverance, Testimony.*

**Scriptures:** Luke 10:27; Romans 5:8; 1 Corinthians 13; 2 Corinthians 5:14; Galatians 2:20; 1 John 4:10, 19.

## 157 LOVE – LACK OF

The night before Frank Vitkovic gunned down eight people and plunged eleven storeys to his death in 1987, his family sat around after dinner, quietly watching TV.

A few months previously he had given up his law studies at Melbourne University and had seen the counsellor. No one knew of the hell going on inside Frank's life. That night he retired to his bedroom to write a two-page note to his family explaining he could not go on.

At 4:25 the next afternoon Frank entered the Australia Post Building in Queen Street. He took the lift to find an old friend and pulled out his gun – a cut-down military weapon – aimed it at his terrified friend and pulled the trigger. When the gun didn't fire, Frank fled. For the next fifteen minutes he went on a killing rampage that put eight people in their graves.

---

157 Adapted from Stuart Rintoul and John Lyons, "Killer who said he was unworthy", *The Weekend Australian* (12–13 December 1987), p. 8.

As he gunned down 19-year-old Judith Morris he said, "Nobody loves me." A few minutes later this unloved man was dead on the pavement below.

*Themes:* *Family life, Killing, Modern life, Murder, Suicide, Violence.*

**Scriptures:** Luke 10:27; 15:11–32; John 3:16; Romans 5:8; 8:31–39; 1 Corinthians 13; 2 Corinthians 5:14; Galatians 2:20; 1 John 4:10, 19.

## 158 LOVE – PRACTICAL

Steve Sjogren tells the story of Rictor. Rictor was going into a neighbourhood at Central Park, Long Island giving away light bulbs, knocking on doors and offering to show God's love in a practical way. Behind one door was a father and a son having a heated conversation. The son had come to Christ and was in a totally shark mode, trying to corner his dad and talk him into coming to Christ. He was doing a pretty good job of getting his father's attention as well as irritating him. Dad had his hand on the doorknob ready to go to the store. In his other hand was a shopping list he was waving at the lad saying, "Son, I'm not going to begin listening to what you Christians have to say until you begin to show the love of God instead of just talking about it all the time." At that instant, as God would arrange it, the doorbell rang. "What do you want?" the father said. Standing in front of him was a girl with a light bulb in her hand saying, "We would like to show you God's love in a practical way by giving you this light bulb." The first item on dad's shopping list was a light bulb.

*Themes:* *Christmas, Evangelism, Families, Fathers, Guidance, Servant evangelism.*

**Scriptures:** Psalms 25:9; 32:8; 48:14; Mark 3:7–12; 6:6–13; Luke 9:1–6; 10:1–20; Acts 1:8; 1 John 4:9–10.

One evening in a country village, a cottage caught on fire. In a few seconds the thatched roof and the timbers were ablaze.

There was no fire engine in the remote place and the villagers stood around helpless. Suddenly a young man who had just arrived upon the scene cried out, "What, can nothing be done to save them?"

When no one responded he jumped through the flames and darted into the house. A moment later he emerged, bearing a child under each arm. He had carefully protected them from the flames by hiding them under his coat; he himself was badly burned.

The parents of the two children died in the fire. There was much sympathy for the two children in the village and several people wanted to adopt them.

When the judge arrived to decide who should adopt the children there were two who petitioned the court. The first was the squire of the village. He had money, position, and a fine house to offer the children. The second petitioner was the man who had rescued the children from the flames.

When the judge asked him what right he had to ask the court for the children he did not answer with words. Instead he held up his hands that had been badly burned and scarred in their rescue and let them do his arguing for him.

*Themes:* *Atonement, Cross, Grief, Jesus – work of, Love, Reconciliation, Redeemed, Rescue, Sacrifice, Salvation, Substitution, Suffering.*

*Scriptures:* Exodus 6:6; Psalms 77:14–15; Matthew 5:4; Mark 10:45; Luke 10:27; 24:21; John 1:29; 8:31–36; 1 Corinthians 1:30; 5:7; 6:19–20; 7:22–23; 13; 2 Corinthians 1:3–4; Galatians 3:13; 4:4–5; 5:1; Ephesians 1:7; 5:2; Titus 2:14; Hebrews 9:15; 1 Peter 1:18–19; 1 John 2:2.

## 160 MAN – A DEFINITION

*His symbol:* YRU1.

*Atomic weight:* 75 kgms (±25 kgms).

*Occurrences:* Wherever there are members of the opposite sex – or large quantities of food and drink.

*Physical properties:* Very active in early development, with great affinity for dirt, grime, etc. In time, displays surface fungus and equalisation of horizontal and vertical dimensions. Hard and brittle on the outside when mature, but still soft as a baby underneath.

*Chemical properties:* Strong orientation to female species where food not available. Turns to jelly when placed alongside stunning sample of female species. Glows brightly when placed in the limelight but becomes invisible when actually needed. Apparently very complex but very easy to analyse as the way to the heart is through the stomach.

*Uses:* Hardly any.

*Caution:* Likely to fall to pieces if dropped, rejected or cut down to size.

*Themes:* Divorce, Family life, Humour, Marriage, Parenting, Woman.

*Scriptures:* Ephesians 5:21 – 6:4; Colossians 3:18 – 4:1.

## 161 MARRIAGE

A young minister was having difficulty getting along with other people, especially his wife and family. He was continually criticising her. Everything was wrong. He was sar-

160 Barry Chant, *Marriage Joy* Seminar (Sydney, Seminar notes, 1993).

castic and demanding, and withdrew from her advances, rejecting her love and affection. He began to realise that he was destroying their marriage.

He went to talk and pray with another minister. Eventually the painful root of the matter came to light. While he was in the armed forces in Korea, he spent two weeks on "R and R" in Japan. During that leave, walking the streets of Tokyo, feeling empty, lonely, and terribly homesick, he fell into temptation and went three or four times to a prostitute. He had never been able to forgive himself. He had sought God's forgiveness, and with his *head* believed he had it. But the guilt still plagued him and he hated himself. When he returned to his faithful fiancée his emotional conflicts increased because he still could not accept complete forgiveness. He felt he had no right to be happy. He said to himself, "I have no right to enjoy my wife. I have no right to enjoy my life. I've got to pay back the debt."

**Themes:** *Forgiveness, Grace, Guilt, Inner healing, Pardon, Prayer, Prostitution.*

**Scriptures:** 1 Kings 8:22–53; Psalms 51; 103:2–3; Jeremiah 31:34; Daniel 9:19; Mark 2:1–12; 11:25; John 8:34–36; Romans 5; 6:23; Ephesians 2:8; 4:32; Colossians 2:13–14; 1 John 2:12.

## 162 MARRIAGE

An American surgeon was completely taken up with his work. His interesting career and brilliant success brought him a feeling of full satisfaction. There was only one thing wrong: his wife was very nervous. So he sent her to a psychiatrist.

One day the psychiatrist came and told the surgeon that he was not giving enough attention to his wife. "You

162 Adapted from Paul Tournier, *Marriage Difficulties* (London: SCM, 1967), p. 57.

should take her out to a show at least once a week," he said. The surgeon decided to take his wife out to the movies every Friday.

A little while later, he met Jesus Christ; he received Christ as master of his life. Immediately he began to listen to his wife in a quite different spirit. He also began to feel responsible for his wife. While he valued the help of the psychiatrist, he knew that sending her to the psychiatrist did not discharge him of his responsibilities. He said this: "We no longer go to the movies every Friday evening. We no longer feel the need of that. Instead, we open up to each other, to say all those things we never dreamt of sharing before, in order to discover and to understand each other and to seek God's leading for our home."

**Themes:** *Divorce, Love, Parenting, Psychiatry, Relationships, Time – use of.*
**Scriptures:** Deuteronomy 24:1–5; Matthew 5:27–29, 31–32; 19:3–12; Mark 10:2–13; Luke 10:27; 1 Corinthians 7:1–11; 13.

## 163 MARRIAGE

Various historical figures have been used in a promotion for the London Underground. One poster shows Henry VIII with the caption: "A return to the Tower of London, please." To which one wit has added: "... and a single for the wife."

**Themes:** *Commitment, Humour, Husbands, Love, Wives.*
**Scriptures:** Deuteronomy 24:1–5; Matthew 5:27–29, 31–32; 19:3–12; Mark 10:2–13; Luke 10:27; 1 Corinthians 7:1–11; 13.

---

[163] Len Evans, "Indulgence", *The Weekend Australian* (22–23 October 1988), p. 18.

## 164 MARRIAGE – RENEWED

The marriage of a Christian man was in a mess. He said this. "It seemed that my wife and I were unable to communicate or relate on any level. I had fallen out of love with her – and to make it worse there was that other woman."

Separation seemed the easy, almost desirable, way out. But God had different plans for them. Through the ministry of others who loved and supported them, they began to learn from God's Word that the only way forward with God is from the place of repentance and that total forgiveness of the past is a liberating experience. He went on to say something very interesting.

"I found that a lifetime of wrong attitudes and reactions had a binding effect on me. I needed long, patient counsel, culminating with prayers of authority, through which I experienced a physical release from a demonic deceit which had convinced me that what God wanted was not right. Now I praise God for insights given, power available and a renewed, revitalised and God-given marriage."

***Themes:*** *Bible, Commitment, Communication, Demonic, Divorce, Inner healing, Love, Renewal, Separation.*

**Scriptures:** Deuteronomy 24:1–5; Matthew 5:27–29, 31–32; 19:3–12; Mark 10:2–13; Luke 10:27; John 14:15–24; Acts 5:29; 1 Corinthians 7:1–11; 13.

## 165 MARTYRDOM

In 1956, five missionaries and their families were the first to penetrate the land of the Auca Indians in Ecuador with the Good News of Jesus.

In a three-month period, during "Operation Auca", the missionaries made weekly flights over the tribal area.

---

165 From Elizabeth Elliot, *Through Gates of Splendour* (London: Hodder and Stoughton, 1957).

They made contact with a loud hailer and often lowered a line with a bucket of gifts on the end. It seemed that relations with the Indians below were sufficiently friendly to land on a river bank in their area.

On Tuesday 3 January 1956, Nate Saint and his missionary colleagues landed at what they called "Palm Beach". They fished in the river, studied their notebooks of Auca phrases and read *Time* magazine as they waited for the Indians to come out of the jungle.

It was not until Friday at 11:15 am that two women and a man they named "George" stepped out of the jungle to meet the white missionaries. The missionaries spent the rest of the day showing the Indians such marvels as rubber bands, balloons, hamburgers, lemonade and even a yo-yo. "George" jumped at the chance to have a ride in the plane.

Towards evening "George" and the younger woman left. The older woman slept by a fire. But she was gone in the morning. The missionaries waited, hoping that they would get an invitation to their village.

On Sunday morning Nate took off and flew over the area. It seemed as if the men were on their way to make contact. At 12:30 pm Nate radioed excitedly to his wife Marj, "Looks like they'll be here for the early afternoon service. Pray for us. This is the day! Will contact you next at 4:30."

So, at 4:30 pm, Marj Saint eagerly switched on the radio receiver. There was no sound from Palm Beach. She waited all night. No sound ever came. The five missionaries had been ambushed and speared to death. And their plane was torn apart.

**Themes:** *Evangelism, Missionaries, Persecution, Sacrifice, Suffering.*

*Scriptures:* Matthew 28:16–20; Mark 6:7–13; Luke 9:1–6; 10:1–20; 24:44–49; Acts 1:8; 4:1–22; 5:41; 6:8 – 8:3; 7:54–58; 9:16, 23–25; 14:5–6, 19; 16:19–24; 21:30–36; 22:20; Revelation 2:13; 6:9–11; 11:2–11; 13:15; 17:6; 18:20; 20:4.

## 166 **MARTYRDOM**

Colin Chapman, in *The Case for Christianity*, quotes Ugandan bishop Festo Kivengere's account of the 1973 execution by firing squad of three men from his diocese:

> February 10 began as a sad day for us in Kabale. People were commanded to come to the stadium and witness the execution. Death permeated the atmosphere. A silent crowd of about 3,000 was there to watch.
>
> I had permission from the authorities to speak to the men before they died, and two of my fellow ministers were with me.
>
> They brought the men in a truck and unloaded them. They were handcuffed and their feet were chained. The firing squad stood to attention. As we walked into the centre of the stadium, I was wondering what to say. How do you give the gospel to doomed men who are probably seething with rage?
>
> We approached them from behind, and as they turned to look at us, what a sight! Their faces were all alight with an unmistakable glow and radiance. Before we could say anything, one of them burst out: "Bishop, thank you for coming! I wanted to tell you. The day I was arrested, in my prison cell, I asked the Lord Jesus to come into my heart. He came in and forgave me all my sins! Heaven is now open, and there is nothing between me and my God! Please tell my wife and children that I am going to be with Jesus. Ask them to accept him into their lives as I did."
>
> The other two men told similar stories, excitedly raising their hands, which rattled their handcuffs. I felt that what I

---

166 From *Leadership* 6 (1, 1985), p. 48.

needed to do was talk to the soldiers, not to the condemned. So I translated what the men had said into a language the soldiers understood. The military men were standing there with guns cocked and bewilderment on their faces. They were so dumbfounded that they forgot to put the hoods over the men's faces.

The three men faced the firing squad standing close together. They looked toward the people and began to wave, handcuffs and all. The people waved back. Then shots were fired and they were with Jesus.

We stood in front of them, our own hearts throbbing with joy, mingled with tears. It was a day never to be forgotten. Though dead, the men spoke loudly to all of Kigezi District and beyond, so that there was an upsurge of life in Christ, which challenges death and defeats it.

The next Sunday, I was preaching to a huge crowd in the hometown of one of the executed men. Again, the feel of death was over the congregation. But when I gave them the testimony of their man, and how he died, there erupted a great song of praise to Jesus! Many turned to the Lord there.

**Themes:** *Capital punishment, Conversion, Death, Encouragement, Forgiveness, Hanging, Heaven, Joy, Murder, Persecution, Sacrifice, Suffering, Testimony.*

**Scriptures:** Acts 5:41; 7:54–58; 9:16; 22:20; Revelation 2:13; 6:9–11; 11:2–11; 13:15; 17:6; 18:20; 20:4.

## 167 MARTYRDOM

On Wednesday 16 October 1555, all Oxford was gathered "in the ditch over against Balliol College", to watch the execution of two bishops who had rejected the Pope's authority. When all was ready, the two bishops were led from their places of confinement; 55-year-old Nicholas Ridley from the mayor's house and 80-year-old Hugh

167 Adapted from R. Demaus, *Hugh Latimer: A Biography* (London: Religious Tract Society, 1869), pp. 520–524.

Latimer from the bailiff's. When they met they embraced each other. Ridley encouraged Latimer: "Be of good heart, brother, for God will either assuage the fury of the flame or else strengthen us to abide it." Ridley went to the stake, knelt by it, kissed it and they both prayed kneeling. When they stood they talked to each other.

For fifteen minutes a Mr Smith preached to the crowd on Paul's words, "Though I give my body to be burnt, and have not love, it profiteth me nothing."

The two prisoners asked if they could say something, but refrained when they were informed that they could only speak if they recanted their errors.

When they were told to get ready, Ridley gave away to the people around him the things he had on him, including some napkins, nutmegs, his sundial and outer clothing. Latimer gave nothing, but very quietly allowed his keeper to pull off his stockings and outer clothing.

The blacksmith chained them to the stake. A bag of gunpowder was tied to each of their necks. A bundle of burning sticks was put at each of their feet. Then Latimer said to Ridley, "Be of good comfort, Master Ridley, and play the man. We shall this day light such a candle, by God's grace, in England, as I trust shall never be put out."

Seeing the fire flaming up towards him, Ridley cried out in Latin, "Into your hand, Lord, I commend my spirit. Lord, Lord, receive my spirit," repeating often the latter part in English.

On the other side of the stake, Latimer was crying out with equal enthusiasm, "O Father in heaven, receive my soul!" After that he stroked his face with his hand and, as it were, bathed them a little in the fire. He soon died, apparently with very little or no pain.

The younger Ridley lingered for some time in excruciating pain, the fire being choked and burning fiercely beneath, while it could not reach any of his vital organs. At last the flame rose and exploded the gunpowder, and his lifeless body fell over the chain at Latimer's feet.

*Themes:* Bishops, Courage, Death, Encouragement, Faithfulness, Heresy, Missionaries, Persecution, Sacrifice, Suffering.

**Scriptures:** Acts 5:41; 7:54–58; 9:16; 22:20; Revelation 2:13; 6:9–11; 11:2–11; 13:15; 17:6; 18:20; 20:4.

## 168 MARTYRDOM *

As the *Washington Post* reported in 1999, the two students who shot thirteen people in Littleton, Colorado, Eric Harris and Dylan Klebold, did not choose their victims at random – they were acting out of a kaleidoscope of ugly prejudices.

Media coverage has centred on the killers' hostility toward racial minorities and athletes, but there was another group the pair hated every bit as much, if not more: Christians. And there were plenty of them to hate at Columbine High School. According to some accounts eight Christians – four Evangelicals and four Catholics – were killed.

Among them was Cassie Bernall. Cassie was a 17-year-old with long blonde hair, hair she wanted to cut off and have made into wigs for cancer patients who had lost their hair through chemotherapy. She was active in her youth group at Westpool's Community Church and was known for carrying a Bible to school.

Cassie was in the school library reading her Bible when the two young killers burst in. According to witnesses, one of the killers pointed his gun at Cassie and asked, "Do you

[168] Charles W. Colson, *Littleton's Martyrs*, BreakPoint Commentary – 26 April 1999. Copyright © Prison Fellowship Ministries.

believe in God?" Cassie paused and then answered, "Yes, I believe in God."

"Why?" the gunman asked. Cassie did not have a chance to respond; the gunman had already shot her dead.

As her classmate Mickie Cain told Larry King on CNN, "She completely stood up for God. When the killers asked her if there was anyone who had faith in Christ, she spoke up and they shot her for it."

Cassie's martyrdom was even more remarkable when you consider that just a few years ago she had dabbled in the occult, including witchcraft. She had embraced the same darkness and nihilism that drove her killers to such despicable acts. But two years previously, Cassie had dedicated her life to Christ, and turned her life around. Her friend, Craig Moon, called her a "light for Christ".

**Themes:** *Courage, Death, Faithfulness, Hatred, Persecution, Sacrifice, Witnessing.*

**Scriptures:** Acts 5:41; 7:54–58; 9:16; 22:20; Revelation 2:13; 6:9–11; 11:2–11; 13:15; 17:6; 18:20; 20:4.

## 169 MATERIALISM

A few miles south-east of modern Naples, on 24 August, in the year 79 AD, Mount Vesuvius exploded. Twenty metres of ash and debris descended and buried the nearby cities of Herculaneum and Pompeii. Seventeen-year-old Pliny, who saw it all, said,

> You could hear the shrieks of women, the wailing of infants and the shouting of men; some were calling their parents,

169 Betty Radice, *Pliny: Letters and Panegyricus*, 2 volumes (London: Heinemann and Cambridge, MA: Harvard University Press, 1969), volume one, p. 445 and Rick Gore, "The Dead Do Tell Tales at Vesuvius", *National Geographic* 156 (May 1984), pp. 557–613. See also Joseph Jay Deiss, *Herculaneum: Italy's Buried Treasure* (New York: Harper and Row, 1985).

others their children or their wives, trying to recognise them by their voices. People bewailed their own fate or that of their relatives, and there were some who prayed for death in their terror. Many besought the aid of the gods, but still more imagined that there were no gods left, and that the universe was plunged into eternal darkness for evermore.

While perhaps 18,000 people escaped, 2,000 people were buried alive in the ash, to be uncovered many years later by the archeologists, just where they were when they died.

A rich and healthy, upper-class, 45-year-old woman, whom the archeologists have called the "Ring Lady", was found where she had been caught fleeing to the wharf to make her escape. She was wearing two gold rings (one set with jasper, the other with carnelian), heavy gold bracelets (in the form of snakes), and gold earrings (probably with pearls).

Not far from her was a lowly helmsman, about the same age as the "Ring Lady". He was poor and the fused six vertebrae in his back are signs of a life of strain from heavy manual labour. Neither wealth nor poverty saved these people from death.

**Themes:** *Death, Fear, Natural Disasters, Poverty, Second Coming, Wealth.*

**Scriptures:** Psalms 34:4; 91; 118:5–6; Matthew 6:19–21, 24–34, 10:28; Mark 10:17–31; 13; Luke 8:22–25; 12:5; 19:1–10; John 11:25–26; 1 Timothy 6:10; 2 Timothy 1:7; Hebrews 13:5–6.

## 170 MINISTERS

A great method for getting the right minister to help a church grow is contained in "The Ultimate Chain Letter" for parishes.

---

170 Adapted from Eddie Gibbs, *I Believe in Church Growth* (London: Hodder and Stoughton, 1981), p. 358.

If you are unhappy with your vicar, simply have your parish secretary send a copy of this letter to six other churches who are tired of their vicar. Then bundle up your vicar and send him to the church on the top of the list in this letter. Within a week you will receive 16,435 vicars and one of them should be all right. Have faith in this chain letter for vicars. Do not break the chain. One church did and got their old vicar back.

**Themes:** *Clergy, Criticism, Discouragement, Encouragement, Leadership, Pastors, Priests.*

**Scriptures:** Psalms 23; 42:6–11; 55:22; Matthew 5:11–12; Acts 6:1–6; 1 Corinthians 9:1–23; 2 Corinthians 4:8–18; 10:1–13:10; Philippians 4:4–7; 1 Timothy 2:2; 3:1–13.

## ⼁⼂⼁ **MIRACLES**

We will call him John. He is only four. But he has a car; a little red one that is pedal-powered. John lives near the rail line that goes through the town.

One day John was keen to take his car across the other side of the rail track and try his car out on the big stretch of clay there. From the window his mother watched everything. All was going well until John found that the ground clearance on his motor was not quite enough to make it across the line. He got stuck and caught on the tracks. His mother was frantic because she could see that a train was coming. However, she had no chance of getting to her son in time.

But the train stopped! It stopped not far from where John was still sobbing and trying to tug his little car off the line. The train driver had been taken seriously and suddenly ill. He had released the pressure on the automatic control lever and the train automatically came to a stop.

---

[171] Based on a story by R. F. Holland, "The Miraculous", *American Philosophical Quarterly* 2 (1965), p. 4.

*Themes: God – his care, God – his sovereignty, Parenting.*
*Scriptures:* Daniel 4:35; Acts 8:26–40; 9:10–19.

## 172 MIRACLES

One Sunday Mr Alvarez went to church. He listened to a talk based on James 5. The preacher emphasised the need to pray for the sick and to anoint them with oil. How much of the message Mr Alvarez understood is unknown. He was not yet a Christian. The next morning, however, he awoke to find his most valuable bull was dead. This was a major tragedy. For a cowboy to lose his prize bull is like an admiral having his flagship sink. As he stared as his dead bull, Mr Alvarez remembered the talk he had heard the night before. He went into the kitchen. He got a can of olive oil. He then walked outside and anointed the immobile shape. He emptied the whole can over the animal. He also prayed. And the bull stood up and walked. When Mr Alvarez told Ed Silvoso about the bull, Ed was somewhat sceptical. Silvoso made the mistake of questioning Mr Alvarez. Mr Alvarez took off his glasses and looked Ed straight in the eye. With a booming voice he said, "Young man, I have been a cowboy for over half a century. I know cows and bulls inside out. If I tell you it was dead, it was dead! Understood." Not surprisingly, Mr Alvarez became a Christian.

*Themes: Conversion, Doubt, Faith, Healing, Humour, Prayer, Signs and wonders, Trust.*

*Scriptures:* Psalms 37:3–5; Proverbs 3:5–6; Matthew 8:5–13; 9:27–31; Mark 1:29–31, 40–44; 2:1–12; 3:1–6; 5:24–34; 7:31–37; 8:22–26; 10:46–52; 11:22–24; Luke 7:1–10; 13:10–17; 14:1–6; John 4:46–54; 9:1–34; James 5:14–15.

## ᕯ‑3 MISSION – COST

It is 25 May 1961. The 43-year-old President John F. Kennedy stands before the joint session of Congress to deliver his dramatic challenge to Americans. He speaks in his crisp New England accent and jabbing the air with his forefinger for emphasis. This is what he says.

> I believe that this nation should commit itself to achieving the goal, before the decade is out, of landing a man on the moon and returning him safely to earth. No single space project in this period will be more impressive to mankind, or more important for the long-range exploration of space; and none will be so difficult or expensive to accomplish... In a very real sense, it will not be one man going to the moon... it will be an entire nation. For all of us must work to put him there... I believe we should go to the moon... Unless we are prepared to do the work and bear the burdens to make it successful, there is no sense in going ahead.

At the conclusion of Kennedy's 47-minute message there was only routine applause. As he left the Congress, members were split over his proposal to spend $40 billion in the decade ahead on the mission to put a man on the moon. But Kennedy turned out to have been successful. The race to the moon had begun. Millions and millions of dollars poured into the programme. In a few years in the mid-sixties over $15 billion a year was being spent on the mission. Men and women from all over America were recruited to join the programme. There were scientists, technical support personnel, people with trades and crafts, clerks and administrators. The best people were giving their best. For one scientist it was so exhilarating he said he would have worked for nothing if he could have afforded it. At one stage NASA was employing 36,000 people in the mission to put a man on the moon. There were another 300,000 sub-contractors dedicated to the task.

Eight years after Kennedy's challenge, Buzz Aldrin and Neil Armstrong were descending towards the moon in the *Eagle*. It was 20 July 1969. A quarter of a million miles away Charlie Duke called from Mission Control. "If you read, you're go for powered descent." Neil said his instrument panel was alive with winking data. Unexpectedly an alarm went off. The computer couldn't cope with all the data. Buzz and Neil eyed the large red ABORT button. But the guidance officers at mission control called that it was an acceptable risk. Five hundred feet above the surface Neil Armstrong took manual control. He wasn't satisfied with the landing zone. He delicately stroked the hand controller. They scooted horizontally across a field of rubbly boulders. They were now short of fuel. They would have to land or abort in 60 seconds. At 30 seconds Neil was still hovering. At 20 seconds they settled silently on the moon. "Houston," Neil called, "Tranquillity Base here. The *Eagle* has landed." Buzz reached across and shook Neil's hand, hard. They had pulled it off.

It took several hours to suit up for the moon walk. They depressurised the module. Neil opened the hatch. Buzz guided him as he backed out on his hands and knees. When he reached the ladder he moved down carefully. "I'm at the foot of the ladder," Neil said. His voice was slow and precise. "I'm going to step off the Lunar Module now..." Through his window Buzz watched Neil. He could see Neil move his blue lunar overshoe from the metal dish of the foot pad to the powdery grey surface. "That's one small step for... man, one giant leap for mankind." Around the world, millions and millions of people stopped to watch the television screen, following the success of one of the greatest human missions of all time. And hundreds of billions of dollars, hundreds of thousands of people had worked to make that mission possible.

**Themes:** *Christmas, Evangelism, Incarnation, Purpose.*

**Scriptures:** Isaiah 9:6–7; 11:1–3; Jeremiah 23:5–6; Micah 5:2; Matthew 1:18–25; 28:18–20; Mark 1:1–3; 3:13–15; 6:7–13; Luke 1:26 – 2:20; 9:1–6; 10:1–20; John 1:1–18; 3:17; Acts 1:8; 13:22–23; Romans 1:3; 8:3; 2 Corinthians 8; 9; Galatians 4:4–5; 1 Timothy 1:15; Hebrews 1:1–13; 2:9–18; 10:4–14; 1 John 2:22; 4:2–3; 2 John 7.

## 174 MONEY

A pillar of orange fire and billows of black smoke poured into the night sky of Austin, Texas, as firemen arrived at a blazing two-storey apartment building. While the fire engines wailed to a halt, people dressed in pyjamas, underwear, and even bed sheets ran from the building. A young fire fighter looked up in horror as a pregnant girl stood screaming inside a second-storey window. Then, responding to urgent cries in Spanish from a young man already on the ground, she jumped, landing with a thud and a whimper.

The firemen hurried to connect their hoses and advance into the searing heat, but experience told them it was too late to save the building or anyone trapped in it. It was an explosive fire, probably started by kerosene or some other flammable substance.

On the ground, a woman and a man came stumbling out, as walking torches. Paramedics ran to cover them with blankets, smothering the flames, trying to comfort them and gently helping them to the ambulances.

"No, no I can't go!" screamed the woman, her face

---

174 Loren Cunningham, *Daring to Live on the Edge: The Adventure of Faith and Finances* (Seattle: YWAM, 1991), p. 49.

charred and streaked with tears, "My baby is in there! I've got to get her out."

But by then their apartment looked like the inside of a furnace. Sadly, a young medic shook his head, and firmly urged the woman towards the ambulance.

It was almost morning before they found the remains of a fifteen-month old girl in the smoking ruin. But before they found the baby's body, the authorities had learned the horrible truth about the cause of the fire.

A man, angry because someone would not repay him $8, had shot a flare gun into the building through a window, igniting some flammable substance. A building was burned to the ground, 48 people were homeless, seven people were hospitalised and a baby was dead – all because of an argument over $8.

*Themes:* *Anger, Greed, Materialism, Tragedy, Wealth.*

**Scriptures:** 1 Samuel 2:29; Job 20:20; Psalms 4:4; 10:3; 57:4; 91; 118:5–6; Proverbs 15:1, 27; 28:25; Jeremiah 6:13; 8:10; 22:17; Ezekiel 16:27; Hosea 4:8; Habakkuk 2:5; Matthew 5:21–24; 6:19–21, 24–34; Luke 8:22–25; 12:15–31; Romans 12:17–21; 1 Corinthians 5:9–11; 6:10; 2 Corinthians 8; 9; Ephesians 4:19, 26–32; 6:4; Colossians 3:8; 1 Thessalonians 2:5; 1 Timothy 2:8; 6:10; Titus 1:7; James 1:19–21; 2 Peter 2:3, 14.

## 17S MONEY

On the weekend of 13–14 February 1993, a man unnamed in press reports was heading for Toulouse on a TGV high-speed train. The train's lavatory had a voracious drainage system which swallowed the man's wallet with a triumphant snap as he was bending to adjust his clothing. As the man tried to retrieve his wallet, the loo's jaws clamped savagely round his wrist. Somehow, he managed to pull the alarm and the train screeched to a halt near Tours. Firemen had to destroy the vicious appliance with metal cutters. France's television viewers saw the unfortunate traveller being carried away on a stretcher, his wallet in one hand and the lavatory bowl still wrapped around his wrist.

**Themes:** *Humour, Materialism, Poverty, Riches, Wealth.*

**Scriptures:** Psalms 37:29; Proverbs 1:19; 15:27; 21:26; 29:25; Matthew 5:22; 6:24; Mark 4:18–19; 10:17–31; Luke 6:24; 12:16–21; 16:13, 19–31; Ephesians 4:28; 1 Timothy 3:3, 8; 6:10, 17–19.

## 176 **NEGATIVITY**

In the late 1600s the French and the English were at war, which involved fighting in the colonies in Canada. Sir William Phips was put in charge of the British naval attack on Quebec. Sir William had arranged to wait off shore until Major Walley had led some men around the rear of the town. But Sir William became impatient of waiting. He started to fire on the city.

The Catholic French in Quebec had hung a massive picture of the Holy Family on the spire of the cathedral. They were hoping it would increase divine aid for their cause. Protestant Sir William was not impressed. It then seemed that every gun on his ships was trained on the cathedral spire. Volley after volley was poured onto that picture. But still it hung there. Meanwhile, Sir William had forgotten about Major Walley. Walley and his men became in great need of food and other supplies. Phips had spent so much of his time and ammunition firing at the saints that he could no longer help Major Walley. Also, he did not have enough ammunition left to fire at the enemy in the ensuing battle. Sir William Phips lost the battle because he had been firing at the saints.

**Themes:** *Enemies, Evil, Good, Life, New life, Old life, Spiritual battle.*

**Scriptures:** Psalms 1; Romans 6:1–14; 7:14–25; 8:31–39; 1 Corinthians 4:16; 9:24–27; 16:13; 2 Corinthians 10:1–6; Galatians 5:16–26; Ephesians 3:16–17; 4:17 – 5:2; 6:10–20; Colossians 3:1–17; 1 Timothy 1:18.

## 177 NEW LIFE

Chester Szuber lives in Berkeley, Michigan. Chester and his wife have six children. The youngest, Patti, was 22. Chester had suffered through three open heart operations and, in August 1994, had been waiting four years for a heart transplant. Without a new heart his life would soon be over.

In August 1994, tragedy struck. While Chester was waiting for a new heart, his daughter Patti was involved in a serious car accident. Patti was rushed to hospital. The family experienced four excruciating days hovering around the intensive care unit. Sadly Patti's brain stopped functioning. Then the family was faced with a momentous decision. It resulted in a wonderful resolution to this tragedy. Before her fatal accident, Patti had signed an organ donor card. She wanted the suitable organs of her body to be used to give life to others. The family had long discussions with a counsellor and members of the medical team. The family decided Patti would have wanted her heart to be given to her father, who desperately needed a new heart. The medical team worked quickly. Patti's heart was taken from her lifeless body and flown to Michigan. Her dad was already in surgery with another medical team waiting. His daughter's heart was stitched into place. With tension rising in the operating theatre, the team watched the new heart start inside Chester.

**Themes:** *Atonement, Cross, Grief, Jesus – work of, Love, Sacrifice, Salvation, Substitution, Suffering.*

**Scriptures:** Psalms 27:14; Isaiah 53; Mark 10:45; Luke 10:27; John 11:50; Romans 3:21–25; 1 Corinthians 13; Galatians 3:13; 1 Timothy 2:6; Hebrews 9:28; 1 Peter 2:24.

## 178 OBEDIENCE *

At the age of 20, in 336 BC, Alexander the Great inherited his father's throne of Macedon in Greece. Two years later he was conquering the world. When he died at the age of 33 he had conquered almost all the known ancient world.

One day Alexander and a small company of soldiers approached a strongly defended, walled city. Alexander stood outside the walls. He raised his voice, demanding to see the king. The king, approaching the battlements above the invading army, agreed to hear Alexander's demands.

"Surrender to me immediately," commanded Alexander.

The king laughed. "Why would I surrender to you?" he retorted. The king went on to say that Alexander was far outnumbered. He was no threat to the king.

Alexander was ready to answer the challenge. He ordered his men to line up in single file. They were then ordered to start marching. They were marching straight towards a cliff that overlooked rocks hundreds of feet below. The king and his soldiers watched in shock and disbelief. One by one, Alexander's soldiers marched without hesitation right off the cliff to their deaths. After ten had died, Alexander ordered the rest of his men to stop and return to his side.

The king and his soldiers surrendered on the spot to Alexander the Great.

*Themes:* *Goals, Humility, Jesus – character, Life, Love, Perseverance, Purpose, Submission, Suffering.*

**Scriptures:** Genesis 22:18; 1 Samuel 15:22–23; Jeremiah 7:22–23; John 14:15–24; Acts 5:29; Romans 5:19; 6:17; 12:1–2; Galatians 2:20; Ephesians 4:32 – 5:2; Philippians 2:5–8; Titus 2:14; Hebrews 5:8–9; 11:8, 17; 1 Peter 1:22; 2:8; 4:2; 1 John 3:23.

---

178 Adapted from Wayne Rice, *Hot Illustrations for Youth Talks* (El Cajon, CA: Youth Specialties, 1994), pp. 22–23.

## 179 **OBEDIENCE \***

Late in the nineteenth century a man was to walk a wire across Niagara Falls with another man on his shoulders. After weeks of preliminary practice, as the final moment for the event drew near, the rope walker cautioned his young colleague in words like these: "We are about to risk our lives. I am to walk the wire. The whole responsibility is mine. You have nothing to do but match my movements. If I sway to the left, let yourself sway with me. If I sway to the right, do the same. Under no circumstances try to save yourself, for there must be only one will in this adventure, and that will is mine. You must submerge yours to ensure harmony, for without perfect unison we are both lost. There is only one thing for you to do – sway with me."

As they drew near the opposite side, the unexpected happened. The long vibration of the wire broke in the centre into two waves, and each of these broke again into two, and so on, in accordance with the law of vibration, until the shortened wavelike movements became so violent that the man could scarcely keep his feet where he placed them. It was a perilous moment, but the feat was accomplished, and the spectacular escapade was a success, holding a place on the first page of the newspapers.

After this, the young man who had played a secondary part settled down to private life, married, became an active leader in Christian endeavour and an elder in a certain church. And he used to say: "I learned more religion on the wire that day than in all my life. I learned that the only sane and safe way to live is to sway with God."

179 Adapted from Frank S. Arnold, Signs of the Times, 24 November 1931, from: Wit & Wisdom E-mail List: wit-wisdom@XC.Org in "Weekend Encounter": owner-weekend-encounter@gospelcom.net

**Themes:** *Courage, Faith, Fear, God – in control, Guidance, Trust.*

**Scriptures:** 2 Kings 18:5, 19–25; Psalms 2:12; 7:1; 9:10; 13:4–5; 16:1; 25:2, 20; 27:14; 31:1; 32:8; 34:4; 37:3–5; 38:15–16; 44:4–8; 56; 62; 73:28; 84:8–12; 91; 94:16–23; 112; 115:9–11; 146:3; Proverbs 3:5–6, 21–27; 4:10–19; 11:28; 28:26–28; 29:25; Isaiah 12:2; 26:3–4; 36:1–10; 63:10–14; Jeremiah 17:7–8; Matthew 10:28; Mark 11:22–24; Luke 7:1–10; 12:5; John 20:24–29; 1 Timothy 4:10; 5:5; 2 Timothy 1:7; Hebrews 11:1–3; 13:5–6.

## 180 OBEDIENCE

Communists demand total obedience of their members. An American student wrote a letter to his fiancée breaking off his engagement.

We Communists... get shot at, hung, jailed, lynched, tarred and feathered, slandered, ridiculed, and fired from our jobs, and in every other way made uncomfortable. A certain percentage of us gets killed or imprisoned; we live in virtual poverty. We turn back to the Party every penny we make above what is necessary to keep alive. We Communists don't have the time or money for many movies or concerts or T-bone steaks or decent homes or new cars. We've been described as fanatics; we are fanatics. Our lives are dominated by one overshadowing factor: the Struggle for World Communism! We Communists have a philosophy of life which no amount of money could buy. We have a cause to fight for, a definite purpose in life. We subordinate our petty personal selves into a great movement for humanity. There is one thing about which I am in earnest: the Communist Cause! It is my life, my business, my religion, my hobby, my sweetheart, my wife, my mistress, my bread and my meat! I work at it in the daytime and dream of it at night! Therefore I cannot carry on a friendship, a love affair, or even a conversation, without relating everything to this force which both guides and drives my life... I have already been in jail because of my ideas, and if necessary I am ready to go before a firing squad.

**Themes:** *Commitment, Goals, Humility, Jesus – character, Life, Perseverance, Purpose, Submission, Suffering, Vision.*

**Scriptures:** Genesis 22:18; 1 Samuel 15:22–23; Jeremiah 7:22–23; 20:9; John 6:29; 14:15–24; Acts 5:29; 6:7; Romans 5:19; 6:17; 9:31 – 10:3, 16; 12:1–2; 1 Corinthians 15:22; Galatians 2:20; Ephesians 4:32 – 5:2; Philippians 2:5–8; 2 Thessalonians 1:8; Titus 2:14; Hebrews 5:8–9; 11:8, 17; 1 Peter 1:15–16, 22; 2:8; 3:1; 4:2, 17; 1 John 3:23.

## ⋀8⋀ OBEDIENCE

During the First World War, a French gunner was directed by his commanding officer to train his gun on a little house in the distance in which he suspected the enemy might be hiding. The soldier obeyed and the little house was blown to bits. Highly pleased with the expert marksmanship, the commander turned to his gunner with a compliment, only to find tears rolling from his eyes. Asked why he wept, the soldier said, "That was my house."

"If you had told me," said the officer, "I might have modified the order."

"A soldier's first duty is to obey orders," came the swift reply.

**Themes:** *Following, Leadership, War.*

**Scriptures:** Genesis 22:18; 1 Samuel 15:22; Jeremiah 7:22–23; John 6:29; 14:15–24; Acts 5:29; 6:7; Romans 6:17; 9:31 – 10:3, 16; 12:1–2; Ephesians 4:32 – 5:2; Philippians 2.5–8; 2 Thessalonians 1:8; Hebrews 5:9; 11:8, 17; 1 Peter 1:15–16; 22; 2:8; 3:1; 4:17; 1 John 3.23.

## ⋀8⋀ OCCULT

A young man was being counselled by a minister as he was emerging from a homosexual affair and was seeking to get his life back into order with Jesus. Something still seemed to be holding him back. During the time of prayer he happened to mention a ring which his former partner had given him as a mark of their relationship and which he was still wearing. It turned out that this ring had been charmed by a medium. The ring was immediately removed and given up. He repented again of his former lifestyle and renounced the ring and all it stood for. From that time onwards he noticed an immediate release and knew he was free from what had held him back in his spiritual growth.

*Themes:* *Demonic, Freedom, Homosexuality, Magic, Repentance.*

**Scriptures:** Exodus 22:20; 32:8; 34:15; Leviticus 18:26, 31; Deuteronomy 18:10–13; 32:17; Luke 4:18; Acts 19:11–20; Romans 8:31–39.

## ⋏8ℨ OPPORTUNITIES – MISSED

In California, a family in the very fashionable community of Hillsborough set out to sing some carols for their neighbours. At the very first house they called, the response was less than the best. A very distraught woman came to the door.

"Look fella," she shouted, "I'm too busy. The plumbing's on the blink. I can't get anyone to fix it, and there is a mob coming for dinner. If you really feel like singing carols, come back about nine o'clock, okay?"

"Yes, ma'am," and, respectfully, Bing Crosby moved his singing troupe along.

*Themes:* *Carols, Christmas, Rejection, Time – use of.*

**Scriptures:** Mark 2:6–12; 4:1–20; 6:1–6; Luke 15:25–32; John 1:11–12.

## ⋏8Ꮞ OPTIMISM

A family had two primary school-aged children. One of the lads was always grumpy and complaining – a real pessimist. The other was always bright and cheerful and could never see anything wrong with anything – a real optimist. The parents were a bit worried about how they would end up coping in life. One Saturday, the father decided to purchase every popular toy he could lay his hands on. He gave them to the grumpy pessimistic child. He also had a truckload of manure up-ended in the shed for the optimist. On Saturday afternoon, the parents found the pessimistic son sitting in his room sobbing away because he was afraid he would break the toys if he played with them. When they went out to the shed, there was the optimistic fellow having a great time burrowing around in the pile of manure. "What are you doing?" the dad asked. "Oh Dad, I just know there's a horse in here somewhere."

**Themes:** *Humour, Life, Parenting, Pessimism, Positive, Praise, Thanksgiving.*
**Scriptures:** Genesis 18:19; Deuteronomy 5:16; 6:4–9; Psalms 34:1; 71:6; Hosea 14:2; Ephesians 5:20; 6:1, 4; Colossians 3:20–21; Hebrews 13:15; 1 Peter 2:5.

## 185 PARABLE – PRODIGAL SON

Feeling footloose and frisky, a feather-brained freshman from Fargo named Fred forced his fond father to fork over the farthings.

Fred flew far to fancy foreign fields finding foolish frivolities, frequent fornication and fabulous feasting with faithless friends and fillies. He frittered father's fortune. Fleeced by his fellows in folly, fully fatigued and facing famine, Fred found himself functioning as a feed-flinger in a filthy farmyard with fungus face and a fist full of fresh fragrant fertiliser. Fairly famishing, Fred fain would have filled his frame with foraged food from fodder fragments.

"Far out and fooey! What a fiasco! My father's flunkies fare far finer!" the frazzled fugitive forlornly fumbled, frankly facing facts.

Freezing, frightened, frustrated by failure, and filled

185 Adapted from Stephen Gaukroger and Mick Mercer, *Frogs in Cream* (London: Scripture Union, 1990), p. 32.

with foreboding, Fred fled forthwith to his Fargo family. Falling at his father's feet, he forlornly fumbled, "Father, I've flunked, and fruitlessly forfeited family fellowship favour."

Fortunately for Fred, the far-sighted father, forestalling further flinching, forgiving and forgetting Fred's failings, frantically flagged the flunkies, "Fantastic! Fetch a fatling from the flock and fix a feast! Furnish Fred with fashionable flannel."

The fugitive's fault-finding brother, Farley, flew into a fury, frowning on this fickled forgiveness of former falderal's fancy footwork. "Fred's a fool," said Farley. But the faithful father figured, "Filial fidelity is fine, Farley, but the fugitive is found! What forbids fervent festivity? Let flags be unfurled! Find the fiddles and flutes! Let fanfares flare!"

Father's forgiveness formed the foundation for Fred the former fugitive's reforming future fortitude.

*Themes:* *Acceptance, Celebration, Failure, Forgiveness, God – Father, God – his love, Humour, Jealousy, Materialism, Parenting, Reconciliation, Repentance.*

**Scriptures:** Exodus 34:6–7; Psalms 51; 103:12; Isaiah 38:17; 43:25; Daniel 9:9; Micah 7:19; Mark 2:1–12; 11:25; Luke 4:18; 10:27; 15:11–32; John 8:1–11; Romans 3:21–31; 1 Corinthians 13; 2 Corinthians 12:7–10; 1 John 1:8–9.

## 186 PARDONED

Queen Victoria was only 18 when she succeeded to the throne of England. Soon afterwards the Lord Chamberlain presented her with several documents that required her signature. Among them was a paper concerning a man who had committed a serious crime. He had been sentenced to

186 Adapted from Walter B. Knight, *Knight's Treasury of Illustrations* (Grand Rapids, MI: William B. Eerdmans, 1963), p. 133.

death. The Queen's signature was required for his execution to be carried out. But the young Queen was hesitant. "And must I become party to his death?" she asked.

"I fear it is so, unless Your Majesty desires to exercise her royal prerogative of mercy!"

To her delight, Victoria was informed that she had the power to pardon the condemned man. She said, "As an expression of the spirit in which I desire to rule, I will exercise my royal prerogative!" She wrote the word "pardoned" on the document and the prisoner was set free.

**Themes:** *Capital punishment, Death sentence, Forgiveness, Freedom, Grace, Mercy, Release.*

**Scriptures:** Exodus 34:6–7; Psalms 51; 103:12; Isaiah 38:17; 43:25; Daniel 9:9; Micah 7:19; Mark 2:1–12; 11:25; Luke 4:18; 15:11–32; John 8:1–11, 31–36; 11:25–26; Romans 3:21–31; 2 Corinthians 12:7–10; 1 John 1:8–9.

## 187 PARDONED

On 30 October 1821, in a Russian hospital for the poor, a son, Fyodor, was born to the chief medical director. When he grew up Fyodor Dostoevsky studied to become a military engineer. But he resigned his commission and began writing.

It was not many years before his writing got him into trouble. Early in the morning of 23 April 1849 he was awakened by the rattling of swords. His apartment was ransacked. Books and papers were confiscated and he was arrested and taken away to the headquarters of the secret police. He was soon under lock and key. Conditions were hard. They had to live with the fleas, lice, cockroaches and rats.

An inquiry into the writings of subversives like

187 Adapted from Geir Kjetsaa, *Fyodor Dostoevsky: A Writer's Life* (London: Macmillan, 1987), pp. 84–89.

Dostoevsky eventually took place. Three hundred people were involved in a 9,000-page report. On 16 November, Dostoevsky received the following sentence. It read, in part: "The military court finds the accused Dostoevsky guilty in that he,... accepted a copy of a subversive letter... Therefore, the military court has... condemned the former... Lieutenant... to... death by firing squad."

Early in the cold, overcast morning, with snow falling intermittently, on 22 December he was brought his clothes and – with 20 others – put into a carriage. When the prisoners emerged from the carriage, they were met by a priest in full burial vestments. He was carrying a Bible and a cross. They stumbled along behind him through the snow. There were 3,000 silent witnesses, for the most part people on their way to work. The atmosphere was tense.

In the middle of the square was a scaffold covered with black cloth. Three stakes had been placed in the frozen ground, and behind the scaffold was a line of carts – apparently laden with empty coffins. The prisoners were placed in two lines on the scaffold facing the troops. By some macabre notion the troops had been selected from amongst Dostoevsky's own regiment, so that he was to be shot by his friends. With rifles loaded the soldiers took aim at the hooded faces. Half a minute of excruciating, terrible suspense passed. Where were the shots?

Suddenly, someone appeared waving a white cloth and the soldiers lowered their rifles. A carriage sped into the square carrying a sealed envelope for the general. The general stepped forward and announced that the Tsar had granted a pardon. Dostoevsky felt a joy in life rush through him once again.

"I cannot remember a happier day... As I walked back

and forth... singing the whole time, singing loudly, I was so glad for the life that had been given back to me."

*Themes:* *Capital punishment, Death sentence, Forgiveness, Freedom, Grace, Mercy, Release.*

**Scriptures:** Exodus 34:6–7; Psalms 51; 103:12; Isaiah 38:17; 43:25; Daniel 9:9; Micah 7:19; Mark 2:1–12; 11:25; Luke 4:18; 15:11–32; John 8:1–11, 31–36; 11:25–26; Romans 3:21–31; 2 Corinthians 12:7–10; 1 John 1:8–9.

## 188 PARENTING

A mother of a rebellious thirteen-year-old boy, who was totally beyond her parental authority, sought help from a Christian professor of child development. The lad would not come home until 2:00 am or later. He disobeyed every request she made of him. The psychologist asked if she could tell him the history of the problem. She said that she could clearly remember when it all started. Her son was less than three at the time. She carried him to his room and placed him in his bed. He spat in her face to demonstrate his usual bedtime attitude. She attempted to explain the importance of not spitting in her face. But her lecture was interrupted by another moist missile. This mother had been told that all confrontation could be resolved by love and understanding and discussion. She wiped her face and began again. At which point the youngster hit her with another well-aimed blast. She began to get frustrated and shook him. But not hard enough to throw off his aim of his next contribution. What could she do? Her philosophy of becoming a parent offered no honourable solution. Finally, she rushed from the room in utter exasperation. And her little conqueror spat on the back of the door as it shut. She lost; he won! She said she never had the upper hand with her child after that night.

*Themes:* *Children, Fathers, Humour, Mothers.*

*Scriptures:* Genesis 18:19; Deuteronomy 5:16; 6:4–9; Ephesians 6:1, 4; Colossians 3:20–21.

## 189 PARENTING

A father had reached a brick wall with Bob, his 17-year-old son. His son had been stealing. One day, when the evidence was incontrovertible, the father was overwhelmed with rage with God. He says, "I told God I hated him. I told him I could take no more. I asked him either to kill me or to kill the boy – I'd really reached the limit. I'd done everything I could, disciplined firmly and consistently, been understanding, established a good rapport with the boy. For years, I'd put up with court appearances, family therapy from psychiatrists, crisis after crisis... I don't know what happened to me or why I reacted so strongly, but inside me all hell broke loose." Then the father said something dawned on him. He realised his discipline was always to control something in Bob's life. It had never occurred to him to punish Bob because justice demanded punishment. The dad said, at this point, he felt scared. For he realised justice would mean a stick to his rear end. Bob was now bigger and stronger than his dad – and a fight would be a disaster. The father is Christian. He said he prayed about it for hours. Eventually he felt at peace. He spoke to Bob. Dad said Bob had to be punished for what he had done wrong. Dad said, to his surprise and relief, his son accepted it like a lamb. The dad said later, "Something happened. It had nothing to do with the physical part but the simple business of coming to terms with justice. He's never been the same since." The dad went on to say that a great change happened in him too. He realised he had been more worried about his pride than in his son knowing justice and logical consequences in his life.

**Themes:** *Control, Discipline, Fathers, Justice, Punishment, Theft.*

**Scriptures:** Genesis 18:19; Deuteronomy 5:16, 19; 6:4–9; Ephesians 6:1, 4; Colossians 3:20–21.

## 190 PARENTING

Jim Cymbala is a minister in Brooklyn, New York. He has been there for over 21 years. Jim and his wife Carol have three children.

Up to the age of 16, Chrissy, their oldest daughter, was a model child. But, then, she drifted away from God. She became involved with a young man who was not a Christian. Eventually she left home and became pregnant.

Jim and Carol went through a dark tunnel of two and a half years. On Sundays, as he went off to preach, Jim would often cry from the minute he left the house until he got to the church door.

After Chrissy had been away for two years Jim spent some time in Florida. As he prayed he said to God, "I've been battling, crying, screaming, arguing, and manoeuvring with Chrissy. No more arguing, no more talking. It's just you and me. I'm just going to pray for my daughter."

Four months later, in February, on a Tuesday, Jim was in the church prayer meeting. Someone passed him a note. It said this person felt deeply impressed that they should stop the meeting and pray for his daughter. Jim struggled to know if this was right.

At that moment, Chrissy was at a friend's home somewhere in Brooklyn, with her baby.

Jim decided to interrupt the meeting. He told the people his daughter was confused and in a mess. She thought up was down, white was black, and black was white. Jim says the room soon felt like the labour room in a hospital. The people called out to God with incredible intensity.

When he got home he told Carol that something had happened in heavenly places.

Thirty-six hours later, Jim was standing in the bathroom shaving. Carol burst in, "Chrissy's here, you better go downstairs."

"I don't know..." he said. For he had intentionally kept his distance from Chrissy for four months, not wanting to argue or push her.

"Trust me. Go downstairs," Carol said.

Jim wiped off the shaving cream. He went down to the kitchen and there was his daughter, 19 years old, and on her knees weeping. She grabbed his leg and said, "Dad, I've sinned against God. I've sinned against you. I've sinned against myself."

A sobbing and sniffing Chrissy went on to explain. God had woken her in the middle of Tuesday night. God showed her that she was heading towards a pit, a chasm, and she was so afraid. Then she said that God showed her that he hadn't given up on her.

As Jim looked into the face of his daughter he saw again the girl they had raised. Chrissy and their granddaughter moved in with Jim and Carol.

Some years later, Chrissy is the music director in the church. And she has got married.

*Themes:* *Anxiety, Confession, Fathers, Parable – Prodigal Son, Prayer, Reconciliation, Repentance.*

**Scriptures:** Matthew 6:25; Mark 1:15; Luke 12:22–31; 15:11–32; Ephesians 6:18; Philippians 4:6.

## ∧९∧ PERSECUTION

Severe persecution came to Korea when it was occupied for a number of years by a neighbouring country. Many of the churches were closed and missionaries told to leave.

Christians were gaoled and some gave their lives for their faith. A small Methodist church, located thirteen miles from my home in the village of Jae-am, was opened up without explanation. Some Christians came joyfully to the church. Then, suddenly, the doors were locked from the outside, petrol was poured around the church and it was set on fire. A squad of police surrounded the building, ready to shoot any who might try to escape through a window. Twenty-nine people died inside the burning building. They died singing the hymn that Korean Christians still love to sing:

> Nearer, my God, to thee, near to thee
> E'en though it be the cross
> Nearer to thee.

After the Second World War, a group of Christians erected a monument and engraved the names of those 29 people who gave their lives for Christ in the church that Sunday. A few years ago, a group of pastors came from the country that had occupied Korea. They visited this village and saw the monument and heard the story behind it. They returned to their home country and raised $25,000. They used this money to erect a church in the place where the old one had burned down. On 27 September 1970, at 3:00 pm, the beautiful church was dedicated. It was my privilege to attend this dedication service. The church was packed out. The group of pastors who had raised the money were there too. As we sang the final hymn, automatically men got up from their seats and embraced one another. They were proving that the past had been forgiven and forgotten.

191 Billy Kim, "God at Work in Times of Persecution (Acts 7:54 – 8:8)", in J. D. Douglas (ed.), *Let the Earth Hear his Voice* (Minneapolis: World Wide, 1975), p. 59.

**Themes:** *Forgiveness, Hate, Joy, Love, Martyrdom, Reconciliation, Sacrifice, Suffering.*

**Scriptures:** Daniel 3:16–18; Matthew 5:43–48; Mark 8:34–38; 11:25; Luke 10:20, 27; John 15:11; Acts 4:1–22; 6:8 – 8:3; 7:54 – 8:8; 9:23–25; 14:5–6, 19; 16:19–24; 21:30–36; 1 Corinthians 4:11–13; 13:3; 2 Corinthians 6:4–5; 11:23–28; 1 Thessalonians 2:9; 2 Thessalonians 3:8.

## ᐊᑌᒿ **PERSEVERANCE ***

In 1968 the Mexico Olympics took place. That year John Stephen Awkhwari was one of the representatives from Tanzania. John was in the marathon. During the race he fell and severely injured a knee and an ankle. By 7:00 pm an Ethiopian had won the race.

Eventually all the other competitors had finished and been cared for. Just a few thousand spectators were left in the huge stadium. A police siren at the gate caught their attention. Limping through the gate came number 36, John Stephen Awkhwari. His leg was wrapped in a blood-soaked bandage. The tiny audience began to cheer the courageous man as he completed the final lap of the race.

Later a reporter asked John the question on everyone's mind, "Why did you continue the race after you were so badly injured?"

The man replied, "My country didn't send me 7,000 miles to begin a race; they sent me to finish the race."

**Themes:** *Endurance, Failure, Goals, Obedience, Pain, Persistence, Suffering.*

**Scriptures:** Luke 10:27; 11:1–13; 18:1–8; Acts 1:14; 2:42, 46; 6:4; 8:13; Romans 12:12; 13:6; 1 Corinthians 13; Galatians 6:9–10; Ephesians 6:18; Colossians 3:24; 4:2; Hebrews 10:32–36; 11:27; 12:1–2; 2 John 8.

## ᐊᑌᒡ **PERSISTENCE**

Samuel Taylor Coleridge (1772–1834) was a great British poet and critic. But he could have been even greater. He left Cambridge University to join the army. He left the army because he could not rub down a horse. He returned to Oxford and left without a degree. He began a paper called *The Watchman*, but it failed after ten issues. It has been said of him, "He lost himself in visions of work to be done, but always remained to be done."

It was said of Coleridge that he had every poetic gift but one – the gift of sustained and concentrated effort. In his head were all kinds of ideas. He told friends his work was: "... completed save for transcriptions. I am on the eve of sending to the press two Octavo volumes." But his work rarely came to anything outside his mind.

**Themes:** *Creativity, Failure, Good works, Laziness, Perseverance.*
**Scriptures:** Matthew 5:14–16; 2 Corinthians 9:8; Galatians 6:9–10; Ephesians 2:1–10; Colossians 1:10; 2 Timothy 2:21; Titus 2:14; 3:1.

## 194 POWER

The Darwin Award is an annual honour given by forensic scientists to "a dim-witted person who has done the human gene pool a great service by killing himself in an extraordinary stupid way". In 1995 it was awarded to a man in Arizona.

In Arizona a police patrol came across a pile of smouldering metal pressed into a cliff. The cliff was at the apex of a tight curve in a two-lane highway. It looked like an aircraft crash sight. But it turned out to be a car. Forensic scientists were called in to reconstruct what had happened. The award winner had got hold of an airforce JATO. A JATO is a jet-assisted take-off solid fuel rocket. It is sometimes attached to military transport planes taking off from short airfields. The Darwin Award winner had driven his Chevy Impala into the Arizona desert. He found a long, straight stretch of road. He attached the JATO to the rear of his Chevy. He jumped in, got up speed and then fired up the rocket. Once a JATO is switched on it cannot be switched off; it simply burns until all the fuel has gone.

As far as can be determined, he was travelling somewhere between 450 and 500 kph when he came to the curve in the road.

**Themes:** *Energy, Direction, "Dunamis", Holy Spirit, Humour, Resurrection.*

**Scriptures:** Luke 4:7, 14, 33; 5:17; 6:8; 10:38; Acts 1:8; Romans 1:16; 1 Corinthians 1:18; 9:23–27; Ephesians 1:19–20; Philippians 3:10; 2 Timothy 1:7–8.

## 195 **PRAYER**

I heard the sad story of a missionary, his wife and three children who went to the Far East. Before they left home their local church gave them full assurance that folk would support them financially and pray for them. In order to help the folk pray intelligently the missionary family sent back tapes and letters telling of their news and needs. Unbeknown to the missionary family, there was only one person in the church family who showed any ongoing interest in them. The missionary adventure turned to disaster. The husband had a great deal of difficulty learning the languages. There was great opposition from the government and non-Christian forces in the country. Then tragically, at the age of only 26, the wife contracted blackwater fever. After a short time she died, leaving him with the three children. He stayed on and completed his first term. When he went home to his church family he was keen to get to the prayer meeting. They prayed for the Sunday School picnic, the new building programme and the women's trip to a conference. The young missionary sat stunned in the back row. At the end of the meeting the minister approached him. The first thing the missionary said was, "Now I understand. This is the reason."

"What on earth are you talking about?" asked the minister. "Those years on the field," said the missionary. "The difficulties, the pain, the lack of results. This is the reason."

*Themes:* *Intercession, Missionaries, Prayer – answered.*

*Scriptures:* Romans 1:8–12; 12:12; 1 Corinthians 14:14–16; Ephesians 1:15–19; 3:14–18; 6:13–18; Philippians 4:6; Colossians 1:9–14; 4:2; 1 Thessalonians 1:2.

## 196 **PRAYER**

In 1727 the Moravian church was part of the Lutheran church in Germany. The Moravians were deeply divided, people were critical of each other and they argued about everything. Their leader, Count Zinzendorf, pleaded for love and unity. On 5 August he spent the whole night in prayer with about twelve or fourteen others. On Sunday 10 August, about midday, the whole congregation was overwhelmed with the powerful presence of God. They continued until midnight in prayer, singing, weeping and praying. Also, the children in the church were touched by God and began to hold their own prayer meetings. On 26 August, 24 men and 24 women agreed to continue praying around the clock, taking an hour each. On 27 August, they agreed to meet weekly where prayer needs would be given out. As a direct result of prayer for God's filling of their lives with the Holy Spirit, the Moravian church sent out over one hundred missionaries in just two decades.

*Themes:* *God – presence of, Intercession, Missionaries, Prayer – answered, Prayer – constant, Prayer – vigil, Revival, Toronto Blessing.*

*Scriptures:* Acts 4:30–31; Romans 1:8–12; 12:12; 1 Corinthians 14:14–16; Ephesians 1:15–19; 3:14–18; 6:13–18; Philippians 4:6; Colossians 1:9–14; 4:2; 1 Thessalonians 1:2; 5:17.

## 197 PRAYER

In 1938, Alf Stanway had just taken over as Principal of an African Christian Boarding School on the coast of Kenya. One of the subjects to be taught was tailoring and the only tailors available were Muslims. All Alf's attempts to find a teacher failed.

During the holidays he was at a conference. He was so worried about the lack of a teacher for his school that he could not concentrate on the task in hand. In desperation he asked God to take away the anxiety. What he did not anticipate was that God took away the anxiety so completely that he forgot all about the issue.

Not until Alf returned to the school and was entering the office did he think of the lack of a tailoring teacher again. And school was due to begin in three days! Alf greeted Joseph the clerk and asked what could be done about a tailor. Joseph simply replied that there was one in the workshop. The man in the workshop had heard of the vacancy and came to investigate. Joseph had given him temporary work until Alf returned from the conference. He was suitable and was hired.

*Themes:* *Answered Prayer, Anxiety, Guidance, Missionaries, Trust, Worry.*
**Scriptures:** Psalms 32:8; 37:3–5; 46; Proverbs 3:5–6; Jeremiah 29:12–13; Matthew 6:19–34; 21:22; Mark 11:24; Luke 11:1–13; 18:1–6; John 15:7; 16:23–24; Philippians 4:6; James 1:5–8; 4:3; 1 Peter 5:6–7; 1 John 3:22; 5:14–15.

## 198 PRAYER

D. L. Moody, the famous American evangelist of the nineteenth century, was in England. He was a young man, and

---

197 Adapted from Alfred Stanway, *Prayer: A Personal Testimony* (Canberra: Acorn, 1991), p. 25.
198 John Woolmer, *Growing in to Salvation* (London: Triangle, 1983), pp. 112–113, his emphasis.

his great work hadn't really begun. He was invited to preach in a large London church. In the morning service, he sensed nothing memorable despite large numbers. In the evening, the whole atmosphere was different. The church was alive in the Spirit! Scores of people answered his call for commitment. The response was so great that he had to minister for several nights. This, humanly speaking, led to the salvation of thousands. Intrigued, he tried to find out what was the difference between the morning and evening congregations.

Eventually he tracked down a bed-ridden woman whose sister came to the church. Every Sunday she would ask her sister about the services. Inevitably she would be given a monotonous and uneventful account. One Sunday the sister mentioned to the bed-ridden woman that a Mr Moody from America had preached that morning. "Ah!" said the bed-ridden one, "I will have no lunch. I must pray." She had once read an article by Mr Moody, and had prayed for *several years* for God to bring him to England to her church. Now her prayer had been answered, and things were going to happen! The results of that prayer were far-reaching for her church, and even more so for the world-wide church – a new spiritual giant was born.

**Themes:** *Conversion, Evangelism, Ministry, Persistence, Preaching.*

**Scriptures:** Jeremiah 29:12–13; Matthew 21:22; Mark 11:24; Luke 11:1–13; 18:1–6; John 15:7; 16:23–24; 17:20–26; Ephesians 6:18–20; Colossians 4:3; 1 Thessalonians 5:25; 2 Thessalonians 3:1; James 1:5–8; 4:3; 1 John 3:22; 5:14–15.

## 199 PRAYER AND FASTING

Minnesota farmers know locust plagues well. Their crops had been destroyed by the voraciously hungry insects in the summer of 1876.

In the spring of 1877 they waited and watched to see

whether or not such pestilence would strike yet again. If it did, the farming future of families would be wiped out permanently.

Acutely aware of the impending disaster, Governor J. S. Pillsbury proclaimed that 26 April would be a day of prayer and fasting to plead with God to save them from calamity. The governor urged that every single person should unite and participate toward this end.

Across the state people responded to their governor's call. In gatherings large and small, Minnesotans assembled to fast and pray.

The next day, as the sun soared in a cloudless sky, with temperatures also rising, the people noticed to their dismay that the dreaded insects started to stir in the warmed soil.

For three days the uninterrupted unseasonal heat caused a vast army of locusts to hatch. It was of such plague proportions as to threaten the entire north-west farm sector.

Then, as the sun departed at the end of the fourth day, there was a sudden climatic change. A blanket of frost flicked across the entire area where the locusts waited for dawn and take-off. Most were killed right where they crouched.

Come summer, instead of scorched stubbled dirt, as far as the eye could see, the wheat crop waved in golden glory.

In the history of Minnesota, 26 April 1877 is recorded as the day when God wonderfully responded to the prayers and fasting of his people.

**Themes:** *Fasting, Miracles, Prayer – answered, Prayer – vigil.*

**Scriptures:** Exodus 34:27–28; 2 Samuel 12:16–24; Ezra 8:21; Psalms 69:10; Isaiah 58:5–12; Jeremiah 14:11–12; Zechariah 7:1–14; 8:19; Mark 2:18–22; Romans 1:8–12; 12:12; 1 Corinthians 14:14–16; Ephesians

1:15–19; 3:14–18; 6:13–18; Philippians 4:6; Colossians 1:9–14; 4:2;
1 Thessalonians 1:2.

## 2OO PRAYER AND FASTING [200]

In a south Asian city a western missionary saw a cow
about to be slaughtered in front of a mosque during the
Muslim festival of Eid ul Adha. He stopped his car, took a
few pictures, then drove home.

But that night the Holy Spirit began to challenge him to
be less a tourist and more a missionary. He was directed
to start praying and fasting, to return to the scene of the
sacrifice and to be a witness to the greater sacrifice of
Jesus.

In the steaming pre-monsoon heat of the next day, he
set off with his shoulder bag full of tracts and gospels to
the same place in the bazaar, near the mosque.

Having sold and distributed much literature, he felt
well satisfied as he returned home that he had done his
"duty". But the Holy Spirit impressed upon him that night
that he was to continue his praying and fasting and to
return to repeat the process in the same place the next
day.

Night after night, as the missionary prayed, the Holy
Spirit repeated his instruction to his obedient servant.

It didn't take long for local opposition to form and even
threaten his life. He was dragged through the market
place, doused in dye, kicked and pushed into a ditch and
stoned. Twice a fanatic tried to kill him with a dagger but
was restrained by his own people.

Finally, two well-trained rabble-rousers were appointed
to stop his witnessing. They approached him directly,
warning him that, should he return again, he wouldn't
leave the bazaar alive.

On the fortieth day of this supernaturally sustained

period of prayer and fasting, directed by what the Spirit was saying, he bade farewell to his wife for what he thought could be the last time. He set out once more with his literature to sell and distribute in the bazaar. No sooner had he arrived than the appointed "crowd conductors" also showed up. They tore up his gospels and his tracts and began to incite the growing crowd to watch the spectacle. Soon there were calls to kill him.

Then, as men moved in to grab him, two unusually tall strangers appeared.

Spearing a path through the crowd, which was now calling for the missionary's blood, they grabbed him, in one swift move, removed him from the crush of people and took him down an alleyway at the end of which was waiting a bicycle rickshaw.

Amazingly, no one had followed them.

Placing the missionary in the rickshaw, the strangers said to him, "It is enough now. Don't come back." God's messengers had saved his servant.

That night the Lord spoke once more, saying, "Now you know how much I love and care for Muslims. It is not my will that any of them should perish without hearing the message of salvation."

With no other tangible resources, other than the practice of sustained prayer and fasting, that missionary went on to be used by God to build what became one of the largest churches in that somewhat hostile environment.

**Themes:** *Angels, Church growth, Fasting, Guidance, Holy Spirit – directing, Miracles, Missionaries, Muslims, Persecution.*

**Scriptures:** Exodus 34:27–28; 2 Samuel 12:16–24; Ezra 8:21; Psalms 69:10; Isaiah 58:5–12; Jeremiah 14:11–12; Zechariah 7:1–14; 8:19; Mark 2:18–22; John 14:26; 16:12–13; Acts 8:1–40; 13:1–3; 16:7; Romans 1:8–12; 12:12; 1 Corinthians 14:14–16; Ephesians 1:15–19; 3:14–18;

6:13–18; Philippians 4:6; Colossians 1:9–14; 4:2; 1 Thessalonians 1:2;
1 John 2:27.

## 201 PRAYER – MEDITATION

A peasant had got into the habit of slipping into a certain church at a certain time of day with clockwork regularity. There, day by day, he would sit and, apparently, do nothing. The parish priest observed this regular, silent visitor. One day, unable to contain his curiosity any longer, he asked the old man why he came to the church, alone, day in, day out. Why waste his time this way?

The old man looked at the priest and, with a loving twinkle in his eye, explained, "I look at him. He looks at me. And we tell each other that we love each other."

*Themes:* Contemplation, Love – for God, Meditation.

**Scriptures:** Deuteronomy 6:5; 10:12; Joshua 1:8; Psalms 1:3; 18:1; 19:14; 25; 40:1–5; 63:5–8; 77:11–15; 104:34; 116:1–2; 119; 130:5–6; 143:5; Lamentations 3:25; Luke 10:27; John 14:15; 21:15–19; 1 Corinthians 13; 1 John 4:19.

## 202 PRAYER – PERSISTENCE

Two African chiefs came to Chalmers the missionary. They asked for Christian teachers for their villages. Chalmers apologised, saying he did not have anyone to send. Two years went by. The chiefs returned to Chalmers to pester him again. Chalmers decided to go himself. When he arrived in one of the villages, he was surprised by what he saw. It was Sunday and all the people were on their knees, in perfect silence. Chalmers asked the chief, "What are you doing?"

"We are praying," he said.

---

[201] Adapted from Joyce Huggett, *Listening to God* (London: Hodder and Stoughton, 1986), p. 64.

"But you are not saying anything," Chalmers returned.

The chief then said, "White man, we do not know what to say. For two years, every Sunday morning we have met here. And for four hours we have been on our knees and we have been praying like that, but we do not know what to say."

*Themes:* *Holy Spirit – directing, Missionaries, Parable – Friend at Midnight.*

*Scriptures:* Luke 11:5–13; 18:1–8; Romans 1:8–12; 8:26; 12:12; 1 Corinthians 14:14–16; Ephesians 1:15–19; 3:14–18; 6:13–18; Philippians 4:6; Colossians 1:9–14; 4:2; 1 Thessalonians 1:2; 5:17.

## 203 PRAYER – PERSISTENCE

A man watched his uncle, Byron, fight a bitter battle with cancer. People from the uncle's church were praying and fasting for him around the clock. All over the world friends of the family were asked to pray for him. But months and then a year went by, and Byron grew steadily worse.

The nephew only visited his uncle once during his illness. He saw that the slightest movement made him weep with pain. The nephew assumed that would be the last time he would see his uncle. Yet, when I heard this story, a year and a half later, Byron was completely free of cancer. He wears the scars of battle; his 5' 10" frame is now 10" shorter. His face has new lines drawn by the pain, and walking is severely limited. But his doctors call his recovery a miracle. What would have happened if people had given up when he wasn't healed the first time they prayed – or the tenth, or the one hundredth?

*Themes:* *Fasting, Parable – Friend at Midnight, Prayer – answered, Prayer – vigil.*

*Scriptures:* Luke 11:5–13; 18:1–8; Romans 1:8–12; 8:26; 12:12; 1 Corinthians 14:14–16; Ephesians 1:15–19; 3:14–18; 6:13–18; Philippians 4:6; Colossians 1:9–14; 4:2; 1 Thessalonians 1:2; 5:17.

## 204 PRAYER – SIMPLE

Three monks lived on an island. Their prayer of intimacy and love was as simple as they were simple: "We are three; you are three; have mercy on us. Amen." Miracles sometimes happened when they prayed in this way.

The bishop, however, hearing about the monks decided that they needed guidance in proper prayer, and so he went to their small island. After instructing them, the bishop set sail for the mainland, pleased to have enlightened the souls of such simple men.

Suddenly, off the stern of the ship he saw a huge ball of light skimming across the ocean. It got closer and closer until he could see that it was the three monks running on top of the water. Once on board the ship they said to the bishop, "We are so sorry, but we have forgotten some of your teaching. Would you please instruct us again?" The bishop shook his head and replied meekly, "Forget everything I have taught you and continue to pray in your old way."

*Themes:* *Bishops, Miracles, Monks, Prayer – answered, Simplicity, Walking on water.*

*Scriptures:* 1 Kings 18:30–40; Matthew 6:1–14; Acts 4:30; Romans 8:26.

## 205 PRAYER – UNANSWERED

Rebecca Templemann is a little girl who goes to church. Rebecca and Megan – her friend from church – caught chicken pox at the same time. Megan recovered very quickly. The church family heard how the Lord had touched the little girl to bring about a speedy recovery. But Rebecca suffered long and hard. There were hundreds of itchy red blisters covering her from scalp to sole. Her dad, Louis Templemann, is the minister of their church family.

One night, when mum was at work as a nurse, Rebecca kept her dad up until 4:30 in the morning, crying and whimpering. He dabbed the raised spots with calamine lotion and tried to encourage her to sleep. Trusting Christ, he prayed for her. But still Rebecca could not sleep.

Eventually dad began to say to the Lord as he lay on his bed, "Lord, what is going on? Megan gets a healing. Why not my Rebecca?"

Then dad sensed God saying this to him: "I have given you a greater miracle. You have been given the honour of showing your daughter the nature of a loving father. By your example you have the privilege of teaching her the nature of God. She is learning that she can call out in her agony to her father. Isn't that worth losing a little sleep?"

**Themes:** *Fatherhood, God – Father, Healing, Lord's Prayer, Suffering.*

**Scriptures:** 2 Samuel 11; Psalms 31:9–10; 32; 34:1; 38; 71:6; Hosea 14:2; Matthew 5:12; Mark 3:35; Luke 11:1–4, 13; Romans 5:3–5; 8:15; 14:7–8; 2 Corinthians 5:15; Galatians 2:20; 4:6; 6:9; Ephesians 5:20; Philippians 1:21; 4:12; Hebrews 10:34; 13:15; James 1:2–4; 1 Peter 1:7; 2:5.

## 206 PRAYER – UNANSWERED

Canon Jim Glennon of Sydney tells his story of prayer for healing in his own life. Jim says that he was in an eye hospital. The ophthalmic specialist came to examine his eye and, as he bent over Jim, he caught sight of his neck and said, "My God, do you know what you have got? You have got multiple skin cancer."

Jim was discharged from the eye hospital and he took time to think about his skin cancer. For he suspected that, as is often the case, a lack of forgiveness can manifest itself in a breakdown in our bodies. He approached the Reverend Tom Jewett and asked for his help. He took Jim Glennon very much by surprise by saying, "Can I come to your home for three days?" "Yes," said Canon Glennon.

"But why do you want to come to my home for three days?" "We want to clear away the barriers to healing," was the reply.

What had to be cleared away was a lack of forgiveness. As he tells the story, Canon Glennon says that he had a series of arguments and disagreements with another member of the Cathedral staff. He was hurt and resentful and had to resign his position even though the problems had not been his own fault. Jim Glennon chose to do something about it and wrote to the person saying that he was sorry for his part in the disagreement. A reply came shortly afterwards. He accepted what Jim had said and saw that it was sincere and wanted to say that he was sorry about his part in the disagreement. In Jim's mind there was a coming together, a forgiveness and a fellowship. He never entertained another resentful thought about him.

Then this is what Jim Glennon says, "I solemnly record that the skin cancer cleared up of its own accord without any medical intervention and never came back."

**Themes:** *Cancer, Forgiveness, Healing, Reconciliation, Sickness.*

**Scriptures:** 2 Samuel 11; Psalms 31:9–10; 32; 38; 51; Mark 2:1–12; 11:25; 1 Corinthians 11:29–32.

## 207 PROMISES – NOT ACCEPTED

Around 1830, Crowfoot was born into the Bear Ghost family of Blackfoot Indians. While still a teenager he won distinction for his bravery and scouting ability. He was soon the great chief of the Blackfoot confederacy of Indian nations in southern Alberta, Canada. In 1884, authorities from the Canadian Pacific Railway sought his permission to take the Atlantic to the Pacific railway line through the territory of his people from Medicine Hat to Alberta. In agreeing during the negotiations Canadian Pacific Railway gave Crowfoot, in return, a life-time rail pass. Crowfoot had a leather case made for the pass. He carried the pass with him, around his neck, wherever he went. However, there is no record of Crowfoot ever using the pass to travel anywhere on Canadian Pacific trains.

*Themes:* Faith, God – his favour, Grace, Leadership, Salvation – rejected, Trust.

**Scriptures:** 1 Kings 8:22–53; 2 Chronicles 6:1–42; Romans 1:16 – 3:20; 3:21–28; 5:2; 10:9; Galatians 2:16; Ephesians 2:1–10.

## 208 PROTECTION

Friday 7 July 1497, a group of Portuguese sailors spent a night in prayer. The next day they had to set out on a voyage to circumnavigate the southernmost tip of Africa. Some 80 million tons of water per second sweep down the east coast of Africa and hit the Atlantic head on. Little wonder the ancient sailors called these dangerous swirling waters, the Cape of Storms.

Vasco da Gama had been sent by the Portuguese king to find the way to India by sea. Da Gama studied the charts and set sail with four ships to round the Cape. On Saturday 18 November the dreaded promontory came into sight. Then, over four days, a number of attempts were made to round the Cape. But the wind was dead ahead and he failed. At last, on Wednesday 22, at noon, he was successful, having the wind astern. As he rounded the Cape da Gama looked landward and cried, "No longer will you be called the Cape of Storms – but now *Buono Esperanza* – the Cape of Good Hope."

*Themes:* God – his care, Persistence, Prayer, Suffering, Thanksgiving.

**Scriptures:** Psalms 4; 5; 6; 12; 13; 23; 25; 28; 31; 35; 40:12–17; 44; 54; 59; 61; 62; 64; 69; 70; 77; 89:46–52; 91; 108; 119:153–160, 169–176; 120; 124;

126; 130; 140; 142; 143; 144; Matthew 5:12; Romans 5:2–5; James 1:2–4; 1 Peter 1:6.

## 209 RANSOM

Nigel is a young man who lives in Britain. On one occasion he went to the United States. He had very little money for the trip. One day he was driving a borrowed car and went through a stop sign. Of course, the police were there waiting for him! Nigel pleaded with the man in blue, saying that he was a tourist and did not have a lot of money. But the policeman would hear none of his excuses and handed him a ticket. The next day, when Nigel arrived home, there was a letter waiting for him. In it was a note from the policeman and a cheque for the amount of the fine.

**Themes:** *Atonement, Cross, Expiation, Freedom, Jesus – work of, Reconciliation, Redeemed, Rescued.*

**Scriptures:** Exodus 6:6; Psalms 77:14–15; Mark 10:45; Luke 24:21; John 1:29; 8:31–36; 1 Corinthians 1:30; 5:7; 6:19–20; 7:22–23; Galatians 3:13; 4:4–5; 5:1; Ephesians 1:7; 5:2; Titus 2:14; Hebrews 9:15; 1 Peter 1:18–19; 1 John 2:2.

## 210 RANSOMED [210]

Eric was the grandson of a motor magnate. At 5:00 pm on Wednesday 13 April 1960 four-and-a-half-year-old Eric Peugeot, his seven-year-old brother Jean-Philippe and an eight-year-old girl were playing in a park next to the Saint-Cloud golf course in a fashionable district on the outskirts of Paris. The chauffeur and a nurse were in a car 20 yards away.

As the three children took turns in going down a slide an ordinary 20-year-old young man came through an opening in a broken wall, took Eric's hand and said, "Come along", just as if they were going for a walk.

The nurse noticed that Eric had gone and rushed to the

slide and found a note on the ground. It was typed in red, warning the family not to contact the police and saying that the child would suffer unless the ransom of 50 million old French francs (equivalent to £35,000 or $85,000) was paid.

That night Roland, the father, went on French radio and said, "My only concern is to get my child back safe and sound."

The next day the father stood under an archway with the ransom money in a folder under his arm. From behind he heard the passwords "Keep the key" and was told not to look around as the money was taken and the person's footsteps could be heard retreating. That night a motorist found little Eric crying on the side of a street in the West End of Paris. There was a wonderfully happy reunion amid much rejoicing. "I am happy, terribly happy," said Eric's father at a press conference at his home.

*Themes:* *Atonement, Cross, Expiation, Freedom, Jesus – work of, Reconciliation, Redeemed, Rescue.*

**Scriptures:** Exodus 6:6; Psalms 77:14–15; Mark 10:45; Luke 24:21; John 1:29; 8:31–36; 1 Corinthians 1:30; 5:7; 6:19–20; 7:22–23; Galatians 3:13; 4:4–5; 5:1; Ephesians 1:7; 5:2; Titus 2:14; Hebrews 9:15; 1 Peter 1:18–19; 1 John 2:2.

## ∠⅄⅄ RECONCILIATION

A tramp in the United States said:

I got off at the Pennsylvania depot one day as a tramp, and for a year I begged on the street for a living. One day I touched a man on the shoulder and said, "Mister, please give me a dime." As soon as I saw his face I recognised my old father. "Father, don't you know me?" I asked. Throwing his arms around me he cried, "I have found you, I have found you. All I have is yours."

The tramp, who became a Christian, went on to say, "Man, think of it, that I a tramp stood begging my father for ten cents, when for 18 years he had been looking for me, to give me all he was worth."

*Themes:* *God – Father, Good Shepherd, Lord's Prayer, Parable – Good Samaritan, Parable – Lost Coin, Parable – Lost Sheep, Parable – Prodigal Son, Salvation.*

**Scriptures:** Isaiah 64:8; Malachi 1:6; 2:10; Luke 11:1–4; 15:1–7, 8–10, 11–32; 10:25–37; 19:10; John 10:1–18; 20:17; Romans 8:17; Galatians 3:26; Hebrews 12:9.

## 212 REJECTION

Jodie Cadman is the street name of a New Zealand girl who came to live in the eastern states of Australia.

At one point in her story she says that she never quite forgot her mother's words she overheard when she was six. This particular day began like any other in her six-year-old world.

It was the Christmas holidays at the end of her first year at school. She woke to a brisk breeze and bright blue skies, and was soon out playing with Susan and Margie Johnson from next door. Jodie's place had a small back-yard. Their games centred around a large white-flowering tree at the foot of the garden. This particular day was unusually hot. At one point, Jodie slipped inside for a drink. She was at the fridge when she realised that her mother was talking to Mrs Johnson in the next room. So she had a listen. Suddenly, she heard her name. She crept a little nearer the wall. Her mother was talking. "I can't bear to touch Jodie. I wish I'd never had a girl. She just revolts me, somehow," her mother said.

---

[212] Adapted from Jeaneatte Grant-Thomson, *Jodie's Story: The Life of Jodie Cadman* (Homebush West: ANZEA, 1991).

Jodie could not move. In a few seconds, her whole world had changed. She huddled, whitefaced and shaking, against the wall, trying not to cry. She hardly heard anything else her mother way saying. There was something about a baby boy that was "stillborn". But then there was a shuffle and a rattle of tea cups so she shakily tiptoed outside.

Susan and Margie must have been sick of waiting, for they had gone home. Never mind, Jodie was relieved. She climbed the old tree and cried and cried until there were no more tears. Eventually it got dark and cool. Jodie went inside for tea. Nobody seemed to notice how quiet Jodie was. The hurt grew inside her like an ulcer and she began to hate both her parents.

"How dare my mother not love me," she thought. "She is my mother."

Jodie noticed more and more that mum cuddled her brothers fondly. She craved the same affection and would run up to her mother, but she would be pushed away.

At one stage she says in the book, "I feel as if I am desperately searching for something and I don't even know what I'm searching for. Maybe it's happiness. Or love, I don't know... Nothing satisfies me. I still feel hollow. Frighteningly hollow. There's still something missing. Something important. Perhaps if ever I found it, I'd know what life was all about and what the point was in it all."

She reached a stage in her life where she wanted God to deal with her feeling of rejection. Friends, Charles and Jill, prayed for her. In the praying, Charles said to her, "God wants you to forgive your mother, Jodie, for everything she did and everything she didn't do."

Jodie's fists were clenched with the familiar anger. "Why the hell should I?" she asked. "She doesn't deserve to be forgiven. She couldn't care whether I forgave her or not." Charles explained a very important biblical principle. That is, God cannot do much with us unless we are prepared to release our revengeful grip on those who have hurt us. When Jodie released her hate and revengeful grip on her mother she said, "I felt an enormous weight lift off me... I felt strangely warm and peaceful inside like I'd never felt before."

Over a period of time she met a number of Christians who really knew what peace was about. It was not a smooth road for Jodie to discover that peace for herself. But by the end of the book she is saying things like, "I love being alive."

The last thing she says in the book is, "It's just so good being able to live peacefully myself and with other people. I'm at peace with God. The anger's gone out of me. I didn't want to live, most of my life. I was running away, searching. I'm glad to be alive now. I just want to thank Jesus for giving me life."

*Themes:* Anger, Forgiveness, Grief, Hate, Healing – inner, Lord's Prayer, Love, Mothers, Parenting, Peace, Reconciliation, Revenge, Violence – domestic.

**Scriptures:** Genesis 18:19; Deuteronomy 5:16; 6:4–9; Matthew 5:4, 22–24, 43–48; 6:5–15; Mark 11:25; Luke 10:27; 11:1–13; John 5:40; 10:10; 14:1–4; 16:33; Romans 5:1–5; 1 Corinthians 13; 2 Corinthians 1:3–4; Ephesians 6:1; Philippians 4:6–7; Colossians 3:20–21.

## 213 REJECTION *

A soldier was returning home from fighting in the Vietnam war. He phoned his parents from San Francisco.

"Dad, I'm coming home, but I've a favour to ask. I have a friend I'd like to bring home with me."

"Sure," he replied, "We'd love to meet him."

"There's something you should know," the son continued. "He was hurt pretty badly in the fighting. He stepped

---

213 Adapted from Wayne Rice, *Hot Illustrations for Youth Talks* (El Cajon, CA: Youth Specialties, 1994), pp. 75–76.

on a land mine and lost an arm and a leg. He has nowhere else to go, and I want him to come live with us."

"I'm sorry to hear that, son. Maybe we can help him find somewhere to live."

"No, Dad, I want him to live with us."

But then the dad said this, "Son, you don't know what you're asking. Someone with such a handicap would be a terrible burden to us. We have our own lives to live, and we can't let something like this interfere with our lives. I think you should just come on home and forget about this guy. He'll find a way to live on his own."

At that point the son hung up the phone. The parents heard nothing more from him. A few days later they received a call from the San Francisco police. Their son had died falling from a building. The police believed it was suicide. The parents were taken to the city morgue to identify the body. They recognised their son at once. But to their dismay they discovered something they did not know: their son had only one arm and one leg.

**Themes:** *Acceptance, Fathers, God – his acceptance, God – his love, Grief, Love, Parenting, Reconciliation.*

**Scriptures:** Matthew 5:4, 43–48; Luke 10:29–37; 11:1–13; John 14:1–4; Romans 5:1–5; 1 Corinthians 13; Ephesians 6:1–4; Colossians 3:20–21.

## 214 REJECTION

For those who have been dumped or rejected by someone there are some practical tips. First, for the women:

1 Go shopping.
2 Eat lots of Häagen-Dazs ice cream.
3 Become a nun.
4 Cry a lot until you look like ET.
5 Call him 1,000 times a day and hang up as he answers.

For men who have been dumped or rejected:

1  Do not listen to country music for at least three months.
2  Refer to "her" not as your "ex" but as Cruella.
3  Avoid the rebound syndrome except for Elle MacPherson or What's-Her-Name from Bay Watch.
4  Return all her gifts COD.
5  Don't slam down the receiver when she rings. Get an air horn ready by the phone.

**Themes:** *Depression, Divorce, Humour, Love, Marriage, Men, Relationships, Women.*

**Scriptures:** Proverbs 31; Matthew 5:4; Mark 10:2–12; 11:25; Luke 10:27; 1 Corinthians 7:1–16; 13; 2 Corinthians 1:3–7; Ephesians 5:21–33; Philippians 4:8.

## ㄥ∩Ƨ **RELATIONSHIPS**

William Inge tells the story of an unhappy quarrelling family in Oklahoma in the early 1920s. The family – the Rubin Flood family – were all insecure, fearful and continually engulfed in self-pity.

The daughter, Reenie Flood, accepted a blind date to a dance at the country club, which was being sponsored by a snobbish socialite family in town. Reenie's date was Sammie Goldenbloom, who was an unwanted orphan. But Sammie was a sensitive boy and a very caring date. Reenie Flood was elated that a person could care for her as did Sammie.

She had danced all evening with Sammie and suddenly realised that no other boy had asked to dance with her. She was concerned that Sammie would think that she was not popular. She decided that she would deceive Sammie into thinking she had been dancing with others. She was actually hiding out with a girlfriend.

While Sammie stood alone, the snobbish socialite sponsor walked over to him and told him how little she thought of him – and of Jews for that matter. Completely humiliated and dejected, Sammie looked for Reenie. Unable to find her, he left. Later he committed suicide.

***Themes:*** *Acceptance, Comfort, Conflict, Courting, Dates, Despair, Families, Persecution, Prejudice, Rejection, Suicide.*

**Scriptures:** 2 Samuel 12; Psalms 6:5–7; 23:4; 46: 55:22; 119:28; Isaiah 25:8; 53:3–4; Hosea 13:14; Matthew 5:4; John 11; Romans 5:1–5; 1 Corinthians 15:54–57; 2 Corinthians 1:3–7; 1 Thessalonians 4:13–18; James 1:2–4; 1 Peter 5:6–7.

## 216 RELATIONSHIPS

We are living through a period of unprecedented change. Part of that change is the changing status and role of women. The following have been suggested as rules for the new role in relationships:

1   The female always makes the rules.
2   The rules are subject to change at any time without prior notification.
3   No male can possibly know all the rules.
4   If the female suspects the male knows all the rules, she must immediately change some or all the rules.
5   The female is NEVER wrong.
6   If the female is wrong, it is because of a flagrant mis-understanding which was a direct result of something the male did or said wrong.
7   If the previous rule applies, the male must apologise immediately for causing the misunderstanding.
8   The female can change her mind at any given point in time.
9   The male must never change his mind without writ-ten consent from the female.

10  The female has every right to be angry or upset at any time.

11  The male must remain calm at all times, unless the female wants him to be angry or upset.

12  The female must under NO CIRCUMSTANCES let the male know whether or not she wants him to be angry or upset.

13  Any attempt to document these rules could result in bodily harm.

14  If the female has PMT, all rules are null and void.

**Themes:** *Conflict, Family, Marriage.*

**Scriptures:** Deuteronomy 24:1–5; Proverbs 31; Matthew 5:4, 27–28, 31–32; Mark 10:2–12; 11:25; Luke 10:27; 1 Corinthians 7:1–16; 13; 2 Corinthians 1:3–7; Ephesians 5:21–33; Philippians 4:8.

## 217 RELIGION – FALSE

Not long after Kay and Shane were engaged, their parents met to discuss arrangements for the wedding. However, Kay's mum Noleen and Shane's dad Terry also fell in love. Noleen and Terry began to meet as often as possible, being consumed with a terrible passion for each other. After the children were married, Terry urged Noleen to leave her husband. But she would not.

Instead, they planned to kill Noleen's husband. Terry gave Paul Buxton £1,000 to carry out the killing. He agreed to give more money later. On the night of the murder, Terry spent the evening out drinking with the victim. When he arrived home that night, Paul Buxton was lying in wait at the top of the stairs. This would have been the sixth attempt to kill Noleen's husband.

As the unsuspecting man reached the top of the stairs he was leaped upon and bludgeoned with a rolling pin. He suffered 29 separate blows to the head. Despite his injuries, he partially undressed and got into bed, where he was later found by the emergency services.

In court, in November 1992, Noleen Hendley, 46 years old, told the Nottingham Crown Court that because of her religious upbringing she would not consider separation or divorce.

**Themes:** *Adultery, Divorce, Ethics, Murder, Selfishness, Sexuality, Sin.*

**Scriptures:** Exodus 20:14; Leviticus 20:10; Deuteronomy 5:18; Proverbs 6:32; Jeremiah 3:8; 5:7; 13:27; Hosea 2:1–5; Matthew 5:7–8; 19:9; Mark 7:21; 10:11, 19; John 8:1–11; 2 Thessalonians 3:6; 2 Timothy 3:5; 2 Peter 2:14.

## 218 REPRESENTATIVE

The Sawi people live in New Guinea. Until recent years they were headhunting cannibals who used the skulls of their victims as pillows.

In the first two months Don and Carol Richardson were in the area to tell them about God's love, they saw fourteen inter-village battles within sight of where they lived. This did not include run-of-the-mill quarrels when, for example, a husband would punish his wife by shooting an arrow through her arm or through her leg.

One day a young fellow from one village called a man, from another village just through the trees, "lizard-skin". Soon there was a man killed and terrible wounds for others. Don pleaded with the fuming men to make peace between the two villages. But the Richardsons got nowhere fast.

That night they decided it was best to leave. Just as Don turned off his lamp there was movement outside their back door. He took a torch to investigate. A large group of leading men had come to plead with Don not to leave

218 Adapted from Don Richardson, *Peace Child* (Ventura, CA, Regal, 1974), pp. 185–201.

them. The speaker steeled himself as he said, "Tomorrow we are going to make peace."

Don and Carol hardly slept that night, wondering what was going to happen. Through most of the night they could hear shrill voices. In the morning, apart from animal noises, it was deathly quiet.

Then they saw a man, with one of his baby sons clinging passively on his back, climb down from his longhouse. His wife was sobbing violently as they walked past the group in the centre of the village. Suddenly, she wiped away the tears from her eyes, grabbed the child and ran off screaming. The man ran after her but one of his older sons stopped him. Now, other women were clutching their babies, crying out.

Don and Carol had no idea what was going on. Then, out of the corner of his eye, Don noticed Kaiyo slip away from the crowd and climb into his home. Kaiyo looked down on his only child, six-month-old Baikadon, lying on the grass mat. The little fellow waved his arms around in anticipation of being picked up. Kaiyo's heart was near to bursting. But he knew that there would be no peace in the village if he did not act. When his wife saw him leap down from the far end of the longhouse and run towards the next village with Baikadon in his arms, she tried to run after him. But she could not keep up. She collapsed on the ground in grief, crying out repeatedly, "Baikadon! Baikadon, my son!"

Kaiyo's chest was heaving as he reached the mass of leading men of the next village. With Baikadon in his arms, he said to one of them, "Will you plead the words of my village among your people?"

"Yes!" was the reply.

"Then," said Kaiyo, "I give you my son and with him my name." He held out his only son. A leading man received him gently and said, "It is enough! I will surely plead for peace between us!" Then there was a great roar from the people as the tension and emotion was released in the two once-warring villages.

Another child, this time from the other village, was brought to Kaiyo's village. In a similar way he was handed over. Young and old from each village filed past the new child in their midst and put a hand on it sealing their acceptance of the peace this child brought. The atmosphere of the villages had been transformed.

Don asked one of the men if such a painful exchange of children was really necessary. He replied, "You've been urging us to make peace – don't you know it's impossible to have peace without a peace child?"

*Themes:* *Atonement, Cross, Jesus – death of, Missionaries, Peace, Reconciliation, Violence, War.*

**Scriptures:** Exodus 6:6; Psalms 77:14–15; Mark 10:45; Luke 15:3–32; 24:21; John 1:29; 14:1–4; 16:33; Romans 5:1–11; 1 Corinthians 1:30; 5:7; 6:19–20; 7:22–23; 2 Corinthians 5:18–20; Galatians 3:13; 4:4–5; 5:1; Ephesians 1:7; 2:11–21; 5:2; Philippians 4:6–7; Colossians 1:19–23; Titus 2:14; Hebrews 9:15; James 4:4; 1 Peter 1:18–19; 1 John 2:2; 4:7–21.

## 219 RESCUED

In March 1991, a Major Lorenzo flew his stolen Soviet-made MiG 23 fighter jet out of Cuba to Florida.

But, in December 1992, Lorenzo flew back to Cuba to rescue his family. Once out over the sea he had to fly the 144 kilometres about three metres above the water to avoid being picked up by the Cuban radar. He landed the four-seater plane on a busy road at a prearranged spot.

Once he got the plane down he faced a number of obstacles. There was a large rock. He had to lift up the left wing

219 Adapted from *The Advertiser* (Adelaide) 10 December 1992, p. 3.

to miss it. There was a bus and a truck heading straight for him. Thankfully, they both pulled off the road. The passengers in the bus watched as the plane drew to a stop.

Mrs Lorenzo said to the children, "It's your dad coming." She grabbed their hands and started running. Lorenzo opened the door and in jumped his wife and Reyniel, eleven, and Alejandro, six. Then Mrs Lorenzo closed the door and the plane took off to freedom.

At a news conference, Lorenzo was surrounded by his family. "I am the happiest man in the world because my family is free," he said. "They are my life."

**Themes:** *Atonement, Christmas, Easter, Evangelism, Family, Freedom, God – love of, Reconciliation, Risk, Salvation.*

**Scriptures:** Luke 10:27; 15:1–7, 8–10; John 3:16; 8:31–36; Romans 5:10–11; 1 Corinthians 13; 2 Corinthians 5:18–20; Ephesians 2:11–21; Colossians 1:19–23; James 4:4.

## 220 **RESCUED**

Scott O'Grady is a young man who flies an F-16 jet for the United States air force. On Friday afternoon, 2 June, he was on a flying mission over Bosnia. Suddenly, a Soviet-made surface-to-air missile sliced his plane in two. His cockpit disintegrated. As he yanked the gold handle of the ejector seat, the explosive bolts hurled off the canopy, singeing his neck and face. A few seconds later he pulled the rip cord of his parachute. Floating down he could see what he feared – a truck of Serbian soldiers waiting for him.

When he hit the ground he tore off his chute and made for the trees. He dropped into a bush and put his face in the dirt. He put his green flying gloves over his head and ears. He didn't want his white skin to be seen. He heard men moving about him – only a few feet away. They were shouting wildly.

O'Grady did not move for five hours. His thirst was overpowering. At nightfall he was finally able to move so he could have a drink from his survival gear. He had a small, simple hand-radio, but he dared not use it. People were so close they would hear his voice or he would easily be traced.

He soon ran out of water. So he prayed for rain. He was rewarded with torrential downpours. But he could not find a creek as he crept about at night. So he used a sponge to sop up water from the ground and squeezed it into his mouth. When he was in survival school he learnt that he could eat ants – but not furry bugs or ones that stung. So he ate ants and grass to stay alive.

As he moved about at night he began using his hand-held radio. But Scott's radio was not powerful. Yet trying to listen to him were NATO jets, spy satellites and a radio beacon. Eventually, United States intelligence picked up snippets of a garbled message they thought might be O'Grady's. It was enough for air force officials to tell his mum that her boy was out there somewhere.

By now O'Grady was running out of time. His radio batteries would last only seven hours. After nearly a week living on ants and grass he was physically weakening. Now he was wringing out his socks for drinking water. Although he didn't know it, he was suffering from hypothermia.

The next Thursday night, at midnight, he was huddled in a rocky field under a clear sky. He heard three clicks on his radio that made his heart race. And then, ever so faintly, came the sound he had been longing for, another American air force pilot's voice: "Basher 52. This is Basher 11 on Alpha." Basher 52 was his call number. Basher 11 was his mate Hanford.

Hanford had been flying for almost an hour searching

for his mate. He had three minutes' fuel left before he'd have had to turn back to base.

"Basher 52 reads you loud and clear," O'Grady was replying to his mate in a hushed cry. But Hanford was wary of traps. So he asked Basher 52 some questions to check that it was O'Grady.

Eventually Hanford said, "Copy that! You're alive. Good to hear your voice." Hanford's voice sounded steady and cool. Actually, he had trouble flying because he was crying.

Immediately, NATO command was notified that O'Grady had been found. They couldn't be sure how much longer O'Grady could survive. So NATO command's solution was a surprise dawn raid to rescue Scott.

Dawn was three hours away when marines began scrambling from their racks. At 5:30 am 40 aircraft and helicopters took to the air. They came from bases in Italy and two aircraft carriers. Some of the planes were designed to jam radio signals. Some planes flew high to direct operations. Some were equipped to knock out ground fire. Then two choppers were each filled with 41 marines.

At 6:35 – just over an hour after take-off – the gunships spotted yellow smoke from Scott's flare signal. Ten minutes later the two helicopters landed. One of them disgorged its 41 marines to form a ring of safety around the pick-up site. But the chopper that was to pick up Scott landed against a rock and a wire fence. Its door was jammed. It had to take off and land again.

Then, dripping wet, waving a pistol, Scott ran from the trees straight to his chopper. He was helped through a side-gunner's hatch. Scott mouthed the words, "Thank you." But he wasn't safe yet.

As the pilots skimmed the ground at 30 metres, gunshots winked off the rotors. By 7:30 the Sea Stallion chopper was landing on the deck of the aircraft carrier *Kearsarge*.

Scott O'Grady had been successfully rescued. One of President Clinton's national security advisers announced the incredible news that the young air force captain had been found and rescued by the marines in a daring raid after six days behind enemy lines. Scott's mum heard the news and fell to the floor.

To bring out that one lost soldier – in all – $6 billion worth of equipment and the attention of United States and NATO high command were brought into operation.

*Themes:* God – Father, God – his love, Good Shepherd, Lord's Prayer, Parable – Good Samaritan, Parable –Lost Coin, Parable – Lost Sheep, Parable – Prodigal Son, People – value of, Salvation, Testimony.

**Scriptures:** Isaiah 64:8; Malachi 1:6; 2:10; Luke 10:25–37; 11:1–4; 15:1–7, 8–10, 11–32; 19:10; John 10:1–18; 20:17; Romans 8:17, 31–39; Galatians 3:26; Hebrews 12:9.

## 221 RESCUED

Gregory Robertson was a parachute safety and training adviser. He was also a veteran of some 1,500 parachute jumps. One day he followed six other skydivers out of a plane 3.22 kilometres above the ground.

When, at 2.75 kilometres, the six attempted to link hands, Debbie Williams accidentally collided with one of the skydivers and knocked herself unconscious. Seeing her plight, Robertson tucked his arms to his sides and, using his shoulders to steer himself, went after Debbie. Plunging downward at 322 kilometres per hour, he was able to catch her. Manoeuvring her into a sitting position, Robertson yanked her rip cord. They were at 823 metres! At 609.5 metres he opened his own chute. Ten seconds later he would have slammed into the ground.

*Themes:* God – Father, God – his love, Good Shepherd, Lord's Prayer, Parable – Good Samaritan, Parable – Lost Coin, Parable – Lost Sheep, Parable – Prodigal Son, People – value of, Salvation.

**Scriptures:** Isaiah 64:8; Malachi 1:6; 2:10; Luke 10:25–37; 11:1–4; 15:1–7, 8–10, 11–32; 19:10; John 10:1–18; 20:17; Romans 8:17, 31–39; Galatians 3:26; Hebrews 12:9.

## 222 RESURRECTION

Nikolai Bukharin was a Soviet politician and Communist theoretician. For a time, he also edited the newspaper *Pravda*.

In the early 1920s, Bukharin was sent from Moscow to Kiev to address a vast anti-God rally. For one hour he brought to bear all the artillery of argument, abuse and ridicule upon the Christian faith till it seemed as if the whole ancient structure of belief was in ruins. At the end there was silence. Questions were invited. A man rose and asked leave to speak, a priest of the Orthodox Church. He stood beside Bukharin, faced the people and gave them the ancient, liturgical Easter greeting, "Christ is risen." Instantly, the whole vast assembly rose to its feet, and the reply came back like the crash of breakers against the cliff: "He is risen indeed." There was no reply; there could not be. When all argument is ended, there remains a fact, the total fact of Jesus Christ.

**Themes:** *Communism, Courage, Easter, Persecution, Suffering.*

**Scriptures:** Psalms 27:14; Matthew 28:1–10; Mark 8:34–38; 16:6; Luke 24:1–12; John 20:1–8; Acts 7:54 – 8:1; 1 Corinthians 15:1–58.

## 223 REUNION

During the Second World War, 17-year-old Leon Frost was on the run from the KGB. At one point he sneaked home and knocked on the door. A voice the other side said, "Who is it?"

"It's your son – Leon," he said, "Open up... " In a second the door was open and mother and son were in each

---

222 Lesslie Newbigin, *A Faith for this One World?* (London: SCM, 1961), pp. 59–60.

other's arms. Then Leon turned to his dad and his thirteen-year-old sister, Irena. He told them he had come home to say goodbye. All Leon took with him was a photo of his brother. Leon made his way to Warsaw, where he was arrested and sent to prison.

At the end of the war there was no way of finding his family. He emigrated to Adelaide and started work at Norwood Engineering. Eventually he married Doris in the Birkenhead Methodist Church.

Leon began trying to track down his family. One day a letter came from the Red Cross. It told of his brother's death during the war. Leon read it without saying anything. The years went by but still he was unable to find his family.

One day Leon's daughter Patti wrote to a newspaper in Poland. A fortnight later a letter arrived. Her eyes widened as she read the contents. She pushed the letter into her dad's hands. It read, "Your parents died in Siberia during the war, but your sister Irena may still be alive, living in England." It was signed by a cousin. Patti wrote another letter. This time to the Red Cross in England. Just weeks later a letter came back. Leon's son Terry rang him. "Sit down, Dad," he said, "I've got great news." Speechless, Leon listened. Irena was alive. She was married with a child and was living in Los Angeles. The Red Cross in England had sent a letter to Irena in Los Angeles. Irena then began phoning every Frost in Australia. Eventually she got Leon's son Terry. Terry gave his father her number. Leon took a deep breath and dialled. A woman's voice answered. "Irena?" asked Leon. "Yes," said the woman. Tears streamed down Leon's face. He had found his sister. "My sister," he said in Polish, "I thought you were dead."

Two months later Irena flew to Australia. At the Mt Gambier aerodrome in South Australia, 72-year-old Leon was waiting. They embraced each other. "This is the happiest day of my life," Leon said. Leon has since visited Irena in California. "I feel so grateful I've had the chance to get to know her again," he said. "I spent so many years believing she was dead. Now I feel a peace I've only ever dreamed of," he said.

**Themes:** *Good Shepherd, Parable – Good Samaritan, Parable – Lost Coin, Parable – Lost Sheep, Parable – Prodigal Son, Reconciliation, Salvation.*

**Scriptures:** Isaiah 64:8; Malachi 1:6; 2:10; Luke 10:25–37; 15:1–7, 8–10, 11–32; 19:10; John 10:1–18; 20:17; Romans 8:17; Galatians 3:26; Hebrews 12:9.

## 224 REUNION

Louis Pasteur (1822–95) was a French microbiologist who discovered vaccines for cholera and rabies. Pasteur and his wife had five children. But three of them died as young children, two in the same year as Pasteur's father died. "They die, one after another, our poor children. You see what a fragile thing it is, this life of ours," he said bitterly. The Pasteurs were left with a son, Jean-Baptiste, and a daughter, Marie-Louise – or "Zizi", as they called her.

Then, in 1870, Pasteur's work was interrupted by the devastating Franco-Prussian war. His son, Jean-Baptiste, had gone to war, but he had not been heard of for some time. In January 1871 a near-starving Paris surrendered. The defeated French troops straggled back in retreat, begging for bread along the way, their uniforms in tatters. Even though they had not heard from Jean-Baptiste for some time the Pasteurs were convinced they could find their son. Pasteur's old friend and neighbour, Jules Vercel, saw him start out, accompanied by his wife and daughter, on Tuesday 24 January, in a half-broken-down old carriage.

On the Friday they reached Pontarlier by roads made almost impassable by the snow, the carriage now a mere wreck. The town was full of soldiers, some crouching round fires in the street, others stepping across their dead horses and begging for a little straw to lie on. Many had taken refuge in the church and were lying on the steps of the altar; a few were attempting to bandage their frozen feet, threatened with gangrene.

Mme Pasteur asked anxiously after her son. "All that I can tell you," a soldier said, "is that out of 1,200 men of that battalion there are but 300 left." As she was questioning another, a soldier who was passing stopped. "Sergeant Pasteur? Yes, he is alive; I slept by him last night at Chaffois. He has remained behind; he is ill. You might meet him on the road towards Chaffois."

The Pasteurs had barely passed the Pontarlier gate when a rough cart came by. A soldier muffled in his greatcoat, his hand resting on the edge of the cart, started with surprise. He hurried down. The family embraced without a word, so great was their emotion.

*Themes:* *God – Father, Good Shepherd, Lord's Prayer, Parable – Good Samaritan, Parable – Lost Coin, Parable – Lost Sheep, Parable – Prodigal Son, Salvation.*

**Scriptures:** Isaiah 64:8; Malachi 1:6; 2:10; Luke 10:25–37; 11:1–4; 15:1–7, 8–10, 11–32; 19:10; John 10:1–18; 20:17; Romans 8:17; Galatians 3:26; Hebrews 12:9.

## 225 **REVENGE**

A woman went to Ibn Saud, the first king of Saudi Arabia. She requested that the man who killed her husband be put to death. The man had fallen from the top of a palm tree when he had been gathering dates and landed on this woman's husband and killed him.

The king said, "It is your right to exact compensation, and it is also your right to ask for this man's life. But it is my right to decree how he shall die. You shall take this man with you and he shall be tied to the foot of a palm tree and then you shall climb to the top of the tree and cast yourself down upon him from that height. In that way you will take his life as he took your husband's. Or perhaps," Ibn Saud added, "you would prefer after all to take the blood money?" The widow took the money.

**Themes:** *Avenger, Humour, Justice, Mercy, Solomon, Vengeance, Wisdom.*

**Scriptures:** Genesis 4:10–16, 23–24; 9:5–6; Leviticus 19:18; Numbers 35:9–15, 16–21, 22–28; Joshua 10:13; Judges 12:3–6; 1 Kings 3:16–28; 2 Kings 9:7; Psalms 94; Matthew 5:38–42; Romans 12:17–19; 13:4; 1 Thessalonians 4:6; Revelation 6:10; 19:2.

## 226 RIVALRY

There's no doubt that *National Geographic* magazine has some incredible stories and pictures in it. In one issue there was a picture of a fossil. It was a fossil of two sabre-toothed cats locked in combat. One of the cats had attacked and bitten deep into the leg of the other. The massive tooth of one was stuck firmly in the body of the other. Of course, neither could feed nor live normally. Because of that vicious attack, they were both destined to die.

**Themes:** *Death, Division, Divorce, Enemies, Fighting, Fruit of the Spirit, Jealousy, Love – of enemies, Marriage, Paul – opponents, Peace, Spirit – fruit of.*

**Scriptures:** Psalms 4:8; 55:18; Isaiah 26:3; Matthew 5:9; Luke 6:27–30; Romans 8:6; 10:15; 12:18, 20; 14:17, 19; 15:13; 1 Corinthians 1:10–17; 7:15; 13; 2 Corinthians 13:11; Galatians 5:19–22; Colossians 3:12–17; 1 Thessalonians 5:13; 2 Thessalonians 3:16; 2 Timothy 2:22; Hebrews 12:14; 1 Peter 3:11.

## 22⁊ SACRIFICE

C. T. Studd was brought up in nineteenth-century luxury. His father was retired and lived in Leicestershire, spending the fortune made as a tea planter in North India. C. T. became captain of the Cambridge University XI and in 1882 he was in Australia, recovering the Ashes.

All of this changed, for he had become a Christian through his father and sensed God's call to the mission field. So, in his early twenties, he was in Shanghai as a missionary. A few years later he was married.

Here is his description of their first home. "The first house we had was a haunted house... It was just bare white-washed walls, and brick floors, but very unevenly bricked, with a fireplace in the centre, and a brick bed. Our mattress was a cottonwool quilt about an inch thick. That was our bed for the first three years, until it became so infested with scorpions that we had to have it pulled down. Then we had a wooden sort of planking.

"For five years we never went outside our doors without a volley of curses from our neighbours."

*Themes:* Contentment, Conversion, Hatred, Joy, Materialism, Missionaries, Persecution, Perseverance, Suffering.

**Scriptures:** John 10:28–30; Acts 9:1–22; 2 Corinthians 1:8–11; 4:1–18; Philippians 4:11; 1 Timothy 6:6–8; Hebrews 13:5; 1 Peter 1:3–9.

## 22♂ SACRIFICE

Princess Alice was the granddaughter of Queen Victoria. It is said that, when William Gladstone was announcing the death of Princess Alice, he told a touching story to the House of Commons in Britain. The little daughter of the Princess was seriously ill with diphtheria. The doctors had told the Princess not to kiss her little daughter and endanger her own life.

Once, when the child was struggling to breathe, the mother, forgetting herself entirely, took her daughter in her arms to comfort her. Gasping and struggling for her life the child said, "Mamma, kiss me!" Without thinking of herself, the mother tenderly kissed her daughter. She caught diphtheria and, after a few weeks, died on Saturday 14 December 1878.

*Themes:* *Easter, Grief, Incarnation, Love, Parenting, Sickness.*
**Scriptures:** Matthew 5:4; Luke 10:27; Romans 4:25; 1 Corinthians 5:7; 13; 2 Corinthians 1:3–4; 5:21; Ephesians 5:2; 1 Peter 2:24.

## 229 SACRIFICE *

Years ago, in a small fishing village in Holland, a young man taught the world about the rewards of unselfish service. Because the entire village revolved around the fishing industry, a volunteer rescue team was needed in cases of emergency. One night the winds raged, the clouds burst and a gale-force storm capsized a fishing boat at sea.

Stranded and in trouble, the crew sent out the SOS. The captain of the rescue rowboat team sounded the alarm and the villagers assembled in the town square overlooking the bay.

While the team launched their rowboat and fought their way through the wild waves, the villagers waited restlessly on the beach, holding lanterns to light the way back.

An hour later, the rescue boat reappeared through the fog and the cheering villagers ran to greet it. Falling exhausted on the sand, the volunteers reported that the rescue boat could not hold any more passengers and they

229 Adapted from Dan Clark in *A Second Helping of Chicken Soup for the Soul: 101 More Stories to Open the Heart and Rekindle the Spirit,* compiled by Jack Canfield and Mark Victor Hansen (Deerfield Beach, Fla. : Health Communications, 1995).

had to leave one man behind. Even one more passenger would have surely capsized the rescue boat and all would have been lost.

Frantically, the captain called for another volunteer team to go after the lone survivor. Sixteen-year-old Hans stepped forward. His mother grabbed his arm, pleading, "Please don't go. Your father died in a shipwreck ten years ago and your older brother, Paul, has been lost at sea for three weeks. Hans, you are all I have left."

Hans replied, "Mother, I have to go. What if everyone said, 'I can't go, let someone else do it?' Mother, this time I have to do my duty. When the call for service comes, we all need to take our turn and do our part."

Hans kissed his mother, joined the team and disappeared into the night.

Another hour passed, which seemed to Hans' mother like an eternity. Finally the rescue boat darted through the fog, with Hans standing up in the bow.

Cupping his hands, the captain called, "Did you find the lost man?"

Barely able to contain himself, Hans excitedly yelled back, "Yes, we found him. Tell my mother it's my older brother, Paul!"

**Themes:** *Atonement, Cross, Grief, Jesus – work of, Love, Reconciliation, Redeemed, Rescue, Sacrifice, Salvation, Substitution, Suffering.*

**Scriptures:** Exodus 6:6; Psalms 77:14–15; Matthew 5:4; Mark 10:45; Luke 10:27; 24:21; John 1:29; 8:31–36; 1 Corinthians 1:30; 5:7; 6:19–20; 7:22–23; 13; 2 Corinthians 1:3–4; Galatians 3:13; 4:4–5; 5:1; Ephesians 1:7; 5:2; Titus 2:14; Hebrews 9:15; 1 Peter 1:18–19; 1 John 2:2.

## 230 SACRIFICE

One day in the summer holidays of 1937 John Griffith, the controller of the great railroad drawbridge across the Mississippi River, took his eight-year-old son, Greg, to work with him. At noon, John put the bridge up to allow ships to pass. He and his son went up onto the observation deck to eat their packed lunches. Time passed quickly. Suddenly, John was startled by the shrieking of a train whistle in the distance. He looked at his watch: it was 1:07 pm. The Memphis Express, with 400 passengers, was roaring towards the raised bridge. He leapt from the observation deck and ran back to the control tower.

Just before throwing the master lever he glanced down for any ships below. His eyes caught sight of something that caused his heart to leap and pound in his throat. His eight-year-old son had fallen into the massive gears that operated the bridge. His left leg was caught in the cogs of the two main gears. Desperately John's mind whirled to devise a rescue plan. But there was no way out.

Again, with alarming closeness, the train whistle shrieked in the air. John could hear the clicking of the locomotive wheels over the tracks. John knew what he had to do.

He buried his head in his left arm and pushed the master lever forward. The massive bridge lowered into place just as the Memphis Express began to roar across the river. When John Griffith lifted his head, his face was smeared with tears. He looked into the passing windows of the train. There were businessmen casually reading their midday papers. There were finely-dressed women in the dining car, sipping coffee, and children pushing long spoons into their dishes of ice cream. No one looked at the control house, and no one looked at the great gear box. With wrenching agony John cried out at the steel train, "I sacrificed my son for you people! Don't you care?"

230 Adapted from Michael P. Green, *Illustrations for Biblical Preaching* (Grand Rapids, MI: Baker, 1989), #1155.

**Themes:** *Atonement, Cross, Expiation, Freedom, Grief, Jesus – work of, Love, Reconciliation, Redeemed, Rescue, Substitution, Suffering.*

**Scriptures:** Exodus 6:6; Psalms 77:14–15; Matthew 5:4; Mark 10:45; Luke 10:27; 24:21; John 1:29; 8:31–36; 1 Corinthians 1:30; 5:7; 6:19–20; 7:22–23; 13; 2 Corinthians 1:3–4; Galatians 3:13; 4:4–5; 5:1; Ephesians 1:7; 5:2; Titus 2:14; Hebrews 9:15; 1 Peter 1:18–19; 1 John 2:2.

## 231 SACRIFICE

Legend has it that Hans and Albrecht, two French goldsmiths, wanted to study painting. The only way they could afford to do so was for one of them to work as a blacksmith while the other went to Venice. Later they would change places.

Albrecht went to Venice and over months and years Hans sent money to his friend. At last Albrecht returned home a rich and renowned painter. Now it was his turn to help Hans.

The two men met in joyous reunion, but, when Albrecht looked at his friend, his eyes filled with tears as he discovered the full extent of Hans' sacrifice. The years of hard and heavy labour had calloused and bruised his friend's sensitive hands. His fingers would never be able to handle a painter's brush.

In gratitude for the sacrifice, that distinguished artist, Albrecht Dürer, used the work-ridden hands of his friend as models to paint the hands of Jesus.

**Themes:** *Gratitude, Love – of others, Substitution, Suffering.*

**Scriptures:** Exodus 6:6; Psalms 77:14–15; Mark 10:45; Luke 10:27; 24:21; John 1:29; 15:12–17; 1 Corinthians 1:30; 5:7; 6:19–20; 7:22–23; 13; Galatians 3:13; 4:4–5; 5:1; Ephesians 1:7; 5:2; Titus 2:14; Hebrews 9:15; 1 Peter 1:18–19; 1 John 2:2.

---

231 Adapted from Mrs Charles E. Cowman, *Harvest Secrets* (London: Oliphant, 1956), pp. 23–24.

## 232 SALVATION – DESIRED

Doctor Chamberlain, a missionary in India, says that one day he was preaching about Jesus by the side of the Ganges river. One of the many people who came to bathe in the river was a man who had journeyed wearily a great distance on his knees and elbows. He came to wash away his continual search for life. He dragged himself to the edge of the river and made a prayer to Gunga. Then he crept into the water. A moment later he emerged. There was no elation, only despair as he lay prostrate on the bank. Nothing had changed. But as he lay there he could hear Chamberlain speaking about Jesus. Chamberlain said the man got up on his knees and clapped his hands and said out loud, "That is what I want! That is what I want!"

**Themes:** *Christmas, Conversion, Despair, Joy, Missionaries, Peace, Religions – other, Searching, Testimony.*

**Scriptures:** Isaiah 9:1–7; Matthew 4:12–17; 28:16–20; Mark 1:14–15; 10:17–31; Luke 4:16–21; 10:20; John 10:10; 14:1–6; 15:11; 16:33; Acts 2:1–42; Philippians 4:6–7.

## 233 SAVED

Normally the flight from Nassau to Miami took Walter Wyatt, Jr. only 65 minutes. But on 5 December 1986, he attempted it after thieves had looted the navigational equipment in his Beechcraft. With only a compass and a hand-held radio, Walter flew into skies blackened by storm clouds.

When his compass began to gyrate, Walter concluded he was headed in the wrong direction. He flew his plane below the clouds, hoping to spot something, but soon he knew he was lost. He put out a Mayday call, which brought

---

232 Adapted from Aquilla Webb, *1001 Illustrations for Pulpit and Platform* (New York and London: Harper and Brothers, 1926), #125.

a Coastguard Falcon search plane to lead him to an emergency landing strip only six miles away.

Suddenly Wyatt's right engine coughed its last and died. The fuel tank had run dry. Around 8:00 pm Wyatt could do little more than glide the plane into the water. Wyatt survived the crash, but his plane disappeared quickly, leaving him bobbing on the water in a leaky life vest.

With blood on his forehead, Wyatt floated on his back. Suddenly he felt a hard bump against his body. A shark had found him. Wyatt kicked the intruder and wondered if he would survive the night. He managed to stay afloat for the next ten hours.

In the morning, Wyatt saw no aeroplanes, but in the water a dorsal fin was heading for him. Twisting, he felt the hide of a shark brush against him. In a moment, two more bull sharks sliced through the water towards him. Again he kicked the sharks, and they veered away, but he was nearing exhaustion.

Then he heard the hum of a distant aircraft. When it was within half a mile, he waved his orange vest. The pilot dropped a smoke canister and radioed the cutter *Cape York*, which was twelve minutes away: "Get moving, cutter! There's a shark targeting this guy!"

As the *Cape York* pulled alongside Wyatt, a Jacob's ladder was dropped over the side. Wyatt climbed wearily out of the water and onto the ship, where he fell to his knees and kissed the deck.

**Themes:** *Atonement, Christmas, Easter, Evangelism, God – his love, Rescued, Salvation.*

**Scriptures:** Isaiah 64:8; Malachi 1:6; 2:10; Luke 10:25–37; 11:1–4; 15:1–7, 8–10, 11–32; 19:10; John 10:1–18; 20:17; Romans 8:17, 31–39; Galatians 3:26; Hebrews 12:9.

Franz-Josef I of Austria was the last emperor of the Habsburg empire, which had its origins in the thirteenth century. Franz-Josef died on 21 November 1916, during the First World War. A few days later, at the funeral on 30 November, the splendorous pageantry of one of the greatest empires Europe had ever known was displayed for the last time. Eight black horses drew the hearse containing the coffin, which was draped in the black and gold imperial colours. The hearse was preceded by carriages filled with wreaths. In turn these carriages were preceded by barouches seating the highest court dignitaries. Behind this procession came the carriages carrying the members of the family and the foreign officials. Mounted guards in their dress uniform escorted the procession along the Ringstrasse, across Vienna, to St Stephen's Cathedral. A band played sombre music.

After the service the cortège covered the few hundred metres to the Capuchin crypt on foot. By the light of flaming torches, the cortège descended the steps of the crypt. At the bottom was a great iron door leading to the Habsburg family crypt. Behind the door was the abbot. With the Grand Master of the court he began the ritual dialogue, established centuries before.

The Grand Master, Prince Montenuovo, cried out, "Open!" The abbot responded, "Who are you? Who asks to enter here?" The Grand Master began to list the emperor's 37 titles, "We bear the remains of his Imperial and Apostolic Majesty, Franz-Josef I, by the grace of God Emperor of Austria, King of Hungary, Defender of the Faith, Prince of Bohemia-Moravia, Grand Duke of Lombardy, Venezia, Styrgia..." And so he continued through the whole 37 titles. However, the abbot called back, "We know him not. Who goes there?" The Prince spoke again. This time he used a much abbreviated and less ostentatious title reserved for times of expediency. But, again, the abbot responded, "We know him not. Who goes there?"

The Grand Master tried a third time. He stripped the emperor of all but the humblest of titles. Going down on his knees, he simply cried out, "We bear the body of Franz-Josef, our brother, a sinner like us all."

At that the door swung open and the abbot said, "Enter then." And Franz-Josef was admitted.

*Themes:* Acceptance, Access, Grace, Heaven, Humility, Salvation, Works.
*Scriptures:* Romans 3:19–31; 5:1–2; Galatians 2:16; Ephesians 2:8–9; 2 Timothy 1:9.

## 235 SECOND COMING

So the story goes, Queen Victoria was out walking one summer afternoon near Balmoral Castle in Scotland.

She wanted a rest and a drink. She passed a couple of houses and knocked on the door of one of them. There was no answer. She knocked a number of times. Still there was no answer. The woman inside was busy and could not be bothered answering the door. The Queen walked on home.

The neighbour across the road saw all this through her front window. In the evening that day, the two women chatted as they pottered in their gardens. With more than a hint of jealousy, the neighbour said, "I see that the Queen called at your place today."

The other woman had no idea and was bitterly disappointed at missing this opportunity of having the Queen to tea. So for the rest of her life that woman waited every day for the Queen to return. She never came.

**Themes:**  *Advent, Angels – entertaining unawares, Christmas, Hospitality, Opportunities missed.*

**Scriptures:**  Genesis 18:1–8; Matthew 25:31–46; Mark 13:32–37; John 1:11–12; 13:20; 1 Thessalonians 5:1–11; 2 Thessalonians 2:1–11; Hebrews 9:28; 13:2; 1 Peter 4:9; 2 Peter 3:1–13.

## 236 SECOND COMING

His parents had gone out and left ten-year-old Michael home with his older sister. She spent the evening in her room reading. Michael could not think of anything to do until he saw the large chiming clock on the mantlepiece over the fire. He took it down. Before he realised what he was doing he had most of the insides out and around him on the floor. He tried hard to remember where everything went and got most of it back in place. However, there were a couple of pieces left over on the floor. It didn't seem to matter as, quite remarkably, the clock went again when he wound it up. But it did not seem to chime on the hour. He hoped his parents would not notice.

Next morning was Sunday and as the family was stirring from sleep the clock in the lounge began to chime. Michael held his breath as the clock struck... One, two, three, four,... nine, ten, eleven, twelve... thirteen, fourteen, fifteen... and still the chiming continued. Twenty-seven, twenty-eight, twenty-nine. Michael was still holding his breath when he heard his mother yell from the bedroom, "Quick, get up, it's later than it has ever been!"

**Themes:**  *Advent, Christmas, Humour, Opportunities missed.*

**Scriptures:**  Genesis 18:1–8; Matthew 24:33; 25:31–46; Mark 8:31–9:1; 13:1–37; John 1:11–12; 13:20; Acts 1:17; Romans 13:11–14; 1 Corinthians 7:29; 1 Thessalonians 5:1–11; 2 Thessalonians 2:1–11; Hebrews 9:28; 13:2; James 5:8; 1 Peter 4:7, 9; 2 Peter 3:1–13; Revelation 1:1; 22:7, 10, 12, 20.

Margaret's parents did not really love her. In fact, they wanted a boy. Margaret's father gave her very little time. As a small girl she would look up to him, but he did not seem to notice her. At other times, when he was in a bad mood, he would push her out of the way.

As she grew up, she used bad language as a way of getting her parents' attention. She told her parents that she hated them. They yelled back that they hated her also. More than once she ran away from home. But she had to come home because she ran out of money. Margaret loved sport and was good at it. But her parents said that she was wasting her time. She ought to be studying. But she could never get high enough marks to please her parents.

The years went by and then, at last, marriage came. She thought that marriage would sort out her life. But marriage only seemed to make things worse. Once the shine had gone out of her marriage, it was hell! There were times when Margaret was belted by her husband for overrunning the tight family budget, or for making mistakes. Their friends noticed, and sympathised. Margaret felt even more sorry for herself and her appearance suffered as her self-esteem dropped. She thought she was going mad.

Interestingly, Margaret is a Christian. With her mind, she accepted that God loved her so much that he gave his only son for her. But, in her heart, she felt that God was remote and had a revulsion for her. Life was a treadmill; there was no joy in it, only painful endurance. Her conclusion was, "I wish I was dead." But then she felt guilty that she had displeased God. If only she could please someone, but she felt she could not.

**Themes:** *Bad language, Commitment, Conflict, Domestic violence, Families, Marriage, Parenting.*

**Scriptures:** Deuteronomy 24:1–5; Matthew 5:27–29, 31–32; 19:3–12; Mark 10:2–13; Luke 10:27; John 14:15–24; Acts 5:29; 1 Corinthians 7:1–11; 13.

## 238 SELF-IMAGE

When David Burns was a student, he kept a journal. It was filled with private memories. Some were painful recollections from childhood – times when he felt hurt, confused, lonely and insecure. He described fragments of dreams and intensely personal feelings of anger and hatred, as well as things he enjoyed such as magic stores and coin shops. Then a terrible thing happened. After dinner one night he realised that he had left his journal in a coat room outside the dining hall. Terrified that somebody might read it and find out the truth about him, he raced back. It was gone. Weeks passed and eventually he gave up all hope of finding it. A month later, he was hanging up his coat in the same place. He saw his brown tattered journal, just where he had left it. Nervously he picked it up and leafed through these private pages. He found a stranger had written this entry: "God bless you. I am a lot like you, only I don't keep a diary, and I'm grateful to know there are others like me. I hope things turn out well for you." Tears came to David's eyes. It had never dawned on him that anyone could have the same worries and inner fears, yet still care about him.

**Themes:** *Anxiety, Fear, Weakness, Worry.*

**Scriptures:** Psalms 55:22; 118:6; Luke 12:22–34; 1 Corinthians 10; 13; 2 Corinthians 12:1–13; Philippians 4:6; Hebrews 13:5; 1 Peter 5:7.

## 239 **SERVANT** *

When Elmer Booze walks on stage for a virtuoso piano performance, nobody applauds. That's because he's not a concert pianist, he's a professional page turner.

Although he has music degrees from two universities, Elmer has been content for many years to sit in the shadows. In Washington, DC, he is a regular at the Kennedy Centre, the National Gallery of Art, the Canadian Embassy, and the Library of Congress. He has turned pages at the White House and at concerts in New York and London.

Many great pianists depend on people like Elmer to make their performance the best it can be. And, while the virtuosos take their bows to the applause of thousands, the Elmers of the world are willing to smile – content with the part they had in the performance.

*Themes:* Body of Christ, Ego, Envy, Fruit of the Spirit, Humility, Jealousy, Parable – Pharisee and the Tax Collector, Pride, Spirit – fruit of.

**Scriptures:** Psalms 5:5; Proverbs 11:2; 15:25; 16:18–19; Mark 7:22; Luke 18:9–14; Romans 1:30; 12:1–8; 1 Corinthians 12:12–31; Galatians 5:16–24; Ephesians 4:4–16; 1 John 2:15–17.

## 240 **SERVICE**

Marion Preminger was born in Hungary in 1913. She was raised in a castle with an aristocratic and wealthy family, surrounded with maids, tutors, governesses, butlers, and chauffeurs.

She attended school in Vienna. At a Viennese ball, she met a handsome young man, the son of a Viennese doctor. They fell in love and, when she was 18 years old, they eloped – but the marriage lasted only one year.

Marion returned to Vienna to begin a life as an actress. While she was auditioning for a play, she met the young German director, Otto Preminger. They fell in love and soon married. When Preminger went to America to begin a career as a movie director, she went with him. After a while, caught up in the superficial excitement of Hollywood, Marion began to live the sordid life that some people live in Hollywood. Preminger divorced her.

She returned to Europe, living the life of a Paris socialite until 1948. Then she read that Dr Albert Schweitzer was making one of his periodic visits to Europe. She phoned his secretary and made an appointment for the next day.

She found Schweitzer playing the village church organ. He invited her to dine at his house. After dinner, Marion knew she had found what she had been looking for. She was with Schweitzer every day during his visit and, when he returned to Africa, he invited her to come to Lamberene and work in the hospital. That was her calling.

There the girl who was raised like a princess became a servant... and changed bandages, bathed bodies, and fed lepers. There she became free.

*Themes:* *Calling, Divorce, Humility, Leadership, Life – purpose, Marriage, Materialism, Money, Purpose.*

**Scriptures:** Deuteronomy 24:1–5; Matthew 5:27–29, 31–32; 19:3–12; Mark 10:2–13; Luke 10:27; John 14:15–24; Acts 5:29; 1 Corinthians 7:1–11; 13; 2 Corinthians 4:1–18; 11:16–23; Philippians 2:1–11.

## 247 SERVICE

Leonard Bernstein was one of America's greatest composers and conductors, directing and conducting the New York Philharmonic Orchestra from 1958 to 1969. His musical *West Side Story* brought him wide acclaim.

An admirer once asked Bernstein what was the hardest instrument to play. He replied without hesitation: "Second fiddle. I can always get plenty of first violinists, but to find one who plays second violin with as much enthusiasm, or second French horn, or second flute, now that's a problem. And yet if no one plays second, we have no harmony."

**Themes:** *Body of Christ, Ego, Envy, Fruit of the Spirit, Humility, Jealousy, Parable – Pharisee and the Tax Collector, Pride, Spirit – fruit of.*

**Scriptures:** Psalms 5:5; Proverbs 11:2; 15:25; 16:18–19; Mark 7:22; Luke 18:9–14; Romans 1:30; 12:1–8; 1 Corinthians 12:12–31; Galatians 5:16–24; Ephesians 4:4–16; 1 John 2:15–17.

## 242  SERVICE *

Dr Frank Mayfield was touring the Tewksbury Institute. On his way out he asked an elderly floor maid, "What can you tell me about the history of this place?"

The maid led him down to the basement, where she pointed to one of what looked like small prison cells, their iron bars rusted with age. "That's the cage where they used to keep Annie" she said.

"Who's Annie?" the doctor asked.

"Annie was a young girl who was brought in here because nobody could do anything with her. The doctors and nurses couldn't even examine her. I'd see them trying, with her spitting and scratching at them. I used to think, 'I sure would hate to be locked up in a cage like that.' I wanted to help her, but I didn't have any idea what I could do. So I just baked her some brownies one night after work. The next day I brought them in. I walked carefully to her cage and said, 'Annie I baked these brownies just for you. I'll put them right here on the floor and you can come and get them if you want.' Then I got out of there just as fast as I could because I was afraid she might throw them at me. But she didn't. She actually took the brownies and ate them.

"After that, she was just a little bit nicer to me when I was around. Sometimes I'd talk to her. Once, I even got her laughing. One of the nurses noticed this and she told the doctor. They asked me if I'd help them with Annie. So that's how it came about that every time they wanted to see Annie or examine her, I went into the cage first and explained and calmed her down and held her hand. Which is how they discovered that Annie was almost blind."

After they'd been working with her for about a year the Perkins Institute for the Blind opened its doors. They were able to help her and she went on to study and became a teacher herself.

Annie came back to the Tewksbury Institute to visit and to see what she could do to help. At first, the Director didn't say anything, but then he thought about a letter he'd just received. A man had written to him about his daughter. She was absolutely unruly – almost like an animal.

He'd been told she was blind and deaf as well as "deranged". He was at his wits' end, but he didn't want to put her in an asylum. So he wrote to ask if they knew of anyone – any teacher – who would come to his house and work with his daughter.

And that is how Annie Sullivan became the lifelong companion of Helen Keller. When Helen Keller received the Nobel Prize, she was asked who had the greatest impact on her life, and she said, "Annie Sullivan." But Annie said, "No, Helen. The woman who had the greatest influence on both our lives was a floor maid at the Tewksbury Institute."

**Themes:** *Calling, Humility, Leadership, Life – purpose, Materialism, Purpose, Servants.*

**Scriptures:** Deuteronomy 24:1–5; Matthew 5:27–29, 31–32; 19:3–12; Mark 10:2–13; Luke 10:27; John 14:15–24; Acts 5:29; 1 Corinthians 7:1–11; 13; 2 Corinthians 4:1–18; 11:16–23; Philippians 2:1–11.

## 243 SEX

Michael is a member of a church youth group. He is 17, doing his final year at high school. Sometimes he drives his dad's car. One night the group went ten-pin bowling. Vicki was on the same bowling team. She went to the same school as Michael and had been at youth group for quite a few weeks. But they had never taken much notice of each other until this particular night. Things moved pretty fast between them and Michael organised it so that no one went back to the church with him except Vicki. They took the long way back to the church and stopped in a poorly lit street near a creek. Neither of them planned it but they had sex in the car. They both felt guilty and that they had blown it badly. They talked about it and agreed not to have sex again. For a while they felt nervous with people, wondering if anyone could tell that they had done it. But all seemed well, and they started going out regularly. A few weeks after the ten-pin bowling night Vicki came up to Michael at school. She was crying. She had discovered that she was pregnant. Michael was stunned and went hot and cold all at once. Vicki said that she could not tell her parents: they would be devastated and might throw her out of the house. She thinks she will get an abortion.

*Themes:* *Abortion, Anxiety, Courting, Dating, Fornication, Worry.*

*Scriptures:* Exodus 20:13–14; Job 31:15; Psalms 22:9–10; 55:22; 71:6; 118:6; 139; Ecclesiastes 11:5; Isaiah 49:1, 5; Jeremiah 1:5; Luke 12:22–34; Romans 1:26–27; 1 Corinthians 6:13; 10;13; 2 Corinthians 12:1–13; Ephesians 5:3; Philippians 4:6; 1 Thessalonians 4:3; Hebrews 13:5; 1 Peter 5:7.

## 244 SEX

An ancient Jewish text has these directions for normal sexual relations. For sailors it is twice a year. For camel drivers it is once a month. For donkey drivers it is once a week. For labourers it is twice a week. For the unemployed it is every day. There are clearly some benefits for the unemployed!

*Themes:* *Humour, Marriage, Unemployment.*
**Scriptures:** 1 Corinthians 7:1–6.

## 245 SEX

Stephanie Marrian, 45, former model and actress, tells her story.

I finally split up with my last partner after twelve months when I found out that he was living with another woman. He was the biggest creep in the world.

We parted in 1990, but it took me until the end of last year to get over the shock.

I felt he'd made a fool of me and I couldn't stand the thought of what the next man might do. The last time we had sex was on his birthday – 24 August 1990 – and it wasn't anything to write home about.

Then last year, I became a Christian. That means I believe sex outside marriage is wrong, so unless I change my views or marry, I'll never have sex again.

I've been celibate before – I was for four-and-a-half years in my mid-20s. I was a topless model at the time, and I couldn't bear the way men assumed that if you went out with them, you would end up in bed. It was the late 70s and it seemed everybody was doing it, but I had old-fashioned ideas

---

[244] See J. Neusner, *The Mishnah* (New Haven and London: Yale University Press, 1988), pp. 388–89) (*Ketuboth* 5.6).

and never got into a casual relationship. I was waiting for Mr Right.

I was 29 when he found me. Before that, the earth never moved for me during sex, but it did with him. Then I ruined it all by having a brief affair. I hoped I could win him back, and so I was celibate for six years, but he married someone else.

I don't miss sex. I guess I have learned to live without it. But, I'm caught in a trap. I don't see any point in getting married unless you intend to have children – and at 45, that's not very likely. So it's quite possible that I'll never have sex again, which is quite a daunting prospect.

Cliff Richard would be my ideal man – so if he ever reads this, perhaps he could contact me.

**Themes:** *Celibacy, Conversion, Divorce, Faithfulness, Fornication, Men, Relationships.*

**Scriptures:** Deuteronomy 24:1–5; Matthew 5:27–29, 31–32; 19:3–12; Mark 10:2–13; Luke 10:27; John 14:15–24; Acts 5:29; 1 Corinthians 7:1–11; 13.

## 246 SEXUALITY

Ryan was 29 and single. He went on a Christian camp where, one night, the speaker gave a meaningful and powerful plea for sexual purity. Just before going to bed a small group of campers gathered for devotions. Ryan had been particularly agitated by the talk that evening. So he used this time for confession and prayer. The group sat in stark silence. He told the members about his sexual desires and his desperate attempts to handle them. He was guilty of neither adultery nor fornication. But he went on, tearfully, to tell his friends that he did make use of pornography and masturbation to meet his sexual needs. When Ryan had finished pouring out his sexual troubles, he asked the group to pray. Specifically he asked them to pray that the Lord would take away his sexual hungers so that he could not be tempted again. At that point one of the group interrupted his pleas. Ryan was rightly told that the sexual drive was a gift from God and that it was not to be taken away but properly handled with God's power.

**Themes:** *Forgiveness, Fruit of the Spirit, Guilt, Lust, Masturbation, Pornography, Spirit – fruit of.*

**Scriptures:** Matthew 5:27–30; Romans 7:14–25; 1 Corinthians 7:8–9; Galatians 5:16–17; Ephesians 2:3; 4:22; Colossians 3:5; 2 Timothy 2:22; Titus 2:11–13; 1 Peter 2:11; 4:3; 1 John 2:15–16.

## 247 SIN – DISCLOSED

In the nineteenth century, the British warship *Sparrow* was pursuing the *Nancy*, a Spanish ship suspected of piracy. When the British boarded the *Nancy* not a shred of incriminating evidence could be found. Nevertheless, the ship was escorted to the port of Kingston in Jamaica.

While this was going on another British ship, the *Abergavenny*, was cruising through the same area. One day, off the coast of Haiti, the officer in charge noticed a dead bullock in the water. It was surrounded by sharks. He ordered the bullock to be towed behind the ship so they could catch one of the sharks. It turned out to be an unusually large shark.

When they opened it up, in the stomach of the big fish was a parcel of papers, tied around with string. The papers had to do with a ship called the *Nancy*. The papers were kept in case they might be useful. They were handed in at the port of Kingston. At this same time, the captain and crew of the *Nancy* were becoming excited about the prospect of being released. But then they were confronted with the papers from the shark: the papers are now in the Institute Museum of Jamaica.

**Themes:** *Confession, God – omniscient, Guilt, Hiding.*

**Scriptures:** Numbers 32:23; Job 26:6; 31:4; Psalms 17:3; 33:13–15; 139; Proverbs 15:11; Jeremiah 12:3; 23:24; Amos 9:2–4; Jonah 1:3; Mark 2:1–12; John 2:24; Hebrews 4:13; 1 John 1:8–9.

## 248 SLAVERY

It is told that once, in the days before the ending of slavery, Lincoln bought a slave girl with the sole purpose of giving her her freedom. She did not realise why he was buying her; she thought that it was simply another transaction in which she was involved as a thing. So he paid the price for her, and then handed her her papers of freedom. She did not even understand. "You are free," he said to her gently. "Free?" she said. "Can I go wherever I want to go now?" "Indeed you can," he said. "Then," she said, "if I am free to go anywhere I will stay with you and serve you until I die."

**Themes:** *Atonement, Cross, Expiation, Freedom, Jesus – work of, Redeemed, Rescue.*

**Scriptures:** Exodus 6:6; Psalms 77:14–15; Mark 10:45; Luke 24:21; John 1:29; 8:31–36; 1 Corinthians 1:30; 5:7; 6:19–20; 7:22–23; Galatians 3:13; 4:4–5; 5:1; Ephesians 1:7; 5:2; Titus 2:14; Hebrews 9:15; 1 Peter 1:18–19; 1 John 2:2.

## 249 SPIRITUAL WARFARE

Carlos Annacondia conducts Christian missions in South America. Some of them are out in the open in a natural amphitheatre. A large stage is erected. Behind the stage a very large marquee is erected. The crowds gather.

There will be tens of thousands of people there. So much has the Spirit of God overshadowed the work of Carlos Annacondia that ropes are put up in front of the

---

[248] William Barclay, *The Plain Man Looks at the Apostles' Creed* (London and Glasgow: Collins/Fontana, 1967), p. 67.

platform to stop people coming forward to submit their lives to Jesus.

Towards the end of the talk Carlos has to ask people to stay where they are until the end of his appeal. At the end of the appeal for people to receive Christ the ropes are lowered and there is a rushing and surge of many hundreds of people seeking the forgiveness of Christ in their lives. They are prayed for and encouraged to go on in their new life in Christ.

Then Annacondia explains that he is going to ask the Holy Spirit to come to release those who are under Satan's bondage. He tells them people will fall down. They are not to touch them. His helpers will deal with them. Then Carlos prays. Again, scores of people right across the crowd fall down as dead or screaming. Then, out from the large marquee come the stretcher bearers. They pick up those who have fallen down and take them back to what is known as the "intensive care unit". There they minister to these folk. Sometimes for six hours they pray, commanding the spirits to leave in the name of Jesus. There is much rejoicing as spirits leave people and they experience the new freedom in Christ.

But all is not plain sailing. As well as the eager crowd, up at the very back Satanists will often set up a booth. Witches will attempt to cast spells or hexes on the meeting. When those on the stage sense Satan's attacks and the curses, they stamp their feet on the floor of the stage. For, underneath, there's a group committed to praying continually for the meeting and that God will change lives.

**Themes:** *Enemies, Evil, Exorcism, Good, Life, Missions, New life, Old life, Revival, Satanists, Spiritual battle.*

**Scriptures:** Psalms 1; Mark 1:21–28; 5:1–20; 7:24–30; 9:14–29; Romans 6:1–14; 7:14–25; 8:31–39; 1 Corinthians 4:16; 9:24–27; 16:13;

2 Corinthians 10:1–6; Galatians 5:16–26; Ephesians 3:16–17; 4:17 – 5:2; 6:10–20; Colossians 3:1–17; 1 Timothy 1:18.

## 250 STRESS

Keith and Colleen are a couple whose family has been under great stress. Shortly after birth their daughter, Cynthia, developed a serious infection. This led to her becoming profoundly deaf in the first month of her life. At first Keith and his wife responded with the question, "Why us?" This is the question of many parents who learn that their child is deaf, blind, disabled, critically ill or injured. Initially Keith and Colleen felt feelings of hope-lessness and helplessness. They prayed fervently that baby Cindy would hear and speak. They felt anger and guilt. They wanted prompt, definitive action from God. When what they wanted did not come over the next year or so, they felt disillusionment. Then one night, many months and many prayers later, it happened. Keith had been away on a business trip. He was returning on the train in a sleeper car. It was cold and wet. When the train stopped suddenly at a siding Keith woke. He looked out the window to see where he was. He saw a full moon shining behind the cross bars of the railroad crossing. Something forced him to fix his eyes on the sign. Soon the crossing sign became a giant crucifix. He was transfixed by what he saw – and heard. From out of the cross came a brilliant light and a remarkably calm voice that said, "Don't despair. Out of the misfortune of your daughter will come benefits for many." Then the voice and the cross disap-peared. Keith was left with an experience of God that changed his attitudes and the stress in his family. That happened just over 30 years ago. Cindy can only hear through lip reading, though she can speak quite well. She became an excellent athlete and has been through tertiary education. Cindy is involved in recreation and health sports for people with disabilities. What was a crippling source of stress for Keith and Colleen, God turned around by giving them peace and a way of carrying the load.

*Themes:* *Anger, Guilt, Illness, Peace, Suffering.*
**Scriptures:** Job; Psalms 23; 2 Corinthians 1:3–7; 4:7–12; 7:6; 12:9; Colossians 1:24; James 1:2–4.

## 251 SUBSTITUTION

At one stage, in India, the British were fighting a native monarch called Tippo Saib. In one of the battles, several English officers were taken prisoner. Among them was a man named Baird who had been severely wounded. One day, an Indian officer brought in fetters to be put on each of the prisoners. The wounded Baird was not exempt from the ordeal even though he was suffering from pain and weakness. A grey-haired officer said to the native official, "Don't think you're putting chains upon that wounded young man." But the Indian said, "There are just as many pairs of fetters as there are prisoners and every pair must be worn."

"Then," said the officer, "put two pairs on me. I'll wear his as well as my own." Baird lived to regain his freedom. But the generous friend died in prison.

*Themes:* *Courage, Cross, Easter, Encouragement, Jesus – death of, Love, Martyrdom, Persecution, Sacrifice, Suffering.*
**Scriptures:** Psalms 27:14; Isaiah 53; Mark 10:45; Luke 10:27; John 11:50; Romans 3:21–25;1 Corinthians 13; Galatians 3:13; 1 Timothy 2:6; Hebrews 9:28; 1 Peter 2:24.

## 252 SUBSTITUTION *

The boy stood with back arched, head cocked back and hands clenched defiantly. "Go ahead, give it to me."

The principal looked down at the young rebel. "How many times have you been here?"

The child sneered rebelliously, "Apparently not enough."

The principal gave the boy a strange look. "And you have been punished each time, have you not?"

"Yeah, I been punished, if that's what you want to call it." He threw out his small chest. "Go ahead, I can take whatever you dish out. I always have."

"And no thought of your punishment enters your head the next time you decide to break the rules, does it?"

"Nope, I do whatever I want to do. Ain't nothin' you people gonna do to stop me either."

The principal looked over at the teacher who stood nearby. "What did he do this time?"

"Fighting. He took little Tommy and shoved his face into the sandbox."

The principal turned to look at the boy. "Why? What did little Tommy do to you?"

"Nothin', I didn't like the way he was lookin' at me, just like I don't like the way you're lookin' at me! And if I thought I could do it, I'd shove your face into something."

The teacher stiffened and started to rise but a quick look from the principal stopped him. He contemplated the child for a moment and then quietly said, "Today, my young student, is the day you learn about grace."

"Grace? Isn't that what you old people do before you sit down to eat? I don't need none of your stinkin' grace."

"Oh, but you do." The principal studied the young man's face and whispered, "Oh yes, you truly do..."

The boy continued to glare as the principal continued, "Grace, in its short definition, is unmerited favour. You cannot earn it; it is a gift and is always freely given. It means that you will not be getting what you so richly deserve."

The boy looked puzzled. "You're not gonna whip me? You just gonna let me walk?"

The principal looked down at the unyielding child. "Yes, I am going to let you walk."

The boy studied the face of the principal. "No punishment at all? Even though I socked Tommy and shoved his face into the sandbox?"

"Oh, there has to be punishment. What you did was wrong and there are always consequences to our actions. There will be punishment. Grace is not an excuse for doing wrong."

"I knew it," sneered the boy as he held out his hands. "Let's get on with it."

The principal nodded toward the teacher. "Bring me the belt." The teacher presented the belt to the principal. He carefully folded it in two and then handed it back to the teacher. He looked at the child and said, "I want you to count the blows." He slid out from behind his desk and walked over to stand directly in front of the young man. He gently reached out and folded the child's outstretched, expectant hands together and then turned to face the teacher with his own hands outstretched. One quiet word came forth from his mouth.

"Begin."

The belt whipped down on the outstretched hands of the principal. Crack!

The young man jumped. Shock registered across his face. "One," he whispered. Crack! "Two." His voice rose an octave. Crack! "Three..." He couldn't believe this. Crack! "Four." Big tears welled up in the eyes of the rebel. "OK stop! That's enough. Stop!"

Crack! The belt came down on the calloused hands of the principal. Crack! The child flinched with each blow, tears beginning to stream down his face. Crack! Crack!

"No please," the former rebel begged. "Stop, I did it, I'm the one who deserves it. Stop! Please. Stop..."

Still the blows came. Crack! Crack! One after another. Finally it was over. The principal stood with sweat glistening across his forehead and beads trickling down his face. Slowly he knelt down. He studied the young man for a second and then his swollen hands reached out to cradle the face of the weeping child.

**Themes:** *Courage, Cross, Easter, Grace, Jesus – death of, Love, Punishment, Sacrifice, Suffering.*

**Scriptures:** Psalms 27:14; Isaiah 53; Mark 10:45; Luke 10:27; John 11:50; Romans 3:21–25; 1 Corinthians 13; Galatians 3:13; 1 Timothy 2:6; Hebrews 9:28; 1 Peter 2:24.

## 253 SUBSTITUTION

Giuseppe Verdi's opera *Rigoletto* has an interesting ending. Rigoletto, the Duke's jester, has a daughter, Gilda, who has become the mistress of the Duke. To say the least, the Duke is a ladies' man and is unfaithful to Gilda. She is heartbroken and has lost the will to live, but not her love for the Duke. Rigoletto schemes to get rid of the Duke. But, rather than see the Duke killed, the girl, dressed as a man, is killed in his place.

Rigoletto had arranged to dump the sack with the body in it into the river. When he hears the Duke still singing inside the inn he frantically cuts open the sack to find his dying Gilda inside the bag instead of the Duke.

**Themes:** *Courage, Cross, Easter, Encouragement, Jesus – death of, Love, Martyrdom, Persecution, Sacrifice, Suffering.*

*Scriptures:* Psalms 27:14; Isaiah 53; Mark 10:45; Luke 10:27; John 11:50; Romans 3:21–25; 1 Corinthians 13; Galatians 3:13; 1 Timothy 2:6; Hebrews 9:28; 1 Peter 2:24.

## 254 SUBSTITUTION

In May 1941 Father Maksymilian Kolbe was arrested by the Nazis and sent to Auschwitz concentration camp. At about three in the afternoon, on almost the last day of July, as men were working digging gravel outside the camp to be used in building more blocks, the sirens began to wail and shriek. A prisoner was missing. After work the whole camp stood to attention until being dismissed to go to bed. There was no meal.

The next day everyone went to work except for Block 14, which had the missing prisoner. They were again put on the parade-ground to stand to attention all day in the sun. The only break came at noon when they were given their soup ration. Quite a few keeled over and were left as they fell.

It was about seven o'clock at night when Lagerführer Karl Fritsch, Commandant Höss' deputy, and Rapportführer Gerhard Palitsch, head of the dreaded Political Department, inspected the silent rows of men. Fritsch barked, "The fugitive has not been found. In reprisal for your comrade's escape, ten of you will die of starvation. Next time, it will be 20." Immediately the selection began. With Palitsch and a prisoner-secretary preceding him, up and down the rows, with pad and pencil to take down the numbers of the condemned, Fritsch meandered slowly to prolong the terror. Then, with a ges-

254 From Patricia Treece, *A Man for Others: Maximilian Kolbe Saint of Auschwitz in the Words of Those who Knew Him* (San Francisco: Harper and Row, 1982), pp. 166–176; also Diana Dewar, *Saint of Auschwitz: The Story of Maximilian Kolbe* (London: DLT, 1982), pp. 110–113; *The Sunday Times* (London) 10 October 1982, p. 18; *The Times* (London) Monday 11 October 1982, p. 1.

ture, he chose his victims. After each row was inspected, the order was given: "Three paces forward." They moved up, leaving an alley between them and the next row so the arrogant Fritsch could stare each of these hapless souls, one by one, straight in the face. Finally the grisly selection was complete. Together the SS officers checked the secretary's list against the numbers of the condemned. As their German passion for accuracy occupied them, one of the victims was sobbing, "My wife and my children!" It was Francis Gajowniczek. The SS ignored him.

Suddenly there was movement in the still ranks. A prisoner several rows back had broken out and was pushing his way toward the front. The watching SS guards raised their automatic rifles, while the dogs at their heels tensed for the order to spring. Fritsch and Palitsch too reached towards their holsters.

It was Kolbe. His step was firm, his face peaceful. Angrily, the block capo shouted at him to stop or be shot. Kolbe answered calmly, "I want to talk to the commander," and kept on walking while the capo, oddly enough, neither shot nor clubbed him. Then, still at a respectful distance, Kolbe stopped, his cap in his hands. Standing at attention like an officer of some sort himself, he looked Fritsch straight in the eye.

"Herr Kommandant, I wish to make a request, please," he said politely in flawless German. Survivors will later say it was a miracle that no one shot him. Instead Fritsch asked, "What do you want?" "I want to die in place of this prisoner," and Kolbe pointed toward the sobbing Gajowniczek. Fritsch looked stupefied, irritated. The prisoner explained coolly that the man over there had a family. "I have no wife or children. Besides, I'm old and not good for anything. He's in better condition," he added, playing on the Nazi line that only the fit should live. "Who are you?" Fritsch croaked. "A Catholic priest." After a moment, the deputy-commander snapped, "Request granted." He kicked Gajowniczek, snarling, "Back to ranks, you."

Prisoners in ranks are never allowed to speak. Gajowniczek later said, "I could only try to thank him with my eyes. I was stunned and could hardly grasp what was going on. The immensity of it: I, the condemned, to live and someone else willingly and voluntarily offers his life for me – a stranger. Is this some dream or reality?"

The block was dismissed and the order was given for the condemned prisoners to march to the basement bunker. The SS guard had snarled, "Strip." The naked victims were in one cell. What kind of martyrdom these men were enduring can be imagined from the fact that the urine bucket was always dry. In their dreadful thirst, they must have drunk its contents. Two weeks went by. The prisoners were dying one after the other, and by this time only four were left, among them Father Kolbe, who was still conscious. The SS decided things were taking too long. One day they sent for the German criminal Bock from the hospital to give the prisoners injections of carbolic acid. Between the injection and death was little more than ten seconds. When Bock got there, Father Kolbe, with a prayer, held out his arm to the executioner. When the fatal injection took its toll, Kolbe was sitting upright, leaning against the wall. His body was not dirty like the others, but clean and bright. The head was tilted somewhat to one side. His eyes were open. Serene and pure, his face was radiant.

*Themes:* *Courage, Cross, Easter, Encouragement, Jesus – death of, Love, Martyrdom, Persecution, Sacrifice, Suffering.*

*Scriptures:* Psalms 27:14; Isaiah 53; Mark 10:45; Luke 10:27; John 11:50;
Romans 3:21–25; 1 Corinthians 13; Galatians 3:13; 1 Timothy 2:6;
Hebrews 9:28; 1 Peter 2:24.

## 255 SUBSTITUTION

On a balmy Saturday afternoon in September 1984, pedestrians near New York's famed Carnegie Hall stared in fascination. Towering over them was one of the world's tallest moving objects: a 200-tonne yellow construction crane whose massive boom reached nearly 20 storeys above the street. The crane sat on the rim of an eight-metre-deep excavation where it was to help erect a 68-storey skyscraper.

Tom O'Brien, one of the area's best crane operators, was in the cabin. Tom's immediate task was to lift a huge steel turntable that would form the base of a smaller crane to be erected on top of a construction tower overlooking the yawning building site. In 22 years of crane driving he had seen two overloaded cranes topple. One operator had been crushed to death in his cab; the other had leaped for his life – to safety. Shortly after 3:00 pm the five men on the tower radioed that all was ready.

Tom gently drew back the lift lever and depressed the power pedal. The diesel engine roared; the wrist-thick, all-steel lifting cable tightened. Tom watched as the load shrank into the blue sky, then swung the boom to the left, over the tower.

Tom had been told that the load weighed 17,000 kilos, well within the capacity of the crane. In fact, someone had apparently miscalculated: it weighed 24,000 kilos. On top of the tower, five men peered up at the load, now hovering over them.

255 Adapted from *Reader's Digest* (November 1985), pp. 132–140.

Tom was the first to know that something was wrong. He sensed the rear of his cab begin to rise. With a groaning of metal, the boom was slowly pitching forward.

The men on the tower thought that the load was being lowered to them; in reality it was falling. If it stayed on course, it would crush them and the tower. And the 75-metre-long boom would slice through the adjacent building like a steel bar smashing teacups.

As the crane continued tilting, Tom felt the sickening sensation of being on a ship's stern, lifted by a giant wave. Every nerve in his body shouted: "Jump!" He tensed to leap through the cab door. But an image flashed before him: shattered buildings avalanching into the street crushing pedestrians, flattening cars and buses, killing scores of people. He might, just might, be able to prevent the carnage. Could he live with himself if he did not try?

On the ground, Tom's friend Roy Ledger, another crane operator, stared in unbelieving horror.

"Oh, God," he thought, "she's going over!"

Yelling, workers around him began scattering. Up in the swiftly tilting cab, Tom O'Brien made his decision. He refused to jump. Instinctively, Tom flicked levers and pedals, trying to swing the load out over the excavation. Hunched in concentration at his post, hands and feet moving like lightning over the controls, he felt himself being thrust high into the air as the screeching, groaning crane tottered on its front end, about to cartwheel. With vast relief, he saw the load crash into the excavation, exactly where he had hoped to place it. Then the boom and cab, with its massive tractor treads, toppled into the pit. The thundering impact could be heard for blocks. People in the street ran in all directions, screaming in panic.

The only person hurt in the tragedy was Tom. He had to have a leg amputated.

**Themes:** *Courage, Cross, Easter, Encouragement, Jesus – death of, Love, Martyrdom, Persecution, Sacrifice, Suffering.*

**Scriptures:** Psalms 27:14; Isaiah 53; Mark 10:45; Luke 10:27; John 11:50; Romans 3:21–25; 1 Corinthians 13; Galatians 3:13; 1 Timothy 2:6; Hebrews 9:28; 1 Peter 2:24.

## 256 SUBSTITUTION

Bob was driving a road tanker through a town. It was a cold, wet night. He glanced in the rear-view mirror and saw flames. They were coming from the side of the tanker. He was carrying an explosive petrol-based chemical. Instead of stopping the truck, he put his foot down hard on the accelerator. He sped through the rain with his hand on the horn until he was clear of the town. By then the cabin was full of flames. He swung the truck into a ditch and fell out. His face and hands and clothes were burning. When the police who were following came they wrapped him in a blanket to put out the flames. He was in shock and in awful pain. A thumb was missing and part of his jaw was gone and his windpipe was burned so that he could no longer breathe. But everyone else in the town was safe.

**Themes:** *Courage, Cross, Easter, Encouragement, Jesus – death of, Love, Martyrdom, Persecution, Sacrifice, Suffering.*

**Scriptures:** Psalms 27:14; Isaiah 53; Mark 10:45; Luke 10:27; John 11:50; Romans 3:21–25; 1 Corinthians 13; Galatians 3:13; 1 Timothy 2:6; Hebrews 9:28; 1 Peter 2:24.

## 257 SUBSTITUTION

I was a prisoner during the war, and the treatment our captors meted out was diabolical... I had been very ill, and the food was poor. One day a crate of bananas was left where we could just reach them – it was a trap.

256 Adapted from B. J. Williams, *Spare Parts for People* (Hove: Wayland, 1978), pp. 37–47.
257 *The Upper Room* (24 October 1980).

I was so hungry that I crept to where they were, and when no one was there I took one. Suddenly two guards pounced on me. I was dragged off to the commandant, who ordered a public flogging as an example. The chaplain knew I would not survive the punishment and begged to take my place. Amused, the commandant agreed and ordered the whole camp to be assembled.

I was compelled to stand nearest the padre to witness the flogging. It was then that I began to understand what Peter meant when he wrote that Christ "himself bore our sins in his own body on the tree".

**Themes:** *Courage, Cross, Easter, Encouragement, Jesus – death of, Love, Martyrdom, Persecution, Sacrifice, Suffering.*

**Scriptures:** Psalms 27:14; Isaiah 53; Mark 10:45; Luke 10:27; John 11:50; Romans 3:21–25; 1 Corinthians 13; Galatians 3:13; 1 Timothy 2:6; Hebrews 9:28; 1 Peter 2:24.

## 258 SUBSTITUTION

On 2 April 1987, two Royal Australian Air Force crewmen died when their F-111 crashed. The residents at Tenterfield in northern New South Wales believe that the airmen delayed ejecting to steer the plane to a deserted paddock. The men were hailed as heroes who were thought to deserve public recognition for their bravery.

The local newspaper editor said, "There's a feeling among the townspeople that we owe a lot of lives to those two. It would have been no trouble for them to eject and not worry too much about where the plane was going to land, and who could have blamed them? But it looks like they stayed in the plane to guide it over the town."

258 Adapted from Mark Ragg, "Dead F-111 Crewmen Hailed as Heroes", *The Weekend Australian* (4–5 April 1987), p. 5.

**Themes:**  *Courage, Cross, Easter, Encouragement, Jesus – death of, Love, Martyrdom, Persecution, Sacrifice, Suffering.*

**Scriptures:**  Psalms 27:14; Isaiah 53; Mark 10:45; Luke 10:27; John 11:50; Romans 3:21–25; 1 Corinthians 13; Galatians 3:13; 1 Timothy 2:6; Hebrews 9:28; 1 Peter 2:24.

## 259 SUFFERING

In the saga of the Cherokee people's *Trail of Tears*, the Cherokee nation, trying to keep peace and self-pride, reluctantly agreed to move from North Carolina to the Okalahoma Indian Territory. It really was a trail of tears as they marched because, between the sickness and the starvation, half of the Cherokee nation didn't make it alive. Funeral after funeral was held for young and old alike. It is one of the sad and grief-filled stories of the injustices against the Native Americans.

There is an interesting side-story to this agonising tale. Every single one of the soldiers assigned as guards for this forced march was converted along the way. No one could remain unmoved or go untouched by the plight of these people as they resolutely followed and left their home for another. But that was not what brought about the conversion of these guards. The guards were all converted by a song that the Cherokee people sang over and over again in the midst of their personal and national tragedy. The title of that song contains all the words that there are. It is a simple song with a simple message, "What can we do for you Jesus? What can we do for you?"

**Themes:**  *Evangelism, Light, Persecution, Singing, Tragedy, Witness.*

**Scriptures:**  Job; Matthew 5:12, 16; 13:43; Acts 5:41; 9:4–5; 14:22; Romans 5:3; 12:12; 2 Corinthians 1:3–7; 11:16–33; Philippians 1:29; 3:10; Colossians 3:24; 1 Thessalonians 1:6; 2 Timothy 3:12; Hebrews 2:18; 4:15; 12:3, 5, 11; 13:13; James 1:2–4; 1 Peter 1:6–7; 2:21; 4:1–2, 12–16; 5:9; 3:17–18.

Joni was a great-looking, blonde teenager. She enjoyed horse riding and had a lovely family and plenty of friends. She had been a Christian for two years. But, as she traced her spiritual progress over this time, she realised that she had not come very far. She felt she was trapped in her emotional sins: anger, jealousy, resentment and possessiveness. She had drifted through her last years of school. Her grades began to drop and she began to fight with her parents. So she became insistent with God, "Lord, if you're really there, do something in my life that will change me and turn me around... I'm sick of hypocrisy! I want you to work in my life for real... Please do something in my life to turn me around!" At last she wanted to be a fully devoted follower of Jesus. A short time later, the storm broke in her life.

On 30 July 1967 Joni Eareckson dived into a shallow lake. She was dragged out by her sister as a quadriplegic. She became bitter and angry with God. She prayed – others prayed for healing – nothing happened. She knows that her accident was not sent from God. But she came to the point of trusting God in the storm of her life as she sought to follow him – especially in talking to others about him. Yet she is able to say, "God is utterly dependable, no matter which direction our circumstances take us." And, she says, "I wouldn't change my life for anything. I even feel privileged."

**Themes:** *Anger, Bitterness, Healing, Jealousy, Possessions, Prayer – unanswered, Resentment.*

**Scriptures:** Daniel 3:16–18; Matthew 5:22–24; 1 Corinthians 13; 2 Corinthians 11:30; 12:9; Philippians 4:13.

260 Adapted from Joni Eareckson, *Joni* (London and Glasgow: Pickering and Inglis, 1976).

## 261 SUNDAY

William Wilberforce was a member of the English parliament in the early years of the nineteenth century. He became famous for convincing parliament to outlaw slavery in the British Empire.

It took Wilberforce 20 years of hard work to construct the coalition of law-makers that eventually passed the anti-slavery bills. The spiritual strength and moral courage of Wilberforce had to be – and was – immense.

There was an important ingredient in his life. It is shown in an incident in 1801. In that year it was rumoured that Wilberforce was to be among the candidates for a cabinet post. He found himself most anxious to gain the appointment. For days it grabbed at his conscious mind, forcing aside everything else. By his own admission, the rising ambition was crippling his life. Sunday brought the cure.

This is what Wilberforce wrote in his journal at the end of that week of furious fantasising and temptations to politic for position: "Blessed be to God for the day of rest and religious occupation wherein earthly things assume their true size. Ambition is stunted." Wilberforce had discovered the importance of Sunday.

**Themes:** *Ambition, Courage, Refreshment, Rest, Sabbath, Slavery.*
**Scriptures:** Exodus 20:8–11; 31:12–17; Leviticus 23:3; Nehemiah 13:15–22; Isaiah 58:13–14; Jeremiah 17:19–23; Mark 2:27; Romans 12:3–8; Revelation 1:10.

## 262 SURRENDER

In 1967, Paul Stanley was an infantry company commander in the Vietnam War. He saw Viet Cong soldiers surrender many times.

On one occasion, after the enemy had withdrawn, Paul

came across several soldiers surrounding a wounded Viet Cong. He was shot through the leg. He was hostile, yet helpless. He threw mud and kicked with his good leg when anyone went near him. Paul joined the circle and looked down at the soldier who was losing blood fast. He looked into his face and saw a 16- or 17-year-old boy.

Paul unbuckled his pistol and belt and hand grenades so he couldn't grab them. Then, speaking gently, he moved towards him. The helpless soldier stared fearfully at Paul as he knelt down. But he allowed Paul to slide his arms under him and pick him up.

As Paul walked along with him towards the helicopter, the young man began to cry and hold him tight. He kept looking at Paul and squeezing him tighter. They climbed into the helicopter and took off. During the ride, the young captive sat on the floor, clinging to Paul's leg. He had never ridden in a helicopter before. He fixed his eyes on Paul. Paul smiled reassuringly and put his hand on the fellow's shoulder.

After landing, Paul picked him up and walked towards the medical tent. As they crossed the field, Paul felt the tenseness leave the boy's body. His tight grasp loosened. His eyes softened and he leant his head against Paul's chest. The fear and resistance were gone. He had finally surrendered.

**Themes:** *Acceptance, Christ – work of, Enemies – love for, Fear, Parable – Good Samaritan, Parable – Lost Sheep, Reconciliation, Rescue, Salvation.*

**Scriptures:** Isaiah 64:8; Malachi 1:6; 2:10; Luke 10:25–37; 11:1–4; 15:1–7, 8–10, 11–32; 19:10; John 10:1–18; 20:17; Romans 5:10; 8:17; 11:28; Galatians 3:26; Philippians 3:18; Colossians 1:21–22; Hebrews 12:9.

## 263 TEMPTATION *

According to tradition, this is how an Eskimo hunter kills a wolf. First, the Eskimo coats his knife blade with animal blood. He allows it to freeze. He then adds layer after layer of blood until the blade is completely concealed by the frozen blood. Next the hunter fixes his knife in the ground with the blade up. When a wolf follows his sensitive nose to the source of the scent and discovers the bait, he licks it, tasting the fresh frozen blood. He begins to lick faster, more and more vigorously. He laps at the blade until the sharp edge is bare. Now feverishly, harder and harder. The wolf licks the frozen blade in the cold Arctic night.

His craving for blood becomes so great that the wolf doesn't notice the razor sharp blade slicing through his own tongue. Nor does he recognise that his insatiable thirst for blood is being satisfied by his own blood. In the morning the wolf is found dead in the snow.

*Themes:* *Character, Enemies, Evil, Life – troubles, Risk, Spiritual battles, Trials.*

**Scriptures:** Exodus 20:20; Deuteronomy 8:2, 16; 13:3; Judges 2:22; 2 Chronicles 32:31; Job 1:12; 2:6; Psalms 1; 26:2; 66:10; 91; 118:5–6; 139:23–24; Isaiah 48:10; Matthew 26:41; Luke 8:22–25; 11:14; 21:9–19; 22:8; 1 Corinthians 10:12–14; Philippians 4:8; 2 Timothy 2:3; Hebrews 4:15; James 1:2–4, 12–15; 4:7; 1 Peter 1:6–7; 4:12–13; 2 Peter 2:9; 3:17.

## 264 TEMPTATION

Frederick Handley Page was a pioneer flyer in the early days of aviation. On one of his long flights in which he was testing an aeroplane, he came down on a field near a city in India; he had to take some rest. When he came back and took off, he had only been flying a short time when he heard a gnawing sound behind him. He knew at once what had happened; a rat had got on board his plane while he was grounded and it was gnawing.

Now those were the days when aeroplanes were not

263 Adapted from Wayne Rice, *Hot Illustrations for Youth Talks* (El Cajon, CA: Youth Specialties, 1994), pp. 87–88.

what they are now; the rat could easily chew through something that could keep him from controlling his flight, and could destroy him.

Suddenly a solution occurred to him. He remembered that rats live in low altitudes. So he pointed the nose of the plane upwards and climbed until the air became so thin he could hardly breathe. He knew he couldn't go any higher or he would black out. So he levelled off and continued to fly at that altitude.

After a while, he didn't hear the gnawing. But he didn't take any chances. He continued to fly at a high altitude for a long time. When he came down at his next stop, he looked in the back to find a dead rat.

**Themes:** *Character, Enemies, Evil, Life – troubles, Old life, Perseverance, Spiritual battles.*

**Scriptures:** Psalms 1; Romans 6:1–14; 7:14–25; 8:31–39; 1 Corinthians 4:16; 9:24–27; 16:13; 2 Corinthians 10:1–6; Galatians 5:16–26; Ephesians 3:16–17; 4:17 – 5:2; 6:10–20; Colossians 3:1–17; 1 Timothy 1:18.

## 265 TEMPTATION

On the morning of 10 April 1963, Lieutenant-Commander John W. Harvey, USA, took the nuclear submarine *Thresher* to sea for post-refit trials. It was the beginning of a most tragic loss of life.

The tear-shaped vessel was 278 feet long with a beam of 31 feet, displacing 3,700 tons when it was on the surface, and cost $45 million. On board were a number of dockyard officials and firms' representatives, making a total of 129.

The shallow diving tests that day were successfully con-

[265] From *The Los Angeles Times* Friday 12 April 1963, pp. 1, 10, 12 and Sunday 14 April 1963, p. 1; Commander Nicholas Whitestone, *The Submarine: The Ultimate Weapon* (London: Davis-Poynter, 1973), pp. 47–50, 118–125; Drew Middleton, *Submarine: The Ultimate Weapon – Its Past, Present and Future* (Chicago: Playboy, 1976), pp. 178–185.

cluded. The next morning the submarine reported that she was starting a dive 270 miles west of Boston to her maximum operating or test depth – unofficially estimated at between 800 and 1,000 feet. The depth of water in this area is 8,400 feet. At 7:52 am she had reached 400 feet and the dive was temporarily stopped for a few minutes for a routine inspection for leaks. At 8:09 am the *Thresher* reported that she was at one half test depth and from then on, for security reasons, all references to depth were reported in terms of test depth. At 8:34 am she was at test depth minus 300 feet and at 8:53 am was "proceeding to test depth". At 9:12 am there was a routine communication check. A minute later a distorted message was received by James Watson, the navigator on *Skylark*, the submarine rescue vessel nearby. James heard the words: "Experiencing minor problem... have positive angle... attempting to blow." Then he heard a sound resembling pressure being blown into the ballast tanks. At 9:17 am a final message reached Watson on the surface. He struggled to make out the words, "Exceeding test depth". Then there was a sound familiar to Watson: sounds of a vessel breaking up, "like a compartment collapsing: a muted dull thud". The *Thresher* had suddenly plunged towards the bottom at a very high speed. It had exceeded its crush limit and imploded.

Later, Admiral George W. Anderson, chief of naval operations, said, "There would be no pouring in of water from ruptured points, no time to dog down [lock] watertight doors, no time for men to scramble to some point of maximum protection aboard. Only instant and complete collapse from all directions with the shock of an explosion."

All that was left of the *Thresher* was debris of twisted steel scattered over an area 1,000 by 4,000 yards.

**Themes:** *Endurance, Limits, Lord's Prayer, Risk, Testing, Tragedy, Trials.*

**Scriptures:** Genesis 22:1; Exodus 16:4; 20:20; Deuteronomy 8:2, 16; 13:3; Judges 2:22; 2 Chronicles 32:31; Job 1:12; 2:6; Psalms 1; 66:10; 91; 118:5–6; 139:23–24; Isaiah 48:10; Matthew 26:41; Luke 8:22–25; 11:14; 21:9–19; 1 Corinthians 10:12–14; Philippians 4:8; 2 Timothy 2:3; James 4:7; 1 Peter 1:6–7; 2 Peter 2:9; 3:17.

## 266 TESTIMONY

One Sunday in a particular church, there was a woman who sang in the choir. She was a former drug addict, now with the HIV virus.

During the service she told the story of how she came to Christ. She described in raw detail the horrors of her former life.

A street person named Roger stood at the back listening closely. After church he approached John, one of the ministry team. John was tired and knew that Roger was going to hit him for money. When Roger got close, the smell took John's breath away: a mixture of urine, sweat, garbage and alcohol.

After a few words, John reached into his pocket and pulled out a couple of dollars for him. John's posture must have communicated the message, "Here's some money. Now get out of here." For Roger looked intently at John, put his finger in his face and said, "Look, I don't want your money. I'm going to die out there. I want the Jesus this girl talked about."

**Themes:** *Acceptance, Conversion, Drugs, Money.*

**Scriptures:** John 2:23; 4:1–42, 53; 6:2, 26; 10:42; 11:45; 12:9, 37; Acts 13:4–12; 14:8–18; 16:16–18; 19:20; 20:7–12; 28:7–10; Romans 4:21; 15:19; 1 Corinthians 2:1–5; 2 Corinthians 12:9–10; 1 Thessalonians 1:5, 9.

In about the year 287, just north of what is now London, there lived a certain man, Alban. Though not a Christian, he gave hospitality to a Christian minister who was running from the Roman persecutors. Instructed little by little by his teaching about salvation, Alban gave up idolatry and became a wholehearted Christian.

After the minister had been staying with Alban for a few days, the Roman ruler heard that a Christian was hiding in Alban's house. He ordered his soldiers to make a thorough search for him there. When they came to the house, Alban immediately offered himself to the soldiers in place of his guest and teacher, having put on the long cloak the minister wore.

The judge ordered Alban to be dragged before the images of the devils in front of which he was standing and said, "You have chosen to conceal a godless rebel rather than surrender him to my soldiers to prevent him from paying the well-deserved penalty for his blasphemy in despising the gods. You will have to take the punishment he has incurred if you attempt to forsake our worship and religion."

The judge went on to ask him, "What is your family and race?" Alban answered, "My parents call me Alban and I shall ever adore and worship the true and living God who created all things." The judge answered very angrily, "If you wish to enjoy the happiness of everlasting life, you must sacrifice at once to the mighty gods." Alban answered, "The sacrifices which you offer to devils cannot help their devotees nor fulfil their desires and petitions.

---

267 Adapted from *Bede: A History of the English Church and People*, translated by Leo Sherley-Price Penguin Classics (Harmondsworth: Penguin, 1955, revised 1968), pp. 44–47, and Bertram Colgrave and R. A. B. Mynors (eds.), *Bede's Ecclesiastical History of the English People* (Oxford: Clarendon, 1969), pp. 29–35.

On the contrary, whoever offers sacrifices to these images will receive eternal punishment in hell as his reward."

Incensed at this reply, the judge ordered Alban to be beaten. Though he was subjected to the most cruel tortures, Alban bore them patiently and even joyfully for the Lord's sake.

When the judge saw that he was not to be overcome by tortures nor turned from the Christian faith, he ordered him to be executed.

Legend has it that as Alban was being led to his execution he came to a rapid river. A great crowd had gathered. St Alban, who desired martyrdom as soon as possible, came to the torrent and raised his eyes towards heaven. It is said the riverbed dried up at that very spot, and provided a path for him to walk on. The executioner who was to have put him to death was among those who saw this. So moved was he that he hurried to meet Alban. The executioner threw away his sword and knelt down at Alban's feet, begging that he might be judged worthy to be put to death either with the martyr, or else in his place.

While there was hesitation among the other executioners, Alban went up the hill with the crowds, and was executed. The soldier who refused to behead Alban was also beheaded there. Alban died on 22 June where St Alban's Cathedral now stands.

*Themes:* *Courage, Enemies – love for, Persecution, Suffering, Patience, Prayer – unanswered, Prisoners, Revenge, War.*

**Scriptures:** Leviticus 19:18; Deuteronomy 32:35; Psalms 27:14; Proverbs 20:22; Daniel 3:16–18; Matthew 5:43–48; Luke 6:27–36; 10:27; 23:34; Acts 7:60; Romans 12:9–21; 1 Corinthians 13; 2 Corinthians 11:30; 12:9; Philippians 4:13; Hebrews 10:30, 36; 1 Peter 3:9.

Chris Frager's dad left home when she was six. She missed him badly. They'd had some good times together. Then her mum was left with her and her three sisters. But mum couldn't cope, and Chris was sent to a children's home until she was twelve. She longed to have a normal home and especially a dad.

She was excited when she heard that mum was marrying again. That would mean she could have a stepdad. But things did not work out. She came to hate the man. One day she told him so. He flew into a cold rage and yelled at her, "Get out!" The next day she was thrown out.

Chris was 17 and did not know where to go or what to do. It was school holidays so she looked for a job. Chris found a job in a hospital where she could live in. Helping dying people took her mind off her problems, and all that was going on inside her. When school started again she had to find somewhere else to live because she went back to working only weekends. Sometimes she was hungry and had to miss school because she did not have the money for the bus fare.

There were some Christians at her school. They started to make friends with her. Exams were looming and they said they were going to have a prayer meeting and breakfast on the beach one morning. They asked Chris to go. She thought a bit of heavenly help for exams wouldn't go astray. In any case, a free meal was what appealed most. The event blew Chris' mind. The group cared for her.

The crunch came one Sunday night. She was invited to church. It was a song which broke her up. The song was about God's love. Chris cried and cried. That night when she got home she thought a lot about God. "What if he is real? What if he really does love me?" she asked herself. It seemed that God was the one solution to the mess she was in and the one who could heal all the hurts from her past. So she said this to God, "God if you're real I want to know it when I wake up in the morning. If not, I'm going to forget about you." When she woke up in the morning, God was just there. She was excited about the reality of God's presence. At school that day she told all her friends that she was a Christian, even though she didn't know what that meant. But from that time her life was changed as nothing else or no one else could change it.

Chris is now married to Rusty Frager. They write, sing and record songs under the Rhema record label.

*Themes: Change, Conversion, Divorce, Family, God – his existence, God – his love, God – his presence, Grace, Parenting, Rejection.*

**Scriptures:** Psalms 100; Luke 10:20; John 3:16; 15:11; Acts 2:1–42; 9:1–19; 10:34–48; 2 Corinthians 5:17; Ephesians 5:21 – 6:4; Colossians 3:18–21; 1 Thessalonians 5:16–18.

## 269 TESTIMONY – MARGARET COURT

Margaret Court had an incredible tennis career in which she won a staggering 66 grand-slam titles. When she started having heart palpitations, she went to her doctor. She discovered she had a torn heart valve. She was told she would be on tablets for the rest of her life. At the age of 38 she faced a life sentence of medication. Margaret met God when she was staying with a family in the United States. She thought the wife was a religious nut. She kept giving Margaret Christian books to read. But, through her illness and this woman, Margaret met God.

Her personal life has been transformed. Interestingly, her heart got strangely better so that she no longer needs her tablets.

269 Adapted from *New Idea* 11 April 1987, p. 8, and 21 April 1990, p. 22.

*Themes:* Conversion, Grace, Miracles, Prayer.

*Scriptures:* Matthew 8:5–13; 9:27–31; Mark 1:29–31, 40–44; 2:1–12;
3:1–6; 5:24–34; 7:31–37; 8:22–26; 10:46–52; Luke 13:10–17; 14:1–6;
John 4:46–54; 9:1–34; James 5:14–15.

## 270 TESTIMONY – WING COMMANDER EDWARD HOWELL

Wing Commander Edward Howell was stationed on Crete
when the Germans invaded and overran the island with
bombs and paratroopers. Howell was badly wounded and
taken prisoner. He spent many months in prison hospitals
in Greece. He discovered the real prison was not the stone
walls around him but the stone walls within. What if there
is a God, he thought? What if this God could set him free
from being his own prisoner? He says:

> I decided to try. As I lay there in the darkness and despair of
> my prison cell, far from home, I gave myself and all I have to
> God – for better or for worse, for richer or for poorer, in sick-
> ness and in health, for ever. I entrusted him with my life, my
> possessions, my career, and my family and friends. I commit-
> ted myself to choose what was right to do and to be, from
> then on, in so far as I could honestly see it. At that moment
> of decision, God spoke to me. It was as though, by that simple
> act of will, I had switched on the light in a dark room. I saw
> the meaning of things for the first time. With an intense
> thrill, my mind told me "God is Love." I began to see what
> that meant for me. My heart filled and overflowed. This was
> home at last, where you loved and were loved beyond all
> knowing. Nothing could ever separate me from it, so long as
> I chose to stay there. I was free at last, and no walls, or sen-
> tries, could take my freedom from me, so long as I chose to be
> free. I found myself praying, a thing I had not done for ten
> years or more... I was ecstatically happy and tears of joy

270 Edward Howell, *Escape to Live* (London: Grosvenor, 1981), quotation from pp. 93–94.

flowed down my face... I was sure and secure in the belief that now I knew the secret of living.

**Themes:**  *Conversion, Freedom, Grace, Joy, Praise.*
**Scriptures:** Luke 10:20; John 8:31–36; 15:11; Acts 2:1–42; 9:1–19; 10:34–48.

## 27٦ TESTIMONY – JEWESS

At the conference on evangelism in the Philippines in 1989, Sue Perlman, a Jewess, told her story.

One day I met a stranger on a street corner in New York City who shattered my misconceptions about the person of Christ. He was the first person really to communicate the gospel to me... He told me that Jesus was not one of *many* paths to God but the *only* way, the *only one* who could forgive my sin...

I reacted in the customary Jewish fashion: "That's a very narrow-minded point of view," I said.

He agreed with me and added, "But it is true!" And something in me knew that I couldn't just dismiss Jesus.

I was invited to attend a church service... Christians began praying for me from that night on, and my defences started crumbling. I didn't want it to be true that Jesus was the Messiah...

But... I realised that to deny the truth would be senseless... I, a Jew, embraced Jesus,... as my Lord and Saviour and so became a completed Jew, in the tradition of Peter, Paul and Priscilla!

**Themes:**  *Conversion, Evangelism, Forgiveness, Grace, Joy, Praise, Prayer, Witnessing.*
**Scriptures:** Mark 11:25; Luke 10:20; John 14:6; 15:11; Acts 2:1–42; 9:1–19; 10:34–48.

---

271 Sue Perlman, "'Uniqueness of Christ' Testimony", in J. D. Douglas (ed.), *Proclaim Christ Until He Comes* (Minneapolis: World Wide, 1990), pp. 312–13.

## 272 TESTIMONY – BOBBY LIMB *

Bobby Limb, the television personality, tells his story as follows:

> It was the late 60s when things weren't going too well for me that I went out to buy my first Bible. I was diagnosed as having cancer. Then my marriage to Dawn was in trouble and we separated. Finally I entered into a disastrous business deal and lost virtually everything.
>
> With nowhere to turn, I started reading my Bible and found it to be a tremendous help and inspiration in those tough times. I could identify with Job and all the terrible things that happened to him and... I, like Job, "desired to speak to the Almighty and to argue my case" with God! On 27 June 1983, I gave my life to the Lord... I am so grateful for God's gift of [love] through my relationship with Christ that I want to share it with others as an expression of thankfulness and obedience.

*Themes:* Cancer, Grace, Miracles, Prayer, Sickness.

**Scriptures:** Matthew 8:5–13; 9:27–31; Mark 1:29–31, 40–44; 2:1–12; 3:1–6; 5:24–34; 7:31–37; 8:22–26; 10:46–52; Luke 13:1–17; John 4:46–54; 9:1–34; 14:1–6; James 5:14–15.

## 273 TESTIMONY – K. N. NAMBUDRIPAD

K. N. Nambudripad is a surgeon, a Hindu by birth.

> In 1959, I was a resident in neurosurgery in Bristol, England. I was lonely and shy. My wife and four children were far away in India. One evening at a cocktail party I was sipping orange juice. A Christian nurse who was also drinking orange juice came to me. In the conversation that ensued she... told me of Jesus Christ, her Saviour. I argued with her and told her my

273 K. N. Nambudripad, "Testimony", in J. D. Douglas (ed.), *Let the Earth Hear His Voice* (Minneapolis: World Wide, 1975), p. 413.

Hindu religion was good enough for me. However, when I went back to my room I began to think about Jesus. As a twelve-year-old boy I had heard of Jesus; I had read about him, and I had been greatly attracted to Jesus as a man.

I began to read the Bible... I was greatly affected by the new reading of this book. I was affected by its authority. I said to myself, "This is not at all like the Hindu books which I am used to. This sounds true. The writers have a real experience of God." I said, "John, who was a fisherman, had an experience of God which I, a Brahmin philosopher, did not have." I said, "I must too have this experience."

It is now fifteen years since that encounter and surrender happened. Many trials and tribulations and difficulties have been my lot. I was put in a psychiatric clinic by my people. I was given electric shock, but the Lord was constantly with me. The Bible became my living friend and reality. I praise his name!

Now my wife and children, who had left me, are back with me and they are Christians. Now depression has left me. I don't get depressed any longer. Jesus keeps me away from depression. I'm never lonely. Jesus is with me. When I operate, he helps me with wisdom and humility. When patients consult me with their tremendous problems, Jesus gives me compassion. Jesus has forgiven my sins; I have no guilt feelings; I can tell it to Jesus. All the Hindu philosophy that I have learned is worthless when compared to the love of Jesus. I now get great joy in serving Jesus in [the] Christian Medical College and Hospital Ludhiana. And when I have free time, I witness in open air meetings to the blessed love of Jesus Christ. He has delivered me. He has saved me.

**Themes:** *Bible – authority of, Conversion, Depression, Evangelism, Forgiveness, Grace, Guilt, Hinduism, Humility, Joy, Loneliness, Praise, Service, Wisdom.*

**Scriptures:** Psalms 32; 34; 100; 121; Matthew 10:16–20; Mark 11:25; Luke 10:20; 18:9–14; John 14:6; 15:11; Acts 2:1–42; 9:1–19; 10:34–48; Philippians 2:3–11; 1 Thessalonians 5:16–18; 2 Timothy 3:16; Hebrews

13:5–6, 15; James 1:5.

## 274 TESTIMONY – J. C. PENNEY

In 1929, the tycoon J. C. Penney's business was secure. But he had made some unwise personal commitments. He became so worried that he could not sleep. Then he developed "shingles". He was hospitalised and given sedatives, but got no relief and tossed all night. A combination of circumstances had broken him so completely, physically and mentally, that he was overwhelmed with a fear of death. He wrote farewell letters to his wife and son, for he did not expect to live until morning.

In the morning he felt drawn to some singing he could hear coming from the chapel. A group was singing, "God will take care of you." There was a Bible reading and a prayer.

"Suddenly something happened," he said. "I can't explain it. I can only call it a miracle. I felt as if I had been instantly lifted out of the darkness of a dungeon into warm, brilliant sunlight. I felt as if I had been transported from hell to paradise. I felt the power of God as I had never felt it before... I know that God with his love was there to help me. From that day to this, my life has been free from worry."

*Themes:* *Anxiety, Conversion, Evangelism, Grace, Joy, Praise, Stress, Worry.*

**Scriptures:** Psalms 46; 55:22; 100; Matthew 6:19–34; Luke 10:20; 12:22–31; John 15:11; Acts 2:1–42; 9:1–19; 10:34–48; Romans 12:12; Philippians 4:6; 1 Thessalonians 5:16–18; Hebrews 13:15; 1 Peter 5:6–7.

---

274 Adapted from S. I. McMillen, *None of These Diseases* (London: Lakeland, 1963), p. 98. Originally in Dale Carnegie, *How to Stop Worrying and Start Living* (New York: Simon and Schuster, 1948), pp. 253–254.

Little Richard was the homosexual king of rock. He was the third of twelve children. He was black in a white society, gay in a straight one and crippled in a world where others walked tall. He had one leg shorter than the other, disproportionate eyes and a head too large for his body.

Cruelly, his father called him "half son". As a result he became a mama's boy with a flair for femininity and a mischievous streak.

His curiosity extended beyond music. Before he reached his teens he was having sex for money with a male friend of the family and masturbating ten times a day. He was nicknamed "Richard the Watcher" because he enjoyed watching others having sex.

After he became a star, Little Richard's after-show orgies were hot stuff even by Hollywood standards. Soon he sank into drugged-out excess, supporting a $1,000 a day cocaine habit. Yet, he says, he still read the Bible while breaking the commandments.

"There was a war going on in my body," he said, "a war between light and darkness." Believe it or not he also said, "I really wanted to be a Christian, but the devil took over till I finally decided that I had to be one or the other..."

That decision came after his brother died of a heart attack at the age of 32. He realised it could be him. Then three friends died. So he allowed God's light to shine in his life. God's light in his life transformed him – not least his homosexuality.

Little Richard says, "The habit [of homosexuality] is too deep for any human being to overcome without God. He gives me the strength not to want a man... "

---

275 Adapted from Vicky Jo Radovsky, "Little Richard: How Rock's Gay Legend Switched on to God", *The Weekend Australian* 8–9 December 1984, p. 7.

**Themes:** *Conversion, Evangelism, Grace, Homosexuality, Jesus – Light, Music industry, Joy, Praise.*

**Scriptures:** Leviticus 18:22; 20:13; 1 Kings 14:24; 15:12; 22:46; Psalms 55:22; 100; Matthew 6:25–34; Luke 10:20; 12:22–31; John 1:5; 3:19; 8:12; 9:5; 15:11; Acts 2:1–42; 9:1–19; 10:34–48; Romans 1:23–27; 12:12; 1 Corinthians 6:9; Philippians 4:6; 1 Thessalonians 5:16–18; 1 Timothy 1:10; Hebrews 13:15.

## 276 TESTIMONY – MITSUO FUCHIDA

It was 7 December 1941. Mitsuo Fuchida's plane climbed steeply. He switched the radio frequency to his home aircraft carrier. Jubilantly he cried, *"Tora! Tora! Tora!"* "Tiger! Tiger! Tiger!" was the code signal for the successful attack he had just led on Pearl Harbour.

Having ascertained that the main force of the American Pacific Fleet of eight warships was at anchor in Pearl Harbour, Mitsuo had lifted the curtain of warfare by despatching that cursed order: "Whole squadron, plunge into attack!"

He described his feeling. "My heart was ablaze with joy for my success in getting the whole main force of American Pacific Fleet in hand, and I put my whole effort into the war that followed, the result of which was that misery which is clear to everyone today." He said that in the following four years of war he faced death several times. But he was miraculously saved every time.

After the war, and 25 years of Navy service, he retired to farming. As he lived in close relation to the earth he was gradually led to think of the presence of God, the creator. He also arrived at the conclusion that the only way for the Japanese to survive and prosper would be for the people to become thoroughly peaceful. He began to write a book, *No More Pearl Harbor*.

He said this, "As my writing progressed, I came to realise that in my appeal for 'No More Pearl Harbor' there must be an assurance of the transformation of hatred among mankind to true brotherly love. So long as mankind remained in opposition to one another within the frame of nationality, the only consequence could be the destruction of civilisation." In the midst of these thoughts Mitsuo went to a Pocket Testament League meeting at Shibuya railway station in Tokyo. There he was handed a pamphlet, "I was a war prisoner of Japan". Mitsuo was captivated by the story. In it Jacob DeShazer told how one day he came to feel a strong desire to read the Bible. Jacob recalled how he had heard about Christianity which could transform human hatred to true brotherly love. In turn, Mitsuo decided to buy and read a Bible. Here is what he later said:

> Before covering the first thirty pages my mind was strongly impressed and captivated. This is it! I was strongly convinced. I concluded that the true realisation of "No More Pearl Harbor" was no other than to expect Christ's second coming and to endeavour to prepare men from all over the world worthy of welcoming Christ's return.
>
> As a first approach towards this, I was convinced that I should first of all become a good Christian... I then opened my heart and accepted Jesus Christ as my personal Saviour on 14 April 1950.

Later Mitsuo said, "I am still in the early stage of Christian growth, but I feel great joy in my daily Bible reading, and my heart is filled with peace as I kneel down to pray."

**Themes:** *Conversion, God – Creator, Grace, Joy, Love one another.*

**Scriptures:** Psalms 32; 34; 100; 121; Matthew 10:16–20; Mark 11:25; Luke 10:20; 18:9–14; John 14:6; 15:11; Acts 2:1–42; 9:1–19; 10:34–48; Philippians 2:3–11; 1 Thessalonians 5:16–18; 2 Timothy 3:16; Hebrews 13:5–6; James 1:5.

## 277 TESTIMONY – SAKAE KOBAYASHI

Sakae Kobayashi was selected to be a Japanese suicide or kamikaze pilot. Like all kamikaze pilots his task was to fly a plane filled with explosives and make a suicidal dive on a target: usually a ship. The day came for his flight, 14 August 1945. He sat in the plane waiting for orders to take off. While the engine was warming a ground crew man ran to tell him that Japan had just surrendered.

This is what Sakae said: "I went home despondent and bitter. My home had been burned, and my mother and grandmother killed. There was no food and no work."

Later Sakae found work in an oil refinery. There he met a Christian girl who led him to Christ. Then Sakae had this to say: "I discovered newness of life which only Christ can bring." Sakae also married the girl he met in the oil refinery.

**Themes:** *Conversion, Evangelism, Grace, Life – purpose, Renewal, Witness.*
**Scriptures:** Luke 10:20; John 8:31–36; 15:11; Acts 2:1–42; 9:1–19; 10:34–48; Romans 14:7–8; Galatians 2:20.

## 278 TESTIMONY – ROSARIO

Rosario is a woman from Peru. She was a terrorist, a brute of a woman who was an expert in several martial arts. In her terrorist activities she had killed twelve policemen. She had heard a little of the story of Jesus and was incensed at the Christian message. When she heard that Luis Palau was conducting a Christian meeting in Lima she set out to kill Palau.

She made her way into the stadium where Palau was speaking. As she sat there trying to work out how she was going to get close to the speaker she began to listen to the message. Instead of shooting Palau she met Jesus.

Ten years later Luis Palau met Rosario for the first

time. In those years she had assisted in planting five churches and had founded an orphanage that houses over 1,000 children.

**Themes:** *Church planting, Conversion, Crusades, Evangelism, Grace.*

**Scriptures:** Mark 1:14–15; Luke 4:18–19; Acts 2:1–42; 3:12–26; 4:8–12; 5:29–32; 10:34–48; 13:1–3, 16–41; 14:15–17; 17:22–31.

## 2̶7̶9̶ TESTIMONY – BILQUIS SHEIKH

Bilquis Sheikh was a high-born Muslim. Her life collapsed when her husband, a high-ranking official in Pakistan, left her. She retreated to the countryside looking for peace. But she did not find it. As she read the Koran she found many references to the prophet Jesus. Out of curiosity she obtained a Bible and began to read it. She found some parts quite compatible with the Koran but in other places there was a clash.

Then Bilquis started to dream. One of the dreams was about a perfume salesman bringing her a golden jar. His perfume glimmered like liquid crystal. He placed the jar by her bed. "This will spread throughout the world," he said. She woke up to find her Bible in the place where the jar had been in the dream. She found some missionaries who interpreted the dream for her. She became a Christian and is living in the United States.

**Themes:** *Bible, Dreams, Grace, Marriage, Peace, Separation.*

**Scriptures:** Daniel 2:1–49; Matthew 8:5–13; 9:27–31; Mark 1:29–31, 40–44; 2:1–12; 3:1–6; 5:24–34; 7:31–37; 8:22–26; 10:46–52; Luke 13:1–17; John 4:46–54; 9:1–34; 14:1–6; James 5:14–15.

*7 January.* I went to see a specialist in Leicester today about a small lump on my neck. He suggested that it should be removed. I'm concerned about the timing as I am anxious not to miss too much of my... course.

*16 March.* I received a very clinical letter this morning asking me to return to hospital for more tests. My mind ran riot. I desperately wanted to know more. I rang my GP and gently he told me what I had already feared – I had cancer...

After I put the phone down... I wanted to tell someone but was on my own in the flat. I'll ring my mother, but how do I tell her? Somehow I found the words. Even over the phone I could feel her acute shock – and I knew Dad's reaction would be worse. Slowly during the day, however, for no apparent reason, the fear has been replaced by a deep peace. I don't understand but I find I can honestly say that I trust God in this.

*20 April.* At last I'm in hospital. All the waiting had become unbearable.

*21 April.* I got up early and took a bath. I lay there for quite a while, thinking and praying. As the time for my operation approached, I was scared but found great assurance in Isaiah 43:1–4. In the evening, just after I returned from theatre, I sensed my parents' concern and love as they held my hand even though I was barely conscious.

*21 September.* I saw my specialist today. He is very pleased with my progress.

*31 December.* Tonight marks the end of a rather special year for me... but I am thankful... thankful because God has provided me with all that I needed. Thankful because of

---

280 Adapted from "Look Back in Wonder", *All Souls Magazine* (January – February 1983), p. 7.

the new perspectives I have gained, but above all I am thankful because in them God allowed me to see and know him as never before – that is very precious.

*Themes:* Cancer, Grace, Miracles, Prayer, Sickness.

*Scriptures:* Matthew 8:5–13; 9:27–31; Mark 1:29–31, 40–44; 2:1–12; 3:1–6; 5:24–34; 7:31–37; 8:22–26; 10:46–52; Luke 13:10–17; 14:1–6; John 4:46–54; 9:1–34; James 5:14–15.

## 281 TESTIMONY – YING GAO

Ying Gao was an eleven-year-old child when the Cultural Revolution began. Her parents held high positions in the Communist party, but were soon accused by the Red Guards of being "capitalist". They were forced out of their home to perform manual labour.

For Ying Gao, who had become an enthusiastic member of the Red Guards, this was the ultimate disgrace, and she denounced her parents both at home and in public. Less than a year later she herself was expelled from the Red Guards because of her "bad family". The family was re-united when she was fifteen, but the hurts were too deep to be reconciled and in any case they were again separated. Ying Gao was just one of fifteen million young people sent to perform manual labour at that time.

By 1976, the Revolution's tenth year, Ying Gao and millions of others had begun to question the truth of the Revolution. She says, "After the fall of Mao and the 'Gang of Four' everything was plain to me and I felt guilty because I had done many wrong things. I became very depressed. I began to look for something to believe in. I had heard about Christianity from western novelists, such as Victor Hugo, and I had the impression that Christianity told people to do good – otherwise I knew nothing."

In 1980 Ying Gao attended a re-opened Beijing church

where a friend's father was a pastor. The first sermon she heard was on reconciliation and being born again. She says, "These words touched a central part of my heart."

On her second visit Ying Gao obtained a Bible and began to study it. She says, "Finally I realised this was exactly what I had been searching for all my life." Ying Gao's father had died and attempts to be reconciled with her mother failed. "She decided to stop being my mother when I became a Christian," says Ying Gao. However, at the time of the Tiananmen Square massacre and just a year before her mother died of cancer, the two were tearfully reconciled.

Today the Revd. Ying Gao serves the largest church in Beijing. She says, "Our needs are for prayer for our pastors – that they will be able to provide nourishment for Christians and not disappoint those who come to the church seeking truth."

*Themes:* *Bible, Born again, Communication, Reconciliation.*

**Scriptures:** Psalms 32; 34; 100; 121; Matthew 10:16–20; Mark 11:25; Luke 10:20; 18:9–14; John 3:10; 14:6; 15:11; Acts 2:1–42; 9:1–19; 10:34–48; Philippians 2:3–11; 1 Thessalonians 5:16–18; 2 Timothy 3:16; Hebrews 13:5–6; James 1:5.

## 282 TITHING

Brian and Kayann were thinking about becoming Christians. One day Kayann said to a friend, "We can't become Christians because I've heard Christians have to give one-tenth of their money to the Church. We can't do that because the bathroom needs tiling."

The friend put it to Kayann that she would discover that if they became Christians and found that God was asking them to give one-tenth of their money to him they would still have money left over for the tiles.

It may have been a year later, after they had become

Christians and were giving one-tenth of their money to the Lord, Kayann and the friend were talking about this conversation and Kayann asked the friend to go and have a look at the bathroom. It was beautifully tiled. That family praised – and indeed still are praising God for his goodness.

*Themes:* *Giving, God – his care, God – his provision, Materialism, Money, Offerings, Sacrificial giving, Wealth.*

**Scriptures:** Psalms 112:9; Isaiah 55:10 – 11; Malachi 3:8–10; Mark 10:17–31; 12:41–44; Luke 19:1–10; Acts 4:32–37; 2 Corinthians 8 and 9; 1 Timothy 6:17–19; Hebrews 13:5.

## 283 TREASURE

Nearly 30 years ago Maurice Wright, a farmer, bought a large painting from a neighbouring farmer for a couple of dollars and hung it in his barn. After collecting cobwebs for several years, the painting was noticed by the farmer's tax accountant. Wondering what it might be worth, he took a colour photograph of it and sent the photo to Christie's, the well-known London auction firm. Subsequently he learned that the painting might be the work of Thomas Daniell, a highly acclaimed nineteenth-century artist.

The painting turned out to be an 1808 Daniell. Art critics had been aware of its existence, but it had come to be known as the "Lost Daniell", its whereabouts having been a mystery for over a century.

Wright sold the painting at an auction – for more than $90,000!

*Themes:* *Gospel – value of, Kingdom of God.*

**Scriptures:** Matthew 13:44–46; Mark 6:1–6; Luke 4:22–30; John 1:11–12; 2 Corinthians 4:7.

Somewhere in New England or upstate New York, late in 1988, there was a clearance sale of unclaimed property. A man bought a painting for $1,000. The painting was in a sorry condition, but he thought it might be worth something, perhaps $1,500. So he took the painting to New York.

The painting measured about two metres by just over two metres. It would not fit in his van. So, with some rope, he tied it on the roof of the van. It was not the kind of painting one would take to the luxurious auction houses in Park Avenue; he dropped it off at Christie's East on 67th Street, where collectibles are sold. He told an attendant that he would accept as little at $1,500 for his find.

Ian Kennedy was Christie's Old Masters' expert. When he saw the picture he knew they had a fabulous picture by Dosso Dossi, one of the better Italian Renaissance paintings in America. It was called *An Allegory of Fortune*, commissioned by Isabella d'Este in the court of Mantua and painted somewhere between 1530 and 1545. But it had disappeared during the nineteenth century.

The painting went on sale in Christie's Old Masters auction on 11 January 1989. It was expected to sell for $600,000 to $800,000.

However, London dealers Hazlitt, Gooden & Fox bought it – dirt, damage and all – for $4 million. It was a record for the artist. Most of the $4 million went to the unidentified man who found it.

Then, two months later, the picture was sold again. This time the Paul Getty Museum purchased the Dosso from the dealers at an undisclosed price.

But the picture was still in a distressing state of repair. Andrea Rothe is the Getty's conservator of paintings. At first she thought it was hopeless to try to restore the picture. One leg of the male figure had been punctured in several places, either during the trip to New York or the warehouse sales. A horizontal row of chips across the centre of the canvas indicated that, at some point many years ago, the canvas had probably been attached by loops to a horizontal crossbar to prevent sagging when it was hung at an angle, she said. Glue used in this process eventually contracted and caused small bits of pigment to fall off. In addition, the painting was so dirty and the background so dark that many of its subtleties were lost.

The restoration turned out to be a three-year project including extensive study. Andrea Rothe finished cleaning the painting only to make a time-consuming discovery. She discovered that the dark-brown background was a sloppily applied, flat coat of paint added later to cover cracks. This addition had to go – microscopic bit by microscopic bit. Andrea said, "It was a slow, tedious process – really mind-boggling." But her work paid off. The original, warm grey background that emerged lends the picture a haunting, atmospheric tone.

She repaired holes, filled cracks, restored losses of paint and gave the painting a coat of varnish. The result is dramatic, but visitors at the museum in Malibu will only see the impact of the finished work: a massive pair of luminous pink-skinned figures who are bathed in eerie moonlight.

**Themes:** *Gospel – its value, Kingdom of God, Parable – Pearl of Great Price, Parable – Hidden Treasure.*

**Scriptures:** Matthew 13:44–46; Mark 6:1–6; Luke 4:22–30; John 1:11–12; 2 Corinthians 4:7.

Ali Sougou was a Muslim in a Muslim country. After he was converted he was arrested and sent directly to prison. He was put in a very small cell. It was so small he could not even kneel down; he had to lean on the wall to sleep. He was fed nothing but rice full of salt and only once a day.

After three months he was taken to a special court arranged by Muslim leaders. They said they did not want him to explain himself or to ask him questions. He was told that he had a choice of three punishments. Ali started to tremble a bit. One choice was to be imprisoned for ever. The second was to be shot. The third was to be deported from the country. As Ali was a family man with eight children and two grandchildren it was a very difficult decision. He had nothing to say. But he felt somebody come from behind, put hands on his shoulders and pull him down. He went down, closed his eyes and prayed loudly. He said, "Lord Jesus, here I am. I need your answer for these people, and I ask this in your precious name. Amen."

The whole gathering stood up. They started shouting, "You people, this man is foolish; let him go away." So they released him.

The first person Ali led to Christ was a police inspector. He was the one who was sent to watch him. This man came to know the Lord after Ali gave him a New Testament to read.

One Sunday the policeman came to Ali and asked him a question. "Brother, I want to ask you a very, very important question. I want to know God the Father, God the Son, and God the Holy Spirit. Do you believe in three gods?"

"No, just one God," Ali said. Then Ali asked him a question. "Brother, tell me, what is your work?

He said, "I'm a police officer."

"Are you married?" continued Ali.

"Oh, yes, I'm married."

"Have you got children?" Ali went on.

"Oh, yes, I have two children," he replied.

Then Ali said, "In the morning when you are in your office, do they call you inspector? Does your wife call you husband? And do your children call you Daddy? But, you are only one person. You are a police officer, a husband, and a father."

The police officer then asked Ali if he could become a Christian.

**Themes:** *Conversion, Evangelism, Stephen, Testimony, Witness.*

**Scriptures:** Matthew 28:19; Luke 10:20; John 8:31–36; 14–16; 15:11; Acts 2:1–42; 6:8–8:3; 9:1–19; 10:34–48; Romans 14:7–8; 2 Corinthians 13:14; Galatians 2:20; 4:6; 1 John 5:7.

# 286 UNITY

In France, during the Second World War, some soldiers carried the body of a friend to a local cemetery to be buried properly. However, they were stopped by the local priest.

The priest could see what was going to happen and so said, "Sorry, boys, you can't bury your friend here if he's not a Catholic."

Although hurt and discouraged the soldiers were not going to give up. They decided to give their friend their own burial service. They dug a grave and buried the body just outside the cemetery fence. Next morning, before they left the area, they went back to the grave to pay their last respects. The site was nowhere to be found. They

---

286 Adapted from John MacArthur, *The Church: The Body of Christ* (Grand Rapids, MI: Zondervan, 1973), p. 22.

looked for an hour, combing the area. Then they went and found the priest, asking him if he could help.

The priest explained, "Well, the first part of the night I stayed awake, sorry for what I had told you. The second part of the night I spent moving the fence."

**Themes:** *Acceptance, Reconciliation, War.*

**Scriptures:** Romans 14:19; 2 Corinthians 13:11; Ephesians 4:3; 1 Thessalonians 5:13; 2 Timothy 2:22; Hebrews 12:14; 1 Peter 3:11; 1 John 4:7–21.

## 287 UNITY

I recently read about the reason migrating geese fly in a "V" formation. Each goose flapping its wings creates an upward lift for the geese that follow. When the geese do their part, the whole flock has a 71-per-cent greater flying range than if each bird were to fly alone.

**Themes:** *Encouragement, Gifts of the Spirit, Loneliness.*

**Scriptures:** Psalms 23; 121; 133:1; Matthew 10:16–20; Romans 12:3–8; 1 Corinthians 10:17; 12:12–26; Galatians 6:2; Ephesians 1:22–23; 4:1–16; Hebrews 13:5–6.

## 288 UNITY

A small child had wandered off in the tall jungle grass near an African village. The little one could not be found anywhere, even though the people searched for the whole of the rest of the day. The next day all the village turned out to hold hands with each other and walk through the grass together in a long line. The child was found. But he was dead: the cold night had been too much for him. In her anguish and through her tears the mother sobbed, "If only we could have held hands sooner."

---

288 Adapted from Michael P. Green, *Illustrations for Biblical Preaching* (Grand Rapids, MI: Baker, 1989), #201.

*Themes:* Encouragement, Gifts of the Spirit, Loneliness.
*Scriptures:* Psalms 23; 121; 133:1; Matthew 10:16–20; Romans 12:3–8;
1 Corinthians 10:17; 12:12–26; Ephesians 1:22–23; 4:1–16; Hebrews
13:5–6.

## 289 **VICTORY**

On Sunday evening, 18 June 1815, a few kilometres south
of Brussels in Belgium, the Battle of Waterloo was over.
The British had won. Wellington needed to send news of
his victory to England. His men set up a series of line-of-
sight communication stations and a coded message was
sent. But only the first part of the message got through.
Halfway through sending the message the fog set in and
the signallers could not see each other. All the English
received was the terrible news, "Wellington defeated..."
However, later the fog lifted and the whole message could
get through, "Wellington defeated Napoleon at Waterloo."

*Themes:* Death, Defeat, Good news, Resurrection.
*Scriptures:* Mark 1:1; 16:1–8; Luke 24:1–12; John 20:1–31 Romans 1:3–4;
1 Corinthians 15; 2 Corinthians 13:4; Ephesians 1:19–20.

## 290 **WAITING**

In 1870 a young lieutenant in Prussia went off to war. As
he left, he told his girl that he would return and they
could get married. The next year, the war with France was
over. The victorious Prussian troops returned tri-
umphantly through the streets of Berlin. And Julie stood
by the gate waiting for her lover to return. "He must
come, he said he would!" she kept saying. In fact, for 40
years, day after day, in all weathers, she waited for him to
return. One day she became ill at the spot where she
waited each day. She had to be taken to hospital, where
she died. Her soldier never did return.

**Themes:** *Hope, Love, Parable – Prodigal Son, Second Coming, Trust.*

**Scriptures:** Mark 13:32–37; Luke 15:11–32; 1 Corinthians 5:5; 15:12–34; 2 Corinthians 1:14; 1 Thessalonians 4:13 – 5:11; 2 Thessalonians 2:2; Hebrews 9:28; 2 Peter 3:10, 12; Revelation 16:14.

## 291 WEAKNESS

Alexander Solzhenitsyn, the Russian dissident, was working twelve hours a day at hard labour. He had lost his family and had been told by the doctors in the Gulag that he had terminal cancer. One day he thought, "There is no use going on. I'm soon going to die anyway." Ignoring the guards, he dropped his shovel, sat down, and rested his head in his hands.

He felt a presence next to him and looked up and saw an old man he had never seen before, and would never see again. The man took a stick and drew a cross in the sand in front of Solzhenitsyn. It reminded him that there is a Power in the world that is greater than any empire or government, a Power that could bring new life to his situation. He picked up his shovel and went back to work. A year later Solzhenitsyn was unexpectedly released from prison.

**Themes:** *Cancer, Cross, Encouragement, Persecution, Power – in weakness, Suffering.*

**Scriptures:** Psalms 34:1; 71:6; Hosea 14:2; Matthew 5:12; Acts 11:22–26; 15:41; Romans 5:3–5; 14:7–8, 19; 1 Corinthians 10:23; 2 Corinthians 5:15; 12:1–13; Galatians 2:20; 6:9; Ephesians 4:29; 5:20; Philippians 1:21; 4:12; 1 Thessalonians 5:11; Hebrews 10:34; 13:15; James 1:2–4; 1 Peter 1:7; 2:5.

## 292 WEALTH

One of the richest men in the world is the Sultan of Brunei, a small state in north-west Borneo. He knows that nothing is beyond his wildest dreams. He took a fancy to polo and bought himself 200 of the best ponies in the world. He wanted an Olympic-sized pool, so he built one. He took up golf and had an international standard 18-hole golf course built outside one of his palaces. His fleet of planes is constantly changing. The latest acquisition is a luxury airbus and a Boeing 757. The British Queen has assets of only $11.6 billion. The Sultan of Brunei's assets are estimated to be $37 billion. His annual income alone is greater than the total assets of all but the very richest people on earth. Put simply, his income is equivalent to $7.3 million a day, or $300,000 an hour. Even while he is asleep he is earning $5,000 a minute, or $84 a second.

**Themes:** *Achievement, Generosity, Greed, Life style, Materialism, Money, Parable – Rich Man and Lazarus, Prosperity, Tithing.*

**Scriptures:** Psalms 37:29; Proverbs 1:19; 15:27; 21:26; 29:25; Matthew 5:22; 6:24; Mark 4:18–19; 8:36; 10:17–31; Luke 6:24; 12:16–21; 16:13, 19–31; Ephesians 4:28; 1 Timothy 3:3, 8; 6:10, 17–19.

## 293 WEDDINGS

You will know that the central figure in any wedding is the mother of the bride. If it wasn't for her, weddings would be so simple – and so dull.

Once there was to be a wedding to beat all weddings. Mother was overcome with joy at the announcement of her daughter's engagement. Nobody knew it, but this lady had been waiting with a script for a production that would have met with Cecil B. de Mille's approval. The father of the bride began to pray for an elopement. His prayers were not to be answered.

Mother had seven months to work, and no detail was left to chance or human error. There were teas and showers and dinners. The bride and groom only met the min-

293 Adapted from Robert Fulghum, *It was on Fire when I Lay Down on it* (London: Grafton/Collins, 1990), chapter one.

ister a couple of times. Mother called weekly. The tuxedos were bought – not rented, mind you. If that was not enough, the engagement ring was returned to the jeweller for a larger stone, quietly subsidised by Mother.

On the day, guests in formal attire packed the church. And the mighty Mother coasted down the aisle with the grandeur of an opera star at a premier performance. Never did a Mother take her seat with more satisfaction. She had done it. She glowed.

The music softened, and nine – nine – chiffon-draped bridesmaids lockstepped down the aisle while the groom and his men made the short march to their positions.

Finally, the wedding march thundered from the 18-piece orchestra. The congregation rose and turned in anticipation.

The bride. She had been dressed for hours, if not days. No adrenalin was left in her body. Left alone in the adjoining reception hall while the march of the bridesmaids went on and on, she had walked among the tables laden with gourmet goodies. She had absentmindedly sampled the little mints, the mixed nuts, the cheese and then the little sausages, and a couple of shrimps and then some paté. To wash it all down and to calm her nerves she had a drink from the punchbowl.

What you noticed as the bride stood in the doorway was not the dress, but her face. It was white. What was coming down the aisle was a living grenade with the pin pulled out.

Just as she walked by Mother, the bride threw up. And I don't mean a polite little ladylike burp in her hanky. She puked. There is no nice word for it. She hosed the front of the church. She hit two bridesmaids, the groom, a ring-bearer and the minister. Drained of everything, the bride went limp in her father's arms. The groom sat down on the floor, too stunned to function. Mother fainted, slumping over like a rag doll.

Then, like a Marx Brothers' fire drill, groomsmen rushed about heroically, flower girls squalled, bridesmaids sobbed, and those with weak stomachs headed for the doors.

Only two people were seen to smile. One was the mother of the groom. The other was the father of the bride. Eventually guests were invited to adjourn to the reception hall for drinks while a clean-up and restoration took place.

Then the cast was reassembled and the deed was done without a hitch.

**Themes:** *Family relationships, Humour, Marriage.*

**Scriptures:** Deuteronomy 24:1–5; Matthew 5:27–29, 31–32; 19:3–12; Mark 10:2–13; 1 Corinthians 7:1–11.

## 294 WOMAN – A DEFINITION

*Her symbol:* WO

*Atomic weight:* 120lbs.

*Occurrences:* Found where ever man is found, seldom in a free state.

*Physical Properties:* Generally rounded in form. Boils at nothing and may freeze at any minute. Melts when treated properly. Very bitter if not used well.

*Chemical properties:* Very active. Possesses great affinity for gold, silver, platinum and precious stones. Violent reactions when left alone. Able to absorb great amounts of food. Turns green when placed beside a better-looking specimen. Ages rapidly without cosmetic attachments.

294 From Barry Chant, *Straight Talk about Marriage* (Unley Park, South Australia: Tabor, 1983), p. 20.

*Uses:* Highly ornamental. Useful as a tonic in the accelerating of low spirits, etc. Equalises the distribution of wealth. Is probably the most powerful income-reducing agent known to man.

*Caution:* Highly explosive when in inexperienced hands.

*Themes:* *Family, Humour, Man, Marriage.*

**Scriptures:** Proverbs 31; Ephesians 5:21–33; Colossians 3:18 – 4:1.

## 295 WORKS

A screaming 19-year-old woman trapped in a car dangling from a freeway in East Los Angeles was rescued in the early hours of the morning.

The woman had fallen asleep at the wheel of her car as she was driving home at 12:15 am. The car went through the guard rail and was left dangling by its left back wheel over the edge of an overpass. Every time the rescuers moved the car she would yell and scream. It took almost two and a half hours for about 25 people – passers by, police, tow truck drivers, fire fighters – as well as their equipment to secure the car and rescue the woman.

Later, Los Angeles County Fire Captain Ross Marshall said something very interesting. "It was kinda funny. She kept saying, 'I'll do it myself'."

*Themes:* *Grace, Law.*

**Scriptures:** Acts 13:39; Romans 1:17; 3:20 – 4:25; Galatians 2:16; Ephesians 2:8–9; 2 Timothy 1:9.

## 296 WORKS

The television programme, *The Marathon Monks of Mount Hiei*, was a fascinating account of Tanno-Ajari's successful attempt to complete 1,000 marathons in seven years. This

---

295 Adapted from *The Los Angeles Times*, 20 November 1988 Part II, pp. 1, 2.

36-year-old monk made the commitment to walk 27,000 miles under penalty of suicide in order to become a living Buddha.

Behind this astonishing physical exertion lies the theory that, in undergoing such austerity, enlightenment can be obtained without subsequent reincarnation.

As if this gruelling pilgrimage was not enough, a nine-day total fast is imposed after the first 700 trips up and down the mountain. Sleep is denied by the constant repetition of 100,000 mantras during this period, which takes the postulant deity two days beyond medical life expectancy.

The programme traced Tanno's journeyings and mortifications over two years until their completion and his proclamation as a god. As only the seventh man to undergo this experience since 1945, he captivated the public imagination.

**Themes:** *Fasting, Grace, Law, Monks, Reincarnation.*

**Scriptures:** Exodus 34:27–28; 2 Samuel 12:16–24; Ezra 8:21; Psalms 69:10; Isaiah 58:5–12; Jeremiah 14:11–12; Zechariah 7:1–14; 8:19; Mark 2:18–22; Romans 1:16 – 3:20; 5:2; 10:9; 2 Corinthians 4:13; Galatians 5:6; Ephesians 2:1–10; Philippians 1:29.

## 297 **WORSHIP**

A few years ago Rod Denton from Clovercrest Baptist, Adelaide, visited Argentina. He wanted to see something of the Christian revival that was sweeping the country. One of the places Rod and a team of 30 visited was Olmos Prison in the city of La Plata.

The prison is a high-security, high-density penal colony of 3,000 dangerous inmates. Prisoners are housed in five-storey rundown squalid buildings with bars on the windows. There are arms and legs poking out of the windows.

As Rod was walking into this massive place he heard a

noise in the distance. As he moved towards the sound it swelled to an incredible symphony of noise, a passionate sound, a strong beat that pierced the air. It sounded like a riot. The closer he got to a large old decrepit building the louder it got.

As Rod entered the building from the heat of the day, before him were 840 prisoners praying and worshipping God in their chapel service. Rod moved among men worshipping Jesus with all their might. There was no overhead projector. Just singing. The men were crying out to God and praising him with all the strength they had. They were lost in wonder, love and praise. In the worship there was an incessant clapping. The team of visitors nearly had to put their hands over their ears. The worship was so loud. Perspiration dripped from the prisoners. They didn't want to stop. Many were prepared to stand for two hours because there were so few chairs in the place. What chairs they had they gave to the visitors.

Rod sat in amazement. It was an awesome moment for him. He had never seen worship like this in all his life. He said he looked into the eyes of some of the prisoners and saw the very presence of Jesus in them.

Later in the meeting they asked for the privilege to pray for the visitors that God would anoint them with the same Spirit of the risen Jesus that was in that place, to take it back to their churches. The small group went and stood at the front. They were not prepared for what happened next.

The 840 prisoners prostrated themselves on the gaol floor for fifteen minutes as they prayed. With tears running down their faces, they cried out to God for him to touch the visitors in a new way. Rod and the others felt the power of God come upon them. Many of the visitors fell to the floor with the power of the risen Jesus.

So powerful is the sense of God's presence in the worship that people walking along outside the prison have fallen to the ground.

At the close of worship on this particular day, they embraced one another. There was a small man of about 60, with a big smile and one tooth. He went up to Rod. Rod wrapped his arms around him and prayed for him.

All too soon they had to leave. They got back into the bus. But they were all silent; no one speaking for many minutes. They had seen something awesome; something they had never experienced before.

**Themes:** *Freedom, Prayer, Prison, Singing.*

**Scriptures:** Deuteronomy 6:1–4; Psalms 95; 96; 97; 98; 100; 122; 149; 150; Isaiah 6:1–4; Mark 12:30; John 4:20–24; 1 Corinthians 14:26–31; Philippians 3:3; Revelation 4; 5; 19:1–10.

## 298 WORSHIP

Under the enormous orange and blue striped canvas of the marquee, the sense of God's presence was giving rise to praise of a very enthusiastic nature; there were smiles everywhere, voices rang out, arms were raised, hands were clapped and even some legs got liberated and danced for joy. In the midst of a group of worshippers sat a severely disabled Christian man in an invalid "buggy". No one could have blamed him for feeling depressed or resentful at those around him who were praising God with agile and healthy bodies, while he could not even stand up. No one would have blamed him for excusing himself from the meeting and trundling off in his electric buggy out into the windy night and back to his room. Apparently nothing of the kind even entered his head, because as the spirit of praise grew stronger those nearby

298 Graham Kendrick, *Worship* (Eastbourne: Kingsway, 1984), p. 99.

were treated to a lovely example of selfless praise. The buggy was well equipped for street use, and there he sat, flashing headlights, stop lights, indicator lights, warning lights; in fact anything that flashed, moved or made a sound was in use as he gave all he had in praise to the Lord he loved!

*Themes:* *Dancing, Praise.*

**Scriptures:** Exodus 15:20; 32:19; Judges 21:19–21; 1 Samuel 18:6; 2 Samuel 6:14; Psalms 100; Ecclesiastes 3:4; Mark 6:21–22; Luke 15:25; John 4:23–24; Acts 2:1–4; 1 Thessalonians 5:16–18; Hebrews 13:15.

## 299 X – RATED

Someone had stolen the vicar's bike. He felt sure that one of his parishioners was the thief. So he decided to preach a sermon on the Ten Commandments. When he came to "Thou shalt not steal", he made a great deal of the commandment, preaching eloquently about the scourge of theft and the collapse of standards in society. However, when he came to the commandment, "Thou shalt not commit adultery", he suddenly remembered where he had left his bike.

*Themes:* *Adultery, Ethics, Humour, Sexuality, Stealing, Ten Commandments, Theft.*

**Scriptures:** Exodus 20:14; Leviticus 20:10; Deuteronomy 5:18; Proverbs 6:32; Jeremiah 3:8; 5:7; 13:27; Hosea 2:1–5; Matthew 5:7–8; 19:9; Mark 7:21; 10:11, 19; John 8:1–11; 2 Peter 2:14.

## 300 X – RATED

Barry Humphries, the actor best known as Dame Edna Everage, tells the following story from his university days:

---

300 Barry Humphries, *More Please* (London: Viking, 1992), p. 118.

The firm of H. J. Heinz had an excellent product called Russian Salad. It consisted largely of diced potato in mayonnaise with a few peas and carrot chips. Surreptitiously spilt and splashed in large quantities on the pavement of a city block, it closely resembled human vomit. It was a simple and delightful recreation of mine to approach a recent deposit of salad in the guise... of a tramp. Disgusted pedestrians were already giving it a very wide berth, holding their breaths and looking away with watering eyes. Not I, as I knelt beside one of the larger puddles, curdled and carrot-flecked. Drawing a spoon from my top pocket I devoured several mouthfuls, noticing out of the corner of my eye, and with some satisfaction, several people actually being sick at the spectacle. I have done this in many parts of the world and only in Fleet Street in the 1960s did I come close to being apprehended by a policeman. He, however, was too profoundly nauseated to take my name, and as he stood gagging on the salad-splattered pavement I made my escape.

*Themes: Humour.*

# INDEXES

*All references apply to story numbers, as opposed to page numbers.*

## BIBLICAL PASSAGES

## Proverbs

## Ecclesiastes

## Isaiah

# Jeremiah

## Mark

## 2 Corinthians

## Galatians

## Ephesians

## NAMES, PLACES AND THEMES